DON [

MUSLIM
INVASION:

The Fuse is Burning!

MUSLIM INVASION:

The Fuse is Burning!

Don Boys, Ph.D.
Ellen Boys, Editor

Muslim Invasion: The Fuse is Burning!

Copyright ©2016, Don Boys, Ph.D.

Don Boys, Ph.D., Author

Ellen Boys, Editor

ISBN 978-1-927684-39-9

First Edition

Book design and typography: David Bolton

Cover art: Bric Bolin, Raleigh, North Carolina

Note: If you would like to have Dr. Boys speak to your organization, write Cornerstone Communications, P.O. Box 944, Ringgold, GA 30736 or e-mail him at DBoysphd@aol.com.

All Scripture quotes are from the King James Version.

Barbwire Books is a subsidiary of Freedom Press Canada Inc.

Dedication

To my wife Ellen, who made this book possible.

Contents

Acknowledgments

Well, my book is finished and it is time to give credit where credit is due. This, I am pleased to do. It is normal procedure to praise the spouse at times like this, and this is no exception. In fact, it is required since my wife Ellen has been invaluable during this process of research, interviews, writing, re-writing, and re-writing. She has been my editor and made me focus on what I was trying to communicate to others. She found many typos, ambiguities, dangling participles (I have a tendency to let them dangle), and inconsistencies. Her editorial expertise is exceptional. It is interesting that my book published in March of 1999 was sent back to us by my publisher with only one correction to be made. When Ellen looked at it, the "correction" was wrong! The publisher agreed with her conclusion. Anyway, keep in mind that a superb editor makes a good book, a better book.

Dr. Harold Willmington graciously wrote of *Muslim Invasion*: "Boys successfully proves that the Koran requires every Muslim to make the nation where he lives a Muslim state under *sharia* law. Every Muslim must participate in *Jihad* which is 'holy fighting in the cause of Islam' according to the Koran. The author delivers fact after fact to prove that Islam is totally opposite to freedom and warns of a massive change coming to America unless concerned patriots act. He provides some practical, common sense solutions to the threat although he believes it will be too late if quick action is not taken and the invasion continues.

"Dr. Boys documents the fact that the Muslim Invasion will change America's culture forever. Every American, concerned about this nation, must be awakened, alerted, and activated to unashamedly 'put America first.' Read *Muslim Invasion: The Fuse in Burning*! and pass it on to friends and neighbors."
Dr. Harold Willmington, Liberty University

Another university professor wrote: "A bold, but necessary read for those interested in the world's Muslim invasion. A MUST read!"
Dr. Pat Taylor, Professor of English and Latin; Tennessee Temple University; University of Tennessee at Chattanooga; Chattanooga State Community College; Dalton State College.

Any errors or omissions are my own and will be corrected in the next edition. Any suggestions or corrections can be sent to DBoysphd@aol.com or to P.O. Box 944, Ringgold, GA 30736.

About the Author

D on Boys was born in West Virginia and received his early education there. He was educated at Moody Bible Institute, Tennessee Temple College, Immanuel College and Seminary, and Heritage Baptist University where he earned his Ph.D. In 1971, he organized a Christian school in Indianapolis and within four years, it was the largest ACE school in the world with over 600 students. While serving as school administrator, Boys was elected to the Indiana House of Representatives, and was identified by the media as the "most conservative member of the General Assembly."

During this time his first book, *Liberalism: A Rope of Sand* was published. Don resigned from the school in 1978 to do preaching, research, and writing. He was under contract to *USA Today* and wrote columns for them from 1985 to 1993. Those columns led to hundreds of talk show appearances where he defended Christian/Conservative positions. He appeared on CNN's "Crossfire"; the "Sally Jessy Raphael Show" (three times); the "Jerry Springer Show" (four times); "NBC Nightly News"; "CBS Morning News"; the "Morton Downey Jr. Show"; the Trinity Broadcasting Network (four times); the BBC, and more than a hundred other television shows.

He also was a guest on many of the major radio shows including the "Pat Buchanan Show"; "Crosstalk" (twice); the "Janet Parshall Show"; "Janet

Mefferd Today"; "Barry Farber Show" (35 times); USA Radio Network (three times) and many other networks.

Don has authored 15 books including *ISLAM: America's Trojan Horse!* published in March of 2003. Among his other books are *Your Health: How to Feel Better, Look Younger, Live Longer; Pilgrims, Puritans, and Patriots: Our Christian Heritage; Boys Big Book of Humor; Is God a Right-Winger?; etc.* Barbwire Books published *The God Haters* in November of 2015 and *Evolution: Fact, Fraud, or Faith?* in April of 2016.

Recently Boys published eBooks available at amazon.com including *The God Haters; Martin Luther King, Jr: Judged by His Character Not His Color!; Did You Know?; Christian Resistance: An Idea Whose Time Has Come—Again!; ISLAM: America's Trojan Horse!* and *Evolution: Fact, Fraud, or Faith?*

In addition to his columns in *USA Today,* he has been published in *USA Today Magazine,* the Chattanooga *Times Free Press, Whistleblower* magazine, the Franklin *Daily Journal,* the *Sword of the Lord; Biblical Evangelist;* and many other periodicals.

His weekly column has been published by WorldNetDaily, Barbwire, Canada Free Press, American Prophet, Before it's News, Patriot Post, Capitol Hill Outsider, Rapture Forums, and many other websites. His very informative websites www.cstnews.com, www.muslimfact.com, and www.thegodhaters.com reach people around the world.

His blog is DonBoys.cstnews.com. Most of his effort is spent as a Christian apologist in books, columns, and on talk shows. Don and Ellen (who edits his books and columns) live in North Georgia, near Chattanooga. E-mail Dboysphd@aol.com.

Foreword

There are about four to seven million Muslims living in America and more than 3,000 Muslim mosques with others planned. In fact, Muslims plan to conquer America. Well, that's not the whole story; they plan to take over the world! And that statement is easily proved, as you will soon discover. We are facing the greatest challenge to our nation that we have ever faced. That includes the War Between the States (or as some call it, "Lincoln's War of Northern Aggression"), our two world wars, and our 90-year conflict with Communism. The enemy is already among us: koranic Muslims and they keep coming!

ISLAM IS A TOTAL ALIEN CULTURE

It must be remembered that Islam is not only a religion, but in its fullest form, it is a complete, total, 100% system of life. Islam has religious, legal, political, economic, social, and military components. Muslims are given specific instruction how to carry out normal, daily bodily functions or suffer penalties for disobedience. Islam totally controls every area of daily living including how you pee!

Keep in mind that the major problem is Islam, not individual Muslims who may be as decent and patriotic as you or I. However, it is Islamic doctrine that turns people into bombs. A problem arises when Muslim apologists declare that wicked people have twisted Koran passages to justify dangerous ideas. That is not true. The footnotes in official Koran translations make it clear that *jihad*, *sharia*, right to lie, and fighting

Christians and Jews are the reality. Moreover, their top scholars support those facts.

One top Egyptian Muslim scholar is Abdel Rahman, known as the "Blind Sheikh" who was found guilty of leading a terror cell that planned the bombing of the Twin Towers in 1993. He is serving life in a federal prison for terrorist crimes against the U.S. as I write. But remember that Abdel is no uneducated nut leading an offshoot of Islam; he is a highly educated Islamic leader. He is a "globally renowned scholar–a doctor of Islamic jurisprudence who graduated from al-Azhar University in Cairo, the seat of Sunni Islamic learning for over a millennium. His area of academic expertise was *sharia*–Islamic law."[1] He teaches that the terrorists are the true Muslims!

Every Muslim is not a terrorist and all Muslims do not encourage terrorism, but a large number of them do. Many were trained that way from infancy. There is a Trojan Horse already within our walls. It is filled with the Muslim extremists that I am concerned about, not those Muslims who are peaceful, kind, law-abiding, and lovers of freedom. However, those Muslims are very quiet in condemning terror.

The fuse is burning and America and the world are holding their breath. The waters may be calm today but that does not mean there are no crocodiles in the water! Get out of the water now and prepare for a difficult tomorrow! We are in a lifetime battle with koranic Muslims. The fuse is burning and the clock is ticking!

IS THIS YOUR DESIRED CULTURE?

Most Americans have difficulty understanding that most Muslims have no concept of freedom, democracy, morality, or civility. There have been many examples of Muslims–in America–who killed their own relatives because they were being too Americanized and not fervent enough for Islam.

Al-Shafie, who died in 820, is considered a founder of Islamic jurisprudence and he clearly demonstrated the backward, bloody, and brutal nature of Islamic culture in contrast to ours. He wrote: "One may eat the flesh of a human body. It is not allowed to kill a Muslim nor a free non-Muslim under Muslim rule (because he is useful for the society), nor a prisoner because he belongs to other Muslims. But you may kill an enemy fighter or an adulterer and eat his body."[2] But it gets worse, if possible.

In November of 1989 a Muslim and his wife murdered their 14-year-old daughter because she was not living according to the strict teaching of Islam. The mother held the girl down while the father stabbed her repeatedly. The Muslim family did not know that the father was under investigation by the FBI, and a bug had been legally planted in the house. The murder was recorded on tape. As the girl struggled and begged her mother to help her, the father said in Arabic, "DIE, DIE QUICKLY, DIE QUICKLY."[3]

There have been honor killings where a wife is killed for adultery, flirting, or being raped, or for asking for a divorce! Daughters have been killed by their brothers for being raped. There is an Egyptian case in which a father actually paraded his daughter's severed head through the streets while shouting, "I have avenged my honor." That culture is in America at this time.

That is the same mentality that drives parents to lead their small children to strap on a bomb and enter a restaurant filled with innocent people. The parents boast about their young martyr and hope their other children will follow his example!

Muslims have a twisted sense of honor that normal people have trouble understanding. They have been taught for a lifetime that only Muslims are going to Heaven and Heaven is guaranteed only if the Muslim kills "unbelievers" while the Muslim commits suicide. Those are the people who are slowly taking control of America. They already hold elective office and many appointed positions that impact your life. They do not have America's best interests at heart since they must honor and obey Allah.

AMERICA LAST

Alas, our nation is being lulled to sleep by leaders whose mantra is "America last," and they have allowed a Muslim invasion to happen. Is the day coming when our glorious Republic will only be remembered as a "noble experiment" between the great oceans? In kindness we are permitting aliens inside our nation who have no intention of being absorbed into our "melting pot." They believe in the "salad bowl" theory. Muslims will not adopt our ways and be assimilated into our culture. They are determined to change our culture, laws, and religion as they have in England, Germany, France, Sweden, and other nations.

I have a question for those who think I am too hard, harsh, or even hateful: What if terrorists detonate a nuclear bomb in one of our major cities resulting in the deaths of 100,000 Americans from the blast with another 300,000 dying of radiation; plunging the stock market to the basement; devastating our economy for a generation; putting millions of people out of work; producing fear and anxiety up and down every street in the nation; would you still think I am too harsh? Many national leaders think the above could happen, or we might have millions infected by a biological or chemical weapon. Keep my question in mind as you read this book. The extremists are here, today!

Arnaud de Borchgrave reported that Islamists in Pakistan expect that "in the next 10 years, Americans will wake up to the existence of an Islamic army in their midst–an army of jihadis who will **force** [my emphasis] America to abandon imperialism and listen to the voice of Allah."[4] Most sleeping Americans are not aware of the danger. I hope to awaken them, anger them, alarm them with this message: There is a dangerous invasion of America–legal and illegal with plans to destroy us. Note that the ten year period of Islamic saturation in America is long past.

It is past time for informed, incensed, indignant Americans to demand that officials stop playing this "Let's stop the terrorists" game and stop the terrorists, at least those here at home.

Islamists have declared war against the U.S. producing a clash of civilizations, cultures, and creeds. Koranic Muslims recognize every non-Muslim as their enemy. They will be patient, even accommodate, acclimate, and acquiesce when they are in the minority to achieve their goal; but once on the rise as in Europe, they will get mean–dangerously mean.

References:

1   Andrew C. McCarthy, Hillsdale College Imprimis, "Islam–Facts or Dreams?" Feb. 2016, p. 2.
2   Al-Kortoby, 716 in volume 1.
3   *People* magazine, Jan. 20, 1992.
4   NewsMax.com website, August 21, 2002.

Introduction

O ur war with terrorism is rooted in the early days of mankind, in the tent of Abraham when he refused to wait for God's promise to provide him a son! At his wife's suggestion (and in keeping with the pagan practice in Sarai's homeland), Abraham took Hagar to bed rather than wait for God's promise to be fulfilled. The result was the birth of Ishmael who, according to Genesis 16:12, would become "a wild man; his hand will be against every man...." This seems to have been played out in history and maybe in the acts of terror perpetrated by Muslim terrorists in recent years and sadly on September 11, 2001 followed by Benghazi, Paris, San Bernardino, Chattanooga, etc. Ishmael is considered the father of the Arabs. Of course, not all Arabs are Muslims but most are.

The Arabs' driving philosophy is condensed by Leon Uris who wrote: "Before I was nine, I had learned the basic canon of Arab life. It was me against my brother; me and my brother against our father; my family against my cousins and the clan; the clan against the tribe; the tribe against the world, and all of us against the infidel."[1] You are the infidel.

Muslim leaders and a cursory reading of the Koran and Hadith support the truth that Muslims are against the world.

ISLAM IS LEGAL IN U.S.

Muslims have a legal right to live in America and to practice their religion (even a perverted religion), and they have a right to think that all other religions are wrong. This is America where First Amendment rights are precious to all of us. I don't want to see anyone's rights abused or denied. After all, if it can happen to you, it can happen to me. Muslims and Methodists, Buddhists and Baptists have a right to believe what they want to believe. If they believe error, then there will be eternal consequences for that error. Of course, that would also be true of me. So be it.

I don't hate Muslims (or anyone else) and I wish them no harm. In fact, I love them as I do all people. I read Islam as **I S**incerely **L**ove **A**ll **M**uslims, and will try to show them by telling them the truth in this book. I have no reason to believe they are not sincere. I am sure many of them want to serve Allah and to be faithful to their "holy" book, as I want to serve Christ and be faithful to the Bible. You see, my convictions are as precious and important to me as theirs are to them. This is America where we can have honest disagreements without being disagreeable. We can contend without being contentious. However, you will discover on these pages that there are many sharp points of disagreement, and I plan to write **bluntly** to make my point.

It is interesting that the Muslim countries do not have freedom of speech, religion, assembly, and press; furthermore, their moderate leaders in those nations have not demanded such freedom since the terror attacks on America! Why are all the "moderates" so quiet on this subject? And why haven't American Muslims demanded freedom in Islamic nations? Is it because they are not moderates? You will be surprised with my exclusive interviews with Muslim leaders reported in this book.

RADICAL ISLAM

After September 11, President Bush told Americans that we are at war. He was correct. It is called *jihad*: a holy war that all Muslims know they are obligated to support, and that war is against Israel, America, and the free world. This war is the most unusual one we have ever fought. The enemy is not associated with one aggressive nation located on a fixed spot on earth. It is also true that Congress must declare war, and they have not done so. That is a mistake and major miscalculation on the part of the administration. The enemy is radical Islamists who want to destroy the U.S., and while we are not at war with Muslims, we are at war with Islam. We are fools if we do not admit that many Muslims are our sworn enemies. In fact, all koranic Muslims are at war with every person on earth who is not a Muslim!

There are 49 nations that have a majority of Muslim citizens and they all have one thing in common: they revere the Koran and many hold the Hadith as sacred as well. The Koran teaches that Allah is God and the world must recognize that fact; furthermore that Mohammed was his prophet. Moreover, all koranic Muslims believe that their sacred duty, their first duty, is to make all nations Islamic. Islam means to "surrender." They will work for surrender, pray for surrender, vote for surrender, lobby for surrender, talk you into surrender, and finally will behead you if you don't surrender.

If I see Muslims (or anyone else) being mistreated, I will come to their defense. No one should be harassed, intimidated, or punished for what he believes. There are many Muslims who are horrified at what happened in the many terrorist attacks. I accept their word that they are sincere. However, out of the millions of Muslims in America, many **do** believe in terror and **do** believe they will go to Paradise as their body bomb goes off or their hijacked plane explodes against a building, killing thousands of "infidels."

We have observed the horror of terrorism many times since the September 11, 2001 attack upon our nation: All over the Middle East, Boston, Fort Hood, Boston, San Bernardino, Paris, Brussels, etc.

Islam has erupted 67% in growth since the 9/11 attack.[2] It is the fastest growing religion in America, third in numbers behind Christians and Jews. All this is a result of legal and illegal immigration, births, and conversions mostly felon conversion in prisons.

Some of our politicians, preachers, and pundits are telling us that there are no differences in religions. One is as good as another. We are told that Islam is a religion of peace. I think those uninformed or dishonest people should stay in their own fields and not pretend to be theologians. Those people have a right to say what they want; however, I reject many of them, and I am compelled to rebuke them as Paul commands in II Timothy 4:2. Christians should be outraged when the pompous pundits equate Allah with the God of the Bible! Since the politicians work for me (I pay their salaries), I demand that they speak the truth or keep quiet on the subject.

ALL TERRORISTS HAVE BEEN MUSLIMS

I shall be accused of being a hater and bigot, but that doesn't negate my major premise that Muslim immigration, legal and illegal, will make us a third-world nation. Our culture is being altered as you read this book.

Muslim clerics will scream at me for being so intolerant; however, I insist that they point out my errors! They will say that I am slandering their religion, but if so, I am "slandering" it with truth and truth is far more important than political correctness.

I would like for a Muslim leader to tell me why he has the right to offend me with lies about Christ's deity, death, and resurrection and I am supposed to sit there and smile like an idiot, but I cannot point out the incredible contradictions, mistakes, and absurdities of Islam without being called a hater and threatened with death.

America opened her doors to Arabs and Muslims, and with the good guys have come the scum (we know that scum comes to the top as does cream). While all Muslims are not terrorists, all the terrorists have been Muslims! As a result of our open doors and porous borders along with an acceptance of Muslims, we have been kicked in the face. Some of our guests have repaid good with evil. It's past time to close our gates for a few years to Muslims and non-Muslims.

Folks, there isn't much anyone can do if there are dedicated, sincere, and fearless Muslims who have decided that we are their enemy. No amount of security measures will ever protect us against terrorist attacks. Those politicians who say we can **ever** be free of terror are dishonest, uninformed, or very naïve. Whatever the reason, they should run, not walk, to hand in their resignations. To say that we will eradicate evil is a silly, nonsensical statement.

PATHETIC U. S. RESPONSE

There is evidence that our government knew of Muslim terrorists many years ago but did nothing about it. We must hold politicians and bureaucrats accountable for their actions and inaction. Don't listen to their rhetoric but watch the reality. Public rhetoric after terrorist attacks attempts to assure Americans that Islam is a religion of peace, and many Americans have adopted that mantra since we **want** to believe it. However, after further attacks, killing thousands or maybe hundreds of thousands, politicians and the media will discard the unwisely adopted mantra that Islam is peaceful as quickly as a low-rated television show. But only after it is too late.

Astute people have noticed that state and federal officials, including Bush, Clinton and Obama always jumped to the defense of Muslims at every attack–even before any facts are known. And often after the facts were known!

It is interesting that Obama spoke at an Egyptian university in 2009, saying, "Islam is not part of the problem in combating violent extremism. It is an important part of promoting peace."[3] The President did not try to document his claim since every Tom, Dick, and Mohammed knew it was bogus. (That's a kind, pussy-footing way of saying Obama was lying through his teeth.)

There are many other examples but the January, 2016 shooting of a Philadelphia police officer is a good example.

Philadelphia Police officer Jesse Hartnett was shot 13 times in his police car by a Muslim follower of ISIS. Amazingly the officer lived. At a news conference the Philadelphia Police Commissioner, Richard Ross, Jr. reported that the perpetrator admitted he did it in the name of Islam since the police force enforces laws that contradict Islamic *sharia* law. Therefore the officer needed to die. While the chief spoke, the mayor, Jim Kenney glared at him. When the mayor spoke, he fussed, fumed, and fidgeted and said, "In no way, shape or form does anyone in this room believe that Islam or the teaching of Islam has anything to do with this... That is abhorrent. It's terrible and it does not represent the religion in any way, shape or form or any of its teachings. And this is a criminal with a stolen gun who tried to kill one of our officers. It has nothing to do with being a Muslim or following the Islamic faith in any way, shape or form."[4] The Honorable Mayor is a jerk, a dishonest jerk. No reporter had the knowledge or courage to ask if that was true, why did the terrorist clearly state that he was motivated by Islam?

Many public officials are making a concerted effort to "run interference" for Islam even if they resort lies to do so. Often it is a matter of them refusing to recognize Islamic terror as Islamic terror as in the killings at Fort Hood by a Muslim fanatic who yelled "Allah is the Greatest" as he shot 13 American soldiers dead and wounded many others. He was **not** tried as a terrorist but for murder and is on death row at Leavenworth Federal Prison.

Defenders of Islam stepped up following the *Charlie Hebdo* massacre in Paris in January of 2015 when the president of France made an international fool of himself when he declared, "Those who committed these acts have nothing to do with the Muslim religion." The fact is, everyone except he, Obama, and some other fanatic leftists know it had **everything** to do with the Muslim religion. Muslim fanatics were agitated that the irreverent magazine had insulted Mohammed.

In this book I will deal with the religion of Islam and the impact it has had on the world and the influence it has and will have on America and Canada. You will be shocked at the magnitude of the Muslim invasion of North America; the hatred toward anything Christian; that many Muslim children are trained from infancy to become killers of "infidels"; at the pugnacious policies of Muslim leaders; at the numerous mistakes in their holy book; at the root cause of Muslims' hatred; at the very real nuclear, chemical, and biological threat to millions of Americans; at how we may respond to major disasters; and finally, at what our response should be to the legal and illegal migrations of Muslims into America.

It is Christ who sets men free, and if we fail to liberate Muslims from Islam, they will be stepping on your face in a very few years. I think you will find this book interesting, informative, and somewhat infuriating, but mainly you will be able to make decisions about your own security and response to the Islamic invasion.

Read on and remember that as you read, the fuse is burning!

References:

1   Leon Uris, *The Haj*, Bantam Books, 1985, Kindle Edition.
2   New York *Daily News*, May 3, 2012.
3   White House News Release, "Remarks by the President at Cairo University," June 4, 2009.
4   New York *Daily News*, Jan. 8, 2016.

Chapter One

Suicidal Slaves to Islam!

It was the best of times; it was the worst of times. History will record that in the summer of 2001, America was in clover. There was high employment, and while the stock market was slipping, few people thought it would hit bottom. Things were looking good for America. We had elected a professing Christian as President who wasn't ashamed of his faith in Christ. All of us received a tax refund with promises of more tax cuts. While there were indications that jobs were going south, we were still the financial power of the earth. Moreover, no informed person questioned our military superiority.

Then on September 11, 2001, the world changed forever when 19 Muslim terrorists from Egypt and Saudi Arabia flew two planes into the twin towers of the World Trade Center in Manhattan and one into the Pentagon in Washington causing over 3000 deaths. Another plane crashed in Pennsylvania before it reached Washington. It is not incidental that those targets represented America's perceived strength: commerce and military. They hit us where we were the strongest. And they made us bleed.

Americans watched in horror as the two massive towers fell, trapping thousands of innocent people inside. There were many acts of courage and some of infamy: police and fire fighters rushed into the burning buildings to save lives and scabs on society robbed the dead and used stolen credit cards to plunder victims' bank accounts. Articles in many national papers on August 6, 2002 revealed: "4,000 use ATMs to steal $15 million." That is literally robbing the dead.

Americans were shocked, startled, and surprised but we should not have been since Muslims had attacked us in 1993 with the first terrorist attack on U.S. soil at the World Trade Center. Even that attack by Muslims did not produce ringing bells, flashing lights, and whining sirens as a warning. Why not? It was because our leaders were deaf, dumb, and blind, or in other words, pluralists, multiculturalists, and humanists. They did not and do not understand that Muslims had started World War III that would last decades!

Informed, thinking, and concerned people should be aware of our imminent danger from Muslim terrorists who are capable of anything. Those who are uninformed, unconcerned, and unaware of the Muslim threat are like a man walking waist-deep through a snake and alligator infested Everglade's swamp. They are going to get bit. We have been bit a number of times but still have not learned. Koranic Muslims are dedicated to killing us and taking control yet they are still defended by American patsies, pacifists, and prevaricators.

If we had been realists and not obsessed with broad-mindedness, pluralism, and political correctness, we would have seen the Islamic attacks coming. Informed people know that Islam plans to accomplish world dominion by sperm, speech, and sword.

PREACHERS: CHEERLEADERS FOR DESTRUCTION

Since the attack, many blinded eyes have miraculously received sight concerning incompetent government and irrational religion, but until I'm proved wrong, I still believe most Americans are using a white-tipped cane as they walk the streets. Before the dust and smoke cleared from the attacks, religious leaders stumbled over each other to get to television cameras to absolve Islam from any guilt. In doing so, they displayed political correctness and personal cowardice. They will be recognized as cheerleaders for our destruction. Those sickly, smiling clergymen wearing pantyhose, silk shorts, lace around their shirts, and sniffing French perfume from frilly handkerchiefs made me ashamed to be an American, let alone a preacher. Most Americans want leaders with hair on their chests, bone in their backs, and a brain in their heads. Many clergymen lack all three.

Leaders who are afraid of adverse public opinion and being labeled "conservative" (gasp!) or "Fundamentalist" (gasp! gasp!) are moral cripples who are not aware of their limp and crooked walk. Such leaders, in crises, are as useless as a milking stool under a bull. When courageous leaders such as Franklin Graham, Jerry Falwell, Jerry Vines, Pat Robertson, and others spoke the truth about the Islamic invasion, unprincipled politicians, preachers, and pundits fled from them like the mythical vampire flees the rising sun. Soft religious leaders are now building bridges (of mist) between Christianity and Islam, and the uninformed who cross that bridge of mist will fall into a noxious swamp of unbelief.

It is astounding that religious leaders would come to the defense of a religion that produced such a massacre of innocent people plus all the beheading and other torturous killings, but men such as the late television preacher Robert Schuller did. He even had a Muslim imam (cleric) on his television show! Just one reason many thinking people considered Schuller to be the biggest phony in America.

Another soft, sensitive, servile preacher is Bill Hybels of Willow Creek Community Church in Illinois, and I think he is President of the League of the Willfully Blind! According to Voice of the Martyrs website, Hybels also had a Muslim leader in his pulpit on October 7, 2001. Faisal Hammouda said, "We believe in Jesus more than you do, in fact." Did Bill correct him with the truth that Muslims do not believe Christ is divine or that he died for our sins? No, Bill Hybels wants everyone to feel warm and fuzzy. He may think he is showing love, but love is not love without truth. Without that truth, his love would encourage Muslims in their unbelief. Our concern should not be inter-religious tolerance but regeneration of the lost. Maybe he should try to "build bridges" between Islam and the thousands of widows and orphans of those who died in the various terrorist attacks since September 11, 2001 to 2016.

TERRORISTS ARE NOT COWARDS

Many pundits, politicians, and preachers called the killers cowards or crazies but they were hardly that. These assassins were dedicated to their cause and their cause was Islam. It does take some courage to follow a plan from which one knows there is no hope of escape. To steer a plane into a building is criminal. It is atrocious; it is hideous, but it is not cowardly. They were sadistic, suicidal slaves to Islam and their number is legion. They plan to destroy our culture as they are doing today in various European nations. According to the Federal Statistical Office of Germany of the 80 million people in Germany in 2010 at least 20% were of "immigrant background." In 2014, more than half the residents of Brussels were of third-world origin. In 2015, 53% of children in schools in Vienna,

Austria, were of "immigrant origin." Only a blind fool says those facts have no changing effect on a society.

Most Islamic killers were not cowardly nor were they deranged. It was murder but not madness. They were all educated young men who worked diligently to complete a dastardly task: to murder innocent people and to spread fear down every street, from the hovels of Appalachia to the palatial mansions of Beverly Hills. They succeeded in accomplishing the worst terrorist attack upon America, but it was not, as some have said, the first Muslim attack upon our nation.

America has had trouble with Muslims since our earliest days when Muslim Barbary Pirates (today's Morocco, Algeria, Libya, and Tunisia) attacked our merchant ships in the Mediterranean Sea, enslaved the crews and held them for ransom or "tribute" as it was called. The Muslim pirates were not cowards but they were thieves. Of course, they got that from Mohammed who was a Prince of Thieves.

MUSLIM PIRATES

Muslims had been attacking European merchant ships since the 13th century. It is believed that perhaps 1.5 million Europeans and Americans were enslaved by Muslims in North Africa between 1530 and 1780! In fact, the complete town of Baltimore, Ireland was taken into Muslim slavery in one night.[1]

American ships were attacked by Muslim pirates starting in 1628 with more attacks continuing to the end of the century when they soon diminished. Large ransoms were paid to attain the release of some of the hostages. Then, in 1783 and 1784 before we had even one warship (while the Muslims had many) the Barbary pirates attacked three American merchant ships. The American seamen were paraded through the streets of Fez and Algiers as Muslims threw rotten vegetables and entrails of butchered animals at them. They were forced to kneel before the emperor who told them, "I'll make you eat stones, Christian dogs," then he sold them into slavery.[2]

The discussion in America was whether to continue paying tribute to the Muslim pirates or fight a war. John Adams was reluctant to go to war and said: "We ought not to fight them at all unless we determine to fight them forever."[3] Man was he right!

James Madison wrote in the *Federalist Papers* that the "rapacious demands of pirates and barbarians"[4] on the sea was a good reason to have a strong central government. Thomas Jefferson refused to be intimidated by them and preferred confrontation with Muslim pirates to blackmail. Our third President called on the U. S. Marines to solve the problem. They did. The problem was solved from the "shores of Montezuma to the shores of Tripoli." Muslims are rather slow but they do understand force. Since that time, the Middle East has become an ugly scab on the face of the world.

BEHIND THE MUSLIM BLACK CURTAIN

The Middle East is a writhing, dangerous snake pit that is a threat to not only the Middle East but also the world. The question is: who is responsible to kill the deadly vipers? I think fellow Muslims should climb into the pit and do the killing; it's time moderate Muslims clean up their own house.

And be assured that after the Sunnis and Shias bomb each other, those remaining will turn their sights on Israel and the free world. U.S. and world officials don't want to admit it but we are in a Hundred Years' War!

Americans need to understand, contrary to all the radical leftist propaganda, that the barbarians are not **at** the gates; they are **inside** the gates. Meanwhile, U.S. politicians and religious leaders stand around sucking their thumbs as a strange wooden horse has been pulled even deeper inside our national borders.

Few people know what lurks behind the black curtain of Islam. Muslim lackeys in America dance, joke, sing, and pretend to be normal Americans; however, they never show the true face of Islam–until they take control. The plan is: take total control of every nation peacefully if possible through conversion, immigration, high birth rate, but with the sword if necessary. If any educated Muslim (or non-Muslim) denies that fact, he is a liar, lackey, or lunatic–literally.

My Medina-approved (publication of Saudi Arabia) Koran, therefore being an official publication, clearly admits in a footnote: "All mankind will be required to embrace Islam with no other alternative."[5] One does not have to be a Muslim scholar to understand that–a World caliphate!

The Council for American-Islamic Relations (CAIR) pretends to be a civil rights group dedicated to improve relations between Muslims and Americans; however, it is a front for implementing *sharia*. It has connections to every other Muslim Brotherhood terrorist group in North America.

The founder of (CAIR), Omar Ahmad, made a damning, infamous statement to a group of Muslims that has come back to bite him in his derrière: "Islam isn't in America to be equal to any other faith, but to become dominant. The Koran, the Muslim book of scripture, should be the highest authority in America, and Islam the only accepted religion on Earth."[6] Omar denies making the contemptible statement that is true to the Koran; however, the reporter and editor stand by the quote. Omar is telling all who listen that the paper recanted the story but that is not true.

Mohamed Akram, a top Muslim Brotherhood operative, wrote a memorandum in 1991 that revealed their purpose. It was an internal correspondence that was meant for the eyes only of the organization's leadership in Egypt. It unambiguously states that the mission of the Muslim Brotherhood in North America is to destroy "Western civilization from within … by [the infidels'] hands and the hands of the believers so that Allah's religion is made victorious over all other religions."[7] Yet, their spokesmen have been White House guests!

Keep in mind that Muslims are permitted to lie if it furthers the Islamic push toward a world caliphate and make no mistake, that's where they are headed.

On April 1, 2016, Muslims marched through Germany yelling, "With Allah's help, we shall conquer you." The German leader proudly opened the gates and the hordes came rushing in and the world is watching Germany die.

And America is marching over the same cliff that Germany marched over.

Ibrahim Hooper, National Communications Director for CAIR declared, "If Muslims ever become a majority in the United States, it would be safe to assume that they would want to replace the U.S. Constitution with Islamic law, as most Muslims believe that God's law is superior to manmade law."[8] That's from the horses' mouth!

WHAT MUSLIMS REALLY WANT

It will be helpful to know what Muslims think, believe, and want when trying to assess their status as citizens and if you want them as neighbors. Obviously, it is not only a small number of Muslims who are violent. Read and weep:

- 83 percent of Palestinian Muslims, 62 percent of Jordanians and 61 percent of Egyptians approve of jihadist attacks on Americans![9]

- 1.5 million British Muslims support the Islamic State, about half Britain's total Muslim population.[10]

- Two-thirds of Palestinians support the stabbing of Israeli civilians.[11]

- 38.6 percent of Western Muslims believe the 9/11 attacks were justified.[12]

- 45 percent of British Muslims agree that clerics preaching violence against the West represent "mainstream Islam."[13]

- One-third of British Muslim students support killing for Islam.[14]

- 80 percent of young Dutch Muslims see nothing wrong with holy war against non-believers. Most verbalized support for pro-Islamic state fighters.[15]

- 81 percent of Muslim respondents support the Islamic State (ISIS).[16]

- 68 percent of British Muslims support the arrest and prosecution of anyone who insults Islam.[17]

- 51 percent of Muslim-**Americans** say that Muslims should have the choice of being judged by *sharia* courts rather than courts of the United States (only 39 percent disagree). Furthermore, nearly 25 percent believed the use of violent *jihad* would be justified in establishing *sharia*![18]

- Nearly one-third of Muslim-**Americans** agree that violence against those who insult Muhammad or the Koran is acceptable.[19]

- 38 percent of Muslim-**Americans** say Islamic State (ISIS) beliefs are Islamic or correct.[20] (Forty-three percent disagree.)

For sure, the fuse is burning.

SHARIA IN YOUR FUTURE

What did Bush, Obama, Clinton, and others say about Islam being a peaceful religion? Obviously, most Muslims want *sharia* law for them and you. *Sharia* can't happen in America we are told; however, it is happening today in Europe! The media reported that a German court approved "Shariah police" permitting them to "patrol" the city streets searching for violators of *sharia* law. Moreover, a judge ruled that Muslim "police" who were arrested in Wuppertal, Germany in 2014 for harassing people entering bars, casinos, and clubs were not guilty.

In London, police substantiated Donald Trump's charge that there are "no-go" zones in English cities and officials in London and Birmingham have told cops not to wear their uniforms while in their cop cars. Officials in Lancashire now ask permission to enter any Muslim area.[21]

Sharia is not compatible with freedom. All over the world Muslims' crude signs expose the fact that they hate democracy: "To Hell with democracy," and "No Democracy–We Just Want Islam!" Mesbah Yazdi said "democracy, freedom, and human rights have no place" in Islam. Muslim cleric Ibrahim Saddiq Conlan said, "Democracy is evil, the parliament is evil and legislation is evil."

Moreover, two Muslim groups in Denmark called on Muslims to boycott their elections explaining, "We are committed to being active participants in our society, but it has to be on Islam's terms, without compromising our own principles and values. Democracy is fundamentally incompatible with Islam, and it is a sinking ship."[22] The Grimshøj Mosque in Aarhus agreed, issuing a statement saying that "people should stay clear of the voting booths. We have concluded that only Allah can pass laws, as he says himself in the Koran that this is so."

So, what would a nation ruled by dedicated Muslims be like and how would it be contrary to the U.S. Constitution? Read, then do something about it.

In court, for a woman to prevail in a rape case she must have four men to testify she was raped. Has anyone asked why four men would permit a woman to be raped? Often the rape **victim** is punished or even killed!

All females will be sexually mutilated by removing the clitoris. This "surgery" is illegal yet common in England and no one has been prosecuted! However, it is illegal to spank a child there and there are numerous prosecutions!

Everyone will be a Muslim or pay an excessive tax.

Any Muslim who wants to convert to Christ will be killed and the one who led him away from Islam will be killed!

A Muslim man can divorce his wife but the wife must have permission to divorce her husband.

No pork, no rock music, no booze, no nudity on television or movies. Well, I didn't say that **everything** about Islam was bad!

No skin will show on female bodies. Ladies will no longer wonder, "What will I wear today?" You **know** what you will wear! It is black and covers your whole body.

There will be no separation of mosque and state. You will be controlled by the Muslim imam down at the local mosque. If you don't go to the mosque, you can be beheaded as was a teenager in Syria in March of 2016. He missed Friday prayers at the mosque! Other teens were killed for listening to popular music!

Your state and nation will be run by Muslim clerics.

There can be no criticism of the Koran or Islam, or even joking about it, under penalty of death!

Four wives will be permissible and, if necessary, they can be legally beaten.

All school children will memorize the Koran and repeat each day, "In the name of God, the Merciful, the Compassionate" and you will hear the call to prayer five times each day from the local mosque. Omar Ahmed the founder of the Council of American Islamic Relations (CAIR). "Islam isn't in America to be equal to any other faith, but to become dominant. The Koran is the highest authority in America and Islam is the only accepted religion on the earth."

Now, in light of the above facts, it would be insane to permit any koranic Muslim to run for **any** U.S. office. The disciples of the illiterate camel-driver want to totally revolutionize your world and they are scheming to accomplish that while Americans sleep.

JIHAD IS HOLY WAR

Leading Muslim mullahs have clearly endorsed war with the non-Muslim world. Every healthy, adult Muslim is obligated to help conquer every country so the Koran (Muslims' holy book along with the Hadith) can be implemented in that society. The *Dictionary of Islam* clearly defines *jihad* as "a religious war with those who are unbelievers in the mission of Muhammad. It is an incumbent religious duty, established in the Quran [Koran] and in the Traditions as a divine institution, enjoined specially for the purpose of advancing Islam and of repelling evil from Muslims."[23]

The purpose of "repelling evil from Muslims" compels Islam to change all societies, which requires forced conversion. It is disingenuous for Muslim clerics to say otherwise. Muslims insist on change of life whether or not there is a change of heart. Christians have no such mandate to use force. Besides, force can never produce genuine conversions to Christ.

Muslims quickly tell all who will listen that *jihad* means inner struggle, but history clearly proves that it means struggle against the non-Muslim world! "*Jihad*, or holy war, means an active struggle, using armed force whenever necessary. The object of *jihad* is not the conversion of individuals to Islam but rather the gaining of political control over the collective affairs of societies to run them in accordance with the principles of Islam. Individual conversions occur as a by-product of this process when the power structure passes into the hands of the Muslim community."[24] The *Encyclopedia Britannica* admitted in their Ready Reference computer edition: "Muslims are enjoined to defend Islam against unbelievers through *jihad*."

So it is no surprise that Muslims, after Mohammed's death, deftly wielded the sword across the Arabian Peninsula, around North Africa and Europe, leaving a prodigious amount of human skulls in their wake. It is no surprise that the butchery is still taking place. It's what all Muslims are taught from birth as they memorize the Koran and hear their Islamic clerics belch out vile, vicious, and vitriolic hatred against all "unbelievers," especially Jews and Christians.[25]

Middle East terrorist Yasser Arafat bellowed: "We know but one word: struggle, struggle. *Jihad, Jihad, Jihad*. When we stop our *intifada,* when we stop our revolution, we go to the greater *Jihad*, the *Jihad* of the independent Palestinian state with its capital Jerusalem." Peace maker? I think not. George Will quoted Arafat's Palestinian television station as it gave Arafat's following instructions: "All weapons must be aimed at the Jews... whom the Koran describes as monkeys and pigs....We will enter Jerusalem as conquerors....Blessings to he who shot a bullet into the head of a Jew."[26] That doesn't sound like "inner struggle" but inner hatred.

Abdallah al-Shami, Muslim terrorist, said "We want this successful operation to prove to the terrorist (Israel Prime Minister, Ariel Sharon) that we can, and we will continue to get him and his fellow pigs and monkeys where it hurts the most."[27] Al-Shami was a senior Islamic *jihad* official who was killed in 2008 by U.S. forces.

TERRORISM IS RELIGIOUS DUTY

The poster boy of terror, Osama bin Laden, put a fine point on terror when he, along with other terrorist leaders, issued this *fatwa* against all Americans: "The ruling to kill the Americans and their allies–civilians and military–is an individual duty for every Muslim who can do it in any country in which it is possible to do it, in order to liberate the al-Aqsa Mosque [in Jerusalem] and the Holy Mosque [in Mecca] from their grip, and in order for their Armies to remove out of all the lands of Islam.... We–with God's help–call on every Muslim who believes in God and wishes to be rewarded to comply with God's order to kill the Americans and plunder their money wherever and whenever they find it."[28]

With a history of terror and blood shedding and major charismatic leaders preaching *jihad,* it is no surprise that "lesser lights" in the Islamic world are parroting the same message. A Muslim sheikh in London praised young boys who are learning to fire Kalashnikovs rifles. On tapes sold in London bookstores Abdullah el-Faisal calls for Muslims to kill "filthy Jews" because they are "evil to the core."[29]

This Apostle of Violence has made two tapes since September 11 calling for all males to train to kill infidels. The bum should be bounced from London, but then I must not suggest that our culture is superior to their seventh-century, desert culture. The sheikh is getting money from the European Development Fund, when I think he should be dropped (by parachute, of course) from a plane onto the Arabian Desert. These zealots are as mean as a menopausal Rottweiler.

Mohammed made it very clear in the Hadith to the most dense Muslim that *jihad* was normal and is required for Islamic followers. Mohammed once was asked: what is the best deed for the Muslim next to believing in Allah and His Apostle? His answer was to "participate in Jihad in Allah's cause" (Al Bukhari vol. 1, book 2, number 25). Mohammed was quoted as saying: "I have been ordered to fight with the people till they say, none has the right to be worshipped but Allah" (Al Bukhari vol. 4, book 52, number 196).

Mohammed also said, "The person who participates in (Holy Battles) in Allah's cause and nothing compels him to do so except belief in Allah and His Apostle, will be recompensed by Allah either with a reward, or booty (if he survives) or will be admitted to paradise (if he is killed)" (Al Bukhari vol. 1, book 2, number 35).

I will return to *Jihad* in later chapters.

SAUDIS SUPPORT TERROR

The royal family in Saudi Arabia has been pumping billions of dollars into extremist Islam **while** they talk about supporting U. S. efforts to wipe out terror! The Saudi royal family not only sees both sides of the issue, they **take** both sides! Of course, much of that money comes from America through purchase of oil. At least the royal family is diversified, since they fund many facets of Islam. They have supported the infamous al-Qaeda network inside the kingdom as well as in the Balkans, Afghanistan, and Somalia. The pitch from analysts is that the royal family doesn't really want to support the terrorists, but since they must live with them, it is only safe to do so. In other words, it is protection money to keep the royal family alive and on the throne.

The Saudis support over 200 Islamic centers, more than 1500 mosques, over 200 colleges, and almost 2,000 schools throughout the world. They have established chairs in various U.S. colleges such as University of California Santa Barbara, Harvard (five million), as well as University of London, University of Moscow, and others. Schools such as Duke University, Johns Hopkins University, Syracuse University, and Howard University have had "research institutes" set up.[30] Question: Would any of those prestigious schools permit the KKK to establish a chair on "Issues of Race"? No, then an honest person must believe those educators are sanctimonious hypocrites!

Former President Bush stated that the U.S. was not only going after the actual terrorists but those who aid and abet them in their terrorism. That includes the nations that sponsor, harbor, or fund them. Did he really mean that? If so, why did he snuggle up to the Saudi leaders? Could it be, dare I say it? Oil!

It is easy to demonize the terrorists in Iraq, Iran, Turkmenistan, Uzbekistan, and all the other "stans," but what about the big oil producers? What about the big boys in China, Russia, and others? Some of the nations that are supposed to be supporting our war are helping our enemies! Americans should demand consistency from politicians.

CAN WE TRUST OUR GOVERNMENT?

There are myths that revolve around Muslim terrorists, Islam, and U.S. activities; thinking people must look with a critical eye to arrive at the truth. We can disagree with our government without questioning its legitimacy, and one can love his country yet fear his government. Can we always trust government? Ask an American Indian. It must also be understood that it is reasonable, not treasonable, to question government. Maybe, if more patriotic Americans questioned the authorities, those authorities might not question us. Only fools accept everything they are told. God tells us in I Thessalonians 5:21 to "prove all things." The following two chapters will help you distinguish myth from reality.

References:

1   Christopher Hitchens, "Jefferson Versus the Muslim Pirates," Spring 2007 issue of *City* magazine.

2   Michael B. Oren, "The Middle East and the Making of the United Sates, 1776 to 1815," Columbia News, accessed April 12, 2016.

3   Letter from John Adams to Thomas Jefferson, July 31, 1786

4   James Madison, *The Federalist*, #41.

5   *The Noble Koran*, King Fahd Complex for the Printing of the Holy Koran, p. 236.

6   Speech by Omar Ahmad, San Ramon Valley *Herald*, July 2, 1998.

7   Mohamed Akram, "The Explanatory Memorandum on the General Strategic Goal of the Group in North America," reported by WND, April 18, 2016.

8   Ibrahim Hooper on the Michael Medved Radio Show, Oct. 2003.

9   World Public Opinion Poll, 2009.

10 ICM Mirror Poll, 2015.

11 Palestinian Center for Policy and Survey Research, 2015.

12 Gallup, 2011.

13 *BBC* Radio, 2015.

14 Center for Social Cohesion, WikiLeaks cable.

15 Motivaction Survey 2014.

16 Al-Jazeera poll, 2015.

17 NOP Research, "NOP Poll of British Muslims," Aug. 8, 2006.

18 The Polling Company CSP Poll, 2015.

19 Ibid.

20 Ibid.

21 WND reported on Dec. 11, 2015.

22 Robert Spencer, *Jihad Watch*, June 6, 2015.

23 Quoted by Ibn Warraq in *Why I Am Not a Muslim*, Prometheus Books, Amherst, NY, 1995, p. 12.

24 *The New Encyclopedia Britannica*, Edition 15, vol. 22, p. 8.

25 *The Philadelphia Trumpet*, vol. 12, number 7, August 2001, p. 5.

26 Quoted by George Will in syndicated column August 18, 2001.
27 *USA Today,* August 10, 2001.
28 *The Banner,* Michigan Conservative Union, Fall 2001.
29 *The American Spectator,* "Watch Your Tongue," March/April 2002.
30 *WorldNetDaily,* Oct. 30, 2001.

Chapter Two

Does God Cause Terror Attacks and other Myths?

Some have suggested that God brought the Muslim terrorist attacks on Paris, Brussels, San Bernardino, Orlando, etc., as His judgment upon mankind for personal and national sins. So, God is to blame for the terror! Others tell us that if God exists He would never bring judgment upon a nation. Still others tell us that God is too puny to intercede on man's behalf or doesn't care what happens to men. What is the fact and what is fallacy? What are some myths being promoted today as they relate to the Muslim plan to produce a world caliphate and can those myths be dangerous to you and America?

God is **never** the author of evil, so He is not the instigator of terror attacks on America. God does permit evil to happen for the present time, but He is never the author of evil. Evil happens because God gave each person a will to decide between right and wrong. When a person chooses wrong, God has no pleasure in his wickedness. God will not forbid a person to take the wrong path, and a person is free to do atrocious acts; but of course, at the end of the chosen path is judgment. All of us will be accountable for our decisions, usually here and always hereafter.

We know that God does not tempt any person, but men are tempted and led astray by demonic influences. Men do evil things, such as killing innocent people, because they are of their father the devil. John 8:44 reveals, "Ye are of your father the devil, and the lusts of your father ye will do. He was a murderer from the beginning, and abode not in the truth, because there is no truth in him. When he speaketh a lie, he speaketh of his own: for he is a liar, and the father of it."

Men kill innocent people because their father (Satan) was a murderer from the beginning. Men do wicked things because they have wicked hearts and out of the heart come the issues of life. Proverbs 4:23 reminds us: "Keep thy heart with all diligence; for out of it are the issues of life." These lost, depraved Muslims are only doing the work of their father. They, like all men, do evil because they think evil, and they think evil because they **are** evil. Proverbs 23:7, "For as he thinketh in his heart, so is he." Without Christ, any of us could do incredibly wicked things.

My talk show opponents have said that God does not exist or if He does, he is a puny, impotent God not deserving of worship and obedience. After all, an all-powerful, all-knowing, and all-loving God would never permit babies to be born blind, crippled, or dead or permit millions to starve in slum conditions. However, they are wrong and Darwin, Voltaire, and thousands of others have "gone down with that ship." They indicted God when He was not guilty.

NOT PUPPETS

Yes, God knew that terrorists were going to kill thousands of innocent people, but He did not create men to be puppets. We each have the ability to choose right or wrong. The Muslim terrorists chose death for themselves and others. That was not God's choice. God loves mankind and reciprocal love is a free choice or it isn't love. True love, human or divine, can never be forced. Who would want a love that was coerced, even if that were possible? When we have a choice, it cannot simply be a choice of good. Evil must be an option; the terrorists **chose** evil. John 3:19 tells us: "And this is the condemnation, that light is come into the world, and men loved darkness rather than light, because their deeds were evil."

God could have created us as puppets or robots that cannot know love or fellowship or make choices. However, since we were created for fellowship with a sovereign God, we must have the ability to refuse love and fellowship and choose between right and wrong. The will to do wrong must be as equally available as the will to do right. Terrorists choose to do wrong, and to blame a sovereign God for man's decision to do evil is unfair, unreasonable, and unscriptural.

The natural laws were established at the Creation and men must live by those laws. If a person jumps or falls from a building, he will fall because the law of gravity demands it. God is not to be blamed. We are all aware of the possibility of falling, so we are careful when we are at high places. God could keep every person from falling when he stubs his toe, but that was not part of the original plan. We are free to fall and to fail.

What kind of existence would we have if we were forced to love, give, and obey, and if there were no possibility of doing wrong because we had been created as fleshly robots? If we never made a mistake? If we always did the right thing because it was impossible to do the wrong thing? We would love God because it would be impossible not to love Him? God chose not to design us that way. He gave us a will to choose, and He longs to have us choose to love and fellowship with Him.

SOCIETY IS NOT CHRISTIAN

In reading the Koran, I have found no place where a person is command-ed to love another! The closest I found was sura 76:8 "And they give food out of **love** for Him to the poor and the orphan and the captive." Love is mentioned 83 times in the Koran and frequently it is used to inform us what Allah does **not** love. He does not love the proud, the boastful, the unbeliever, etc.

No, God did not stop the terrorist attacks, but that was **not** because He was helpless or wanted the attacks to occur. Those men chose to attack because of their sinful nature. God only permitted them to exercise their free will. If something or someone much higher than himself does not guide man, he will often do wrong and he will be held accountable.

If a person is a Muslim, he will act like a Muslim and will attempt to follow the tenets of the Koran and the Hadith. It will not be surprising if that person is violent. If a person is a Christian, he will attempt to follow the principles of the Bible. He will realize that he is a new creature in Christ and is expected to live Christ-like. He will want to do right and not wrong. He will want to love and not hate. He will want to give rather than take. He will want to forgive rather than hold a grudge. In this day when old truths have been ridiculed, revised, and rejected, the Bible stands as it has for centuries as a trustworthy guide to the lost, as encouragement to the lonely, and a map for the pilgrim. Furthermore, it is an indictment of the liberal.

Our society is not Christian, but it has been "Christianized." Men have an imperfect view of the Bible, self, Christ, life, death, etc., but there are flashes, from time to time, of awesome Bible truth and Christian living.

Muslims have little conception of Bible principles and Godly living. That is why many Muslims are not appalled at beheadings, chopping off limbs, yanking out tongues, and prying out eyes. And beatings are an honorable way of following Allah. They have known that as standard operating procedure, so they shrug their shoulders and walk away.

Therefore, it is a myth to think that God caused the terrorist attacks; or that He was too weak to do anything about it; or that if He exists, He would have forbidden it to happen.

ARE ALL RELIGIONS EQUAL?

Another myth is that one religion is as good as another, that all are equal. What is really meant is that truth doesn't matter, and in fact, religion doesn't matter. Follow any religion you want and if you are sincere, then truth is totally irrelevant. That sounds so tolerant, so broadminded, and so kind; however, it is so untrue. If there is a sovereign God (and there is), then He is concerned with truth and wants His creatures to know the truth. He surely does not want us to be involved with error. Truth sets us free. It's God's heaven and He can tell us the prerequisite for entry.

The perpetrators of the above myth want us to believe that the religion of a small Amazon tribe that worships the rivers, snakes, the Sun, etc., and who, at times, eat their fellow men, is just as acceptable, right, and civilized as the teaching of the Word of God that has stood the test of time. Alternatively, the suggestion that Muslims, following an immoral slaveholder, killer, and desert thief, even compares to Christians is falsehood, foolishness, and folly.

Listen as a church full of **changed** Christians sing, "How Great Thou Art" and then watch Muslims hoot and holler as they throw stones at the devil! But the plan is in place to consider all religions equal, that is, except evangelical and fundamental Christianity! We are the ones the multiculturalists love to hate. They tolerate everyone except us; after all, toleration has its limits!

CATHOLIC STATEMENT

The Roman Catholic Church issued a statement on Islam that is tolerant, gracious, and kind but without any regard for truth. It makes everyone, especially those who constructed the Trojan Horse, feel so warm, fuzzy, and good. The Catholic statement[1] says, "For the Muslim, Allah is none other than the God of Moses and Jesus." Now the authors of that statement and the editor who approved it are either dishonest or uninformed. Moreover, it may only be that they are uninformed. Islam teaches that Christ is not Deity; that He did not die on the cross; that He is not part of the Trinity. It is bad enough that Muslims make Christ a mortal man, but that very mortality would also make Him a liar or a lunatic. I believe He was neither; He was, is, and always will be Lord.

The Catholics also said, "One can therefore understand the Muslims' protest at the all too frequent custom in European languages of saying 'Allah' instead of 'God' [implying a difference when referring to the god of Islam]." Again, this statement makes the Muslims feel good and accepted by civilized people and it makes the Catholics feel good in being so kind and ecumenical, but to say there is no difference in Allah and the God of the Bible is contrary to the facts of history. The Bible clearly teaches about those who reject the doctrine of Christ in II John 1:9: "Whosoever transgresseth, and abideth not in the doctrine of Christ, hath not God."

In another chapter, I go into more detail on this subject but suffice it to say that Allah was a pagan god known throughout the Middle East hundreds of years before Mohammed was born! Allah was one of 360 pagan gods worshiped in Mecca. It's a matter of history, and all the subterfuge by Muslims and the sentimentalism of Catholics will not change the facts, since facts are very stubborn.

The bleating heart sentimentalists continue: "In fact, Islam was hardly any more fanatical during its history than the sacred bastions of Christianity whenever the Christian faith took on, as it were, a political value." Many will be surprised that I agree with that statement. I agree because they are not referring to Bible Christianity but to Roman Catholicism. Moreover, the Catholic Crusades and the Inquisition are two of the most disgraceful events in history.

Now we are all aware of the deplorable history of the Crusades (see chapter 13), but just to keep the record straight, it was the popes, priests, and prelates of the Roman Catholic Church who traveled across Europe to plan, preach, and promote the Crusades. I'm not mean, or malicious, or mad (well, maybe a little), but I do insist on the truth. You don't find Bible-believing Christians participating in the Crusades and loping off the heads of Jews and Turks, nor are Christians steering planes into buildings or exploding bombs in civilian areas. Just as terror is born and bred in Muslim homes and mosques, the Crusades were born and bred in the Roman Catholic Church.

Finally, the Roman Catholic Church statement tries to convince us that those who believe "Islam is a hide-bound religion, which keeps its followers in a kind of superannuated Middle Ages" are a bunch of bigots. Wait a minute. Isn't it obvious that Islam is a seventh-century culture right off the desert? They insist that women wear a veil or the burqa (that would be reasonable for desert life); that "justice" is done by chopping off hands and feet, tearing out tongues, beheading people for minor crimes, and even for converting to another religion. Of course, it is a religion and culture of the Middle Ages, and even the Roman Catholic Church cannot change that fact.

INTOLERANT CHRISTIANS

Some liberal, mythmaking "Christians" tell us that Islam is not that much different from Christianity and there is much we can learn from it. One man said that if a monk from the sixth-century Byzantine Empire were to come back today, he would find much more that was familiar in the practices and beliefs of a modern Muslim than he would find in a contemporary American evangelical church. Such a man is obviously uninformed as to Islam, evangelicalism, or both. Even Billy Graham said, "I think we're closer to Islam than we really think we are..."[2] Graham was wrong.

Television preacher Robert Schuller said that it wouldn't bother him if he came back in a hundred years and found all his descendants were followers of Mohammed! Let me remind him that Muslims have always denied the deity and Gospel of Christ and the Trinity. To suggest that there is any comparison of Islam and Bible Christianity is insensitive, incredible, and insane.

We are seeing Bible-believing Christians demonized in the media to make Muslims appear more acceptable. It is another myth that Bible-believers are an aberration of Christianity. The fact is we are the mainstream; however, there is a continuing trend to demonize conservative Christians.

NO CHRISTIAN TERRORISTS

The term "fundamentalism" is almost always used in a pejorative and negative way. It is incredible that many educated people don't know what it means: it simply means to get back to the fundamentals! Consider a basketball team that has lost every game during the season and the coach decides that the team must "get back to fundamentals," so he starts a session with his team around him by saying, "This is a basketball. This is a dribble. This is how you pass." That is back to basics.

That is what a Fundamentalist is without going into the historical background of the origination of the word which is not necessary here. There are fundamental Jews, fundamental Muslims, and fundamental Christians. Keep in mind that since all Muslims say they believe in the Koran and the Hadith, they are all supposed to be fundamentalists!

There is a definite separation of "Christians." There are non-believing liberals who do not accept the Bible as the Word of God and those of us who do. If unbelieving liberal preachers had any character, they would admit they are not Christians, and resign their pulpits to sell insurance. After all, they took vows to teach and defend the Word of God.

Christians are often presented as being uneducated, unsophisticated, and unreasonable, but our critics don't understand that we believe that we have an obligation to obey the Bible; consequently, we may appear inflexible, intolerant, and insensitive to others. One thing is sure: we don't kill innocent people. Moreover, the "nuts" who beat their kids to death and say "God told me to do it," are not Fundamentalist Christians. Should we be tolerant of those people? After all, who are we to make a judgment and discriminate? Of course, we are to discriminate between truth and error.

Some have used a few extremists in the abortion movement to tar everyone who takes a pro-life position. First, some of those abortion terrorists have never been involved with the pro-life movement, and none to my knowledge has professed faith in Jesus Christ. They are simply "fruitcakes" who care about unborn babies being ripped from the womb. What our enemy has done is to consider a very few fringe individuals and based on those, indicted the whole class of pro-lifers and Fundamentalists. No, it isn't fair or honest, but no one has ever accused the radical left crowd of being fair and honest, have they?

You see, if there is no eternal God who has established absolute authority, then it doesn't matter what you believe. And when a person doesn't believe in the true and living God, he will believe almost anything. If it is true that a sovereign God (as taught in the Bible) really exists, then every person will be held accountable as to what he or she does with His message. It would not be loving and kind if I led people into an error that damns them for eternity. So I am a lover not a hater.

Remember that it is God's Heaven, and He has the right to set the requirement for admission, and that requirement is the New Birth by placing faith in the atoning work of Christ. It doesn't really matter what theologians, philosophers, and others think about that requirement. It is settled in Heaven! They don't have to accept it, but if not, they won't gain entrance to Heaven. Rather narrow, isn't it? That's what God called it!

Look folks, let's cut to the chase. Is Jesus Christ who He said He was? Is He God? If so, then there are no concessions, no compromises, and no collaboration with teachers of error. It is astounding that educated people cannot understand that simple fact. Do they want us to say, "Jesus Christ is not God"? Well, we cannot say that because He **is** God. Do they want us to say, "Well, Christ is God, but we will overlook that fact and sit down with others who say He was a liar or lunatic"? Do patrons of pluralism think we are total idiots? Christ is not a liar or lunatic but Lord of all!

EXCLUSIVE TRUTH

II John 9-11 give Christians some parameters and principles to follow in our everyday living: "Whosoever transgresseth, and abideth not in the doctrine of Christ, hath not God. He that abideth in the doctrine of Christ, he hath both the Father and the Son. If there come any unto you, and bring not this doctrine, receive him not into your house, neither bid him God speed: For he that biddeth him God speed is partaker of his evil deeds." As a Christian I may choose to disobey that clear passage, but if I profess to love and follow Christ, I should obey it even if I am accused of being unloving, unkind, unbending. So be it. Just because we don't recognize other religions as true does not mean we would hinder their preaching, teaching, growing, and doing their thing. That doesn't mean that we must revise our theology, knowing we would be accepting error just to be tolerant of others to make them feel better.

David Limbaugh wrote, "The left is always complaining about hate speech because such speech is likely to lead to violence. If incitement to violence is the test for hate speech, is it not hate speech to contend falsely that Christianity or other religions, because they claim to have exclusive truths, advocate the extermination of other faiths? Is it not hate speech for the left to engage in such sloppy comparisons as equating Bible-believing Christians with Muslim terrorists?"[3]

Great question, David! Christians are not fools or fanatics but followers of Christ who must have the pre-eminence in all things. Thinking, informed, and honest people will not fall for myths. They know the reality: that conservative Christians, while not perfect, are the backbone of this nation and have been since the *Mayflower* with about 100 people bobbed on the waves in the bay at Plymouth.

NO SEPARATION OF MOSQUE AND STATE

What most Americans don't understand is that with the religion of Islam comes the culture of the desert and Islamic law known as *sharia*. When Islam takes over a country, it imposes not only the religion of Islam but also all the laws, customs, and mores that have developed since the seventh century. One custom is the desert code of loyalty. An Arabian proverb says, "My brother and I against our cousin, but my cousin and I against a stranger." There is much loyalty to people–very select people, but little loyalty to principle.

There is also religious exclusivity in Islam. No Islamic nation permits religious freedom. The Saudi Arabia royal dictatorship prohibits all non-Muslim religious activity. There are fewer than five Roman Catholic priests in the country, and they must work *incognito*. There are no churches in the land! Saudi citizens are paid $3,000 for reporting a home Bible study to the authorities, and Americans who convert to Islam are paid about $22,000.00. Saudis who convert from Islam are killed.[4]

What has Islamic law and religion produced in many Middle East countries besides a divisive, dominate, deadly theocracy? Then former President of Pakistan, Pervez Musharraf, made a very revealing statement about this: "The Muslim umma (community) is one-fourth of humanity, but we are the poorest, the most illiterate, the most backward, the most unhealthy and indeed the most deprived and weakest of the human race."[5] I would have added the word, "depraved" as well. So, when a nation installs Islam as their religion, they get the "whole package." Muslims don't separate mosque and state.

GOD JUDGES NATIONS

Yes, there are many myths but one of the easiest to explode is that God does not judge the nations that reject His Gospel and the Bible. One thing is sure: God has never said, "Oops!" "Come to think of it," or "On second thought." None of the terrorist events surprised God because He is an all-knowing, all-powerful, and yes, all-loving God. He is sovereign and does not answer to any entity. The Apostle Paul wrote in I Timothy 6:15-16: "Which in his times he shall shew, who is the blessed and only Potentate, the King of kings, and Lord of Lords." Now since God is sovereign,

He not only has the authority but the right to judge nations. Is He judging America at this time by permitting terrorist attacks?

One of our great early leaders, George Mason, aptly wrote: "Every master of slaves is born a petty tyrant. They bring the judgment of heaven on a country. As nations cannot be rewarded or punished in the next world, they must be in this....Providence punishes national sins by national calamities."[6] Thomas Jefferson suggested the same possibility when he wrote, "Indeed I tremble for my country when I reflect that God is just, that his justice cannot sleep forever."[7]

All Christians are aware that God brought judgment upon the whole world with the Flood of Noah. Genesis 6:17 reveals this fact: "And, behold, I, even I, do bring a flood of waters upon the earth, to destroy all flesh, wherein is the breath of life, from under heaven; and everything that is in the earth shall die." That was the ultimate judgment upon all people.

Uninformed people cannot visualize God who would bring judgment resulting in the deaths of people, especially innocent children; however, those people have not considered or don't understand a holy God who, by His very nature, must punish sin.

Muslim leaders, U.S. politicians, media personalities, ecumenical preachers, and others are disseminating these and other myths as they seek to "build a bridge between Islam and Christianity," but their bridge is one way, and it leads to Islam. The following allegory, written by Jalal-ud Din Rumi, the beloved Muslim thirteenth-century Sufi, illustrates the pernicious propaganda that is being peddled by preachers, politicians, and pundits in the free world. Jalal-ud lived in a city whose population was almost equally divided among Christians, Muslims, and Jews. When asked about those three incompatible religions he told his now famous story about a city where **every person was blind**:

One day the news came that an elephant was passing outside the city, so the townsfolk decided to send a delegation to report back as to what an elephant was. Three men left and stumbled forwards until they found the beast. They felt the animal and headed back to report. The first man said: "An elephant is like a vast snake!" The second man was indignant at hearing this: "What nonsense!" he said. "I felt the elephant and what it most resembles is a huge pillar." The third man shook his head and said: "Both these men are liars! I felt the elephant and it resembles a broad, flat fan." All three men stuck by their stories and for the rest of their lives refused to speak to each other. Each professed that they and only they knew the truth. Of course all three blind men had a measure of insight. The first felt the trunk of the elephant, the second the leg, the third the ear, but not one had begun to grasp the totality or the greatness of the beast. If only they had listened to one another, they might have grasped the true nature of the beast. But they were too proud and preferred to keep to their own half-truths. "So it is with us," said Jalal-ud Din. "We see the Almighty one way, the Jews have a slightly different conception and the Christians a third. To us, all our different visions are irreconcilable. But what we forget is that before God we are like blind men stumbling around in total darkness...."

However, Christians are not blind. God does not leave us "like blind men stumbling," but opens our eyes of understanding to see Him. (See Luke 24:31.) The above writer was a better storyteller than theologian. I am interested in truth, not political correctness, unity, diversity, pluralism, multiculturalism, ecumenicity, or making Muslims feel warm and fuzzy. Love without truth can be dangerous. The fact is all three men were wrong about the elephant as men are today about religion.

Christians must correct the myths with the truth of Scripture as the following chapter attempts to do. It's good to know that the facts, while always uncompromising, are on our side.

References:

1   Catholic Statement, Vatican Office for Non-Christian Affairs, "Orientation Between Christians and Muslims."

2   Dave Hunt, *Judgment Day*, 2005, p. 132.

3   *WorldNetDaily*, Jan. 4, 2002.

4   Tom Bethell, *The American Spectator*, "Saving Faith at State," April, 1997.

5   Associated Press, quoted in The Sword and Staff, March, 2002.

6   George Mason, Speech on the floor of the Constitutional Convention, 1787.

7   Thomas Jefferson, Notes of the State of Virginia," Query XVIII, 1781.

Chapter Three

Mythmakers are Mythtaken!

Since the terrorist attacks on America, especially on September 11, there have risen some myths about God and His dealing with men. Some tell us that if God really exists, He would not permit such tragedies to occur. Others tell us that God was responsible for the attack. Then still another myth is that God does not use such events to bring a nation to repentance, but those mythmakers are mythtaken.

The Bible and history are replete with examples of the judgment of God upon the various nations so can America expect to escape the same judgment? It is a **fact**, not a myth, that other nations have not escaped His judgment, as a cursory examination of early civilizations will show.

There were two impressive centers of civilization in mankind's early history: Ur and Babylon. Civilization moved from Ur, (located 200 miles north of the Persian Gulf) and Babylon (located between the Tigris and Euphrates Rivers) to Judea and to Nineveh, respectively, and eventually to Egypt, Greece, and Rome.

Thousands of miles of the Tigris and Euphrates Rivers permitted farmers along their banks to produce prodigious amounts of produce and provided the avenues of commerce for most of the Fertile Crescent. The area became the garden and granary of western Asia.

During the time of Abraham, the Sumerian city of Ur was a center for trade from the Persian Gulf as ships sailed up the Euphrates bringing gold, copper ore, ivory, hardwoods, and other items from Egypt, India, and Ethiopia. Excavations of Ur have proved that it was settled at least 3,000 years B.C. and had developed "a high culture."[1] Intricate and impressive carvings, pottery, and gold headdresses have been uncovered in the Royal Cemetery. Graves were discovered that contained wealthy occupants, each holding a heavy gold cup to his or her mouth. In time, Ur was eclipsed by other city-states as power shifted from place to place.

EARLY BABYLON

Standing on the sandy shores of the Euphrates amid the wastes of ancient Babylon (known as Babel in Genesis 10:10, and ruled by Nimrod), one would never imagine that there stood the epitome of civilization 700 years before Christ! The various settlements and cities were unified and became Babylonia with headquarters in Babylon.

Hammurabi united lower Mesopotamia with its capital in Babylon, and he changed it from an insignificant river town to the capital of an empire. He ruled from 1795 to 1750 B.C. and introduced his famous code, said to be given by the Sun god himself.

Babylon, the first city to have 200,000 residents, reached its zenith under the 43-year reign of Nebuchadnezzar. Soon Babylon controlled all the trade in western Asia, and with the additional funds Nebuchadnezzar built a magnificent city. Daniel quoted him as saying, "Is not this great Babylon that I have built?"[2] Herodotus (born about 484 B.C.) visited Babylon about 150 years after Nebuchadnezzar died, describing it as standing in a spacious plain and surrounded by a wall about a hundred yards high! He said that a four-horse chariot could be driven along the top of the walls. The Euphrates, lined with stately palms, ran through the center of town and was spanned by a bridge that permitted its citizens to live on either side of the river. The city was built of brick faced with yellow, blue, and white enamelled tiles, most of which were emblazoned with, "I am Nebuchadnezzar, King of Babylon."[3]

The most impressive sight when approaching the city was a 650-foot ziggurat that was "probably the Tower of Babel."[4] Six hundred yards north of Babel was one of Nebuchadnezzar's palaces and the Hanging Gardens that he had built for one of his wives who was homesick for the mountains. The Greeks considered the Hanging Gardens one of the Seven Wonders of the World. There had never been a city to equal Babylon in grandeur and few to this day!

An official census taken about 900 B.C. revealed that the Babylonians worshiped about 65,000 gods! Ishtar was one of those gods. She was sometimes presented as a bisexual deity and sometimes as a nude, offering herself as a willing sexual object to her subjects who called her "The Virgin," "The Virgin Mother," and "The Holy Virgin." "Virgin" only meant that she had not been soiled by marriage! None of the hundreds of gods could give any assurances of life after death! The Babylonian citizen could not trust his gods beyond the grave! Moreover, those gods did not produce pure, decent, or magnanimous living. Such worship produced correct ritual rather than a good life.[5]

WICKEDNESS OF BABYLON

The wickedness was so bad that even Alexander the Great, who was an adulterer and bisexual (who died drunk in the palace of Nebuchadnezzar) was shocked by the wickedness of the city![6] Herodotus revealed that every native woman in Babylon was required, once in her life, to go to the Temple of Venus and have sexual intercourse with a stranger! Wealthy women (attended by many maids and eunuchs) would ride up to the Temple in luxury carriages, enter the Temple, and wait for a stranger to throw a piece of silver (of any value) into her lap. She could not refuse anyone for any reason. The two would then go off together in or outside the Temple for their tryst. At the conclusion of the liaison, she would enter her carriage and return home, having obeyed the law and satisfied Venus.[7] Since she had satisfied the law, she could not be required to participate any further in the one-time prostitution. Such was the status of women (and morality) in Babylon.

Herodotus also revealed that when Babylon was besieged it was common for the men to strangle their wives to keep them from eating their stored provisions.[8] After all, a man can't fight if he is hungry! Such wickedness was followed by even more in the form of effeminate degeneracy. Young men dyed and curled their hair, wore perfume and rouge, wore necklaces, bangles, earrings and pendants.[9] (We're on our way!) After Babylon was conquered by the Persians, it got even worse when women of every class thought it only courtesy to reveal their bodies to as many men as possible. Herodotus even said, "Every man of the people, in his poverty prostituted his daughters for money."[10]

Durant's summation is appropriate to the U.S. as we face the greatest challenge of our history from invading Muslims. He wrote, "Morals grew lax when the temples grew rich; and the citizens of Babylon, wedded to delight, bore with equanimity the subjection of their city by the Kassites, the Assyrians, the Persians, and the Greeks."[11]

WORSE THAN WORTHLESS

Is that the danger Americans face? Have we grown lax in our wealth, good times, and easy living depending on our missiles, bombs, and planes to protect us? Will we calmly, dispassionately permit our society, our culture to be taken over by a foreign element that uses undisguised threats to accomplish their desires? Others appeal to our sense of fairness and assure us that Muslims are not interested in capturing our nation. Should we believe them? At least, should we not inquire deeply into what specific Muslims believe to assure ourselves that they are not part of an international religious conspiracy? Are we so fearful of being considered bigots and haters that we reject our culture, our civilization, and our convictions? If so, maybe we deserve to lose and become absorbed in the pagan Islamic culture.

The greatness of Babylon had been deteriorating for many years as they indulged themselves in all desires, lost interest in maintaining their strength to repel aggressors, permitted the family to continually dissolve, and fanned themselves under stately palms. They tried one god after another, then an assortment of gods; but none could provide peace, piety, or power over degrading, debilitating, and destructive wickedness. The pagan priests had them in a lock box from which they could not escape. Only the priests could provide revelation and that was worse than worthless. Finally, the soul, whether good or evil, at death would drop into Hades where it would suffer in outer darkness forever. Is it any surprise that Babylonians gave themselves to revelry, rioting, and ravenous behavior? Is the world not doing the same thing in our day?

BABYLON CRUMBLED

Babylon began to crumble. Nebuchadnezzar was now dead and Nabonidus ruled, or actually, he played at ruling. Nabonidus was more interested in excavating the desert than in executing directives. While Nabonidus was digging in the sand, his son Belshazzar ruled as co-regent, but Belshazzar had not learned, as had Nebuchadnezzar, that God can put down the mighty. Because of Nebuchadnezzar's pride, God took away his senses and he lived with the beasts of the field until God returned his understanding. Then he said: "Now I Nebuchadnezzar praise and extol and honour the King of heaven, all whose works are truth, and his ways judgment: and those that walk in pride he is able to abase."[12] Nebuchadnezzar learned that God will bring judgment upon people to bring them to Himself.

Belshazzar gave a lavish party for a thousand of his lords and ladies and it was a wild night of desecration, debauchery, and death. Belshazzar purposefully sought to offend God by drinking wine from the sacred vessels that had been taken from the Temple when Jerusalem was sacked. During the revelry, the king suddenly dropped his golden goblet of wine and pointed to the fingers of a man's hand, writing on the wall. The king lost control of his body as his mind troubled him, his face was contorted and his knees smote against each other. That broke up the party.

The official court clergy were called but didn't have an interpretation for the supernatural phenomenon. Then the queen reminded Belshazzar about Daniel; so when all else failed, they called the preacher! Daniel came before the king, told him to keep his gifts of gold, then listed the royal transgressions. (Daniel was not interested in climbing the corporate ladder.) Daniel said that the meaning of the writing was: "MENE; God hath numbered thy kingdom, and finished it. TEKEL; Thou art weighed in the balances, and art found wanting. PERES; Thy kingdom is divided, and given to the Medes and Persians."[13] Translation: "King, you are dead meat." That judgment was fulfilled that very night.

The Persians were at the gates of the city, but it was still a mighty city, so the wily Medes and Persians diverted the river Euphrates (that flowed through the city), and the army marched up the riverbed under the massive walls to take the city: "In that night was Belshazzar the king...slain." Thus ended the world empire of Babylon. Historians write of the military conquests, but they are really writing about the judgment of God upon a civilization. Often one wicked nation is allowed to bring down another wicked nation–all in God's plan.

DANIEL AND HIS FRIENDS

Daniel and his three friends were brought into this wicked Babylonian atmosphere when Nebuchadnezzar was at his height of power. They spent the rest of their lives there, five hundred miles from Jerusalem, away from home, and they stayed true and pure, positive, and productive for a lifetime! While Daniel and his friends served in prominent places during the reign of Nebuchadnezzar, the king wanted them to convert to his religion. That is what the third chapter of Daniel is all about. It is one of the most famous Old Testament stories. Nebuchadnezzar set up a massive idol on the plain and required all political leaders of his empire to come for the dedication of the image of gold. As every Sunday school pupil knows, Shadrach, Meshach, and Abednego (their Babylonian names) refused the king's command and were thrown into the fiery furnace, but God brought them out of the fire without the odor of smoke on their clothes. However, this incident is far more than three young men who stood on their principles and were willing to die for them.

Nebuchadnezzar's threat to force everyone to submit to him was not as simple as preachers have made it for over 2000 years. Too often, we look at this incident through modern eyes and miss its subtleties. People of that day did not consider the worship of the golden image religious oppression. By worshipping the image, the worshippers were not forbidden to worship any other god. They were not required to renounce their favorite god. They simply had to add another god to their pantheon. No big deal.

In fact, heathens thought it only proper to show reverence to any and all gods. If the king wanted another god, so be it. They would pay homage to his god. After all, the king felt rather strongly about it, and bowing before the king's image would save their lives. It would also be a good career move to placate the king. After all, what's one more god? Notice that all the people from the other nations obeyed the king's command. They did that because they did not serve the one, true, sovereign God. The three young Hebrews thought that it was important to stand for what you believe, and this "mature" Gentile believes the same!

Standing on principle exacts a price as the Hebrews discovered. The reigning despots of that day didn't think it was outrageous that all citizens be required to worship the official god of the nation where they lived. Citizens could then add as many gods as they wanted. Most despots have understood that religion could act as glue that would hold society together. Daniel and his three friends were saying: "The state-approved gods are false gods and must be rejected. Worship must be directed to the only true God under heaven." That exclusivity was not permitted, and trouble resulted. Such persons were "atheists" attacking the state. The three Hebrews were not only refusing to worship a false god, but they were also refusing to recognize the authority of the king! Bad news.

CONFRONTATION

This enforced religious conformity is where early Christians had their trouble. They were not required to forsake the worship of Christ. All they were required to do was to burn a little incense to Caesar. Of course, in doing so, they were affirming that Caesar was lord, and no Christian could, in good conscience, admit that. Christians believed that there was but one true God who desired, deserved, and demanded exclusive worship. That produced a major confrontation resulting in thousands of believers being thrown to the lions, burned at the stake, broken on the rack, drawn and quartered, drowned, lynched, crucified, and killed in other ingenious ways.

Christians in the Roman Empire basically claimed that the pagan gods were worthless, and everyone should recognize Christ as King of kings and Lord of lords. That amounted to heresy in Caesar's court, and it amounts to heresy today. We don't have problems when we say that Jesus Christ is Savior, but when we say that He is the **only** hope for this world, that He is the **only** way to Heaven, then we have trouble. We are saying that other religions are not valid, that their doctrines are untrue, and we become politically incorrect. We become *persona non grata* in most areas of society.

Basically Nebuchadnezzar was saying: (1) all the gods worshipped by others were to be recognized; (2) other gods could be introduced by authority of the State; (3) the gods which the government approved were to be honored by everyone whatever their religious persuasion; (4) if any person denied the new god instituted by the State and refused homage, that person would be recognized as an enemy of the State.[14]

This is where we are in this Age of Terror. Men have lost confidence in the Bible as the authoritative Word of a sovereign God and are now guided by how they "feel" about things. Truth is not required, received, or respected. Peoples' feelings are more important than truth. We are told that reality is that America is now a pluralistic society (and it is), and we must all live together peacefully (and we must). Furthermore, we are told that Christianity has "had its place in the sun" but that is now past, and that a sovereign God must step aside, or at best, share the spotlight with other gods. That we will not do.

MYTH OR REALITY

The myth is that God (if there is a God) does not involve Himself in the affairs of men. Most people want to believe that God is a benevolent grandfather (somewhere in Heaven) who is forever indulgent with his erring grandchildren, and that He would never bring judgment upon them or their nations. Therefore, modern men have convinced themselves that this myth is reality.

As with Nebuchadnezzar's image, all gods worshipped by others must be recognized by everyone, and government will endorse all gods (except the God of the Bible because He is exclusive). Anyone who refuses to acknowledge the gods will be considered a religious terrorist who wants to force his intolerant views on everyone. Such a person will be considered an enemy of the state. Babylon was an early pattern for Mecca and the 360 gods worshipped by the desert Arabs.

The Hebrews had been in Egypt for over 400 years, and the cup of God's wrath was slowly filling. When Moses was 80 years old, God called him to lead the Hebrews out of the land of bondage to the land of blessing. In a confrontation with Pharaoh, God brought 10 judgments upon the nation resulting in Pharaoh and his army being drowned in the Red Sea. Obviously, God does bring judgment upon nations. God brought judgment upon the cities of Sodom and Gomorrah for their vile sin of sodomy. God did not hate them, but He surely hated their sin. Their unrepentant hearts resulted in God's judgment that totally destroyed the cities.[15]

There are many examples of God sending judgment upon Israel because of national rebellion. Numbers 21 is a good example where God infested their camp with poisonous snakes and many of the people died. Those bitten could be healed if they cast their eyes upon a brazen serpent on a pole in the midst of the camp. If they looked, they lived. If not, they died. Jesus mentioned that example in John 3 when He likened Himself to that serpent of brass. In John 12:32, Christ promised: "And I, if I be lifted up from the earth, will draw all men unto me." Just as during that time of wilderness judgment, if men look to Christ, they live. If they don't, they die. It is a personal choice.

Americans can "buy into" the myth that God does not bring judgment upon nations (or individuals) if they choose, but they must understand that such a belief has consequences. Ask Nebuchadnezzar and Belshazzar!

References:

1   Charles F. Pfeiffer and Howard F. Vos, *The Wycliffe Historical Geography of Biblical Lands*, Moody Press, 1970, p. 14.

2   Daniel 4:30.

3   This was a shock to Bible critics who claimed for hundreds of years that Nebuchadnezzar was fictitious!

4   Will Durant, *The Story of Civilization*, Simon and Schuster, New York, 1935, Book 1, p. 224.

5   Ibid., p. 240.

6   Ibid., p. 244.

7   Ibid., p. 245.

8   Ibid., p. 248.

9   Ibid., p. 248.

10 Ibid., p. 248.

11 Ibid., p. 248.

12 Daniel 4:37.

13 Daniel 5:26-28.

14 Albert Barnes, *Barnes' Notes on the Old Testament*, Baker Book House, Grand Rapids, First pub. 1831, p. 212.

15 *The Stringer Report*, Phil Stringer, June, 1997.

Chapter Four

Creating Terrorists Around the Globe!

Islam is a religion in which Allah requires you to send your son to kill and die for him, but Christianity is a faith in which God sent His Son to die for you. That is a paraphrase of former Attorney General John Ashcroft whose courageous and accurate statement hit the bull's eye and caused howling and gnashing of teeth from the Redwoods of California to the vacant lot in Manhattan. Some of the "moderate" Muslims went after him with a hatchet seeking his scalp as they did after his suggestion that all foreigners coming to America from the Middle East be finger-printed and photographed. What's wrong with that? Some will tell us that many Muslims are moderate so it would be intimidating and unfair to them. Too bad, how do all Americans feel knowing that Muslim men massacred about 3,000 innocent people, including a few Muslims? More-over, they admit their plan is to conquer America and the world and are creating terrorists all over the globe at this time to accomplish that task

A good definition of a Muslim wearing a moderate facade is a man who doesn't have the ability to act ruthlessly to seize control **today**. I have spoken to Muslims who are critical of any terrorist acts for any reason; however, the mosques are full of men who do believe in using terror as a weapon. I have talked to them. Many Muslim leaders publicly abhor terror while they privately applaud it. So a moderate Muslim true to the Koran is an oxymoron. It's like being a moderate child molester or moderate Nazi. If a Muslim believes what traditional Muslims believe, he is an extremist, not a moderate; and those Muslims who are really moderate will be the first to die when the true Muslims take control as we are seeing with ISIS in the Middle East.

Most non-Muslims do not understand the seventh-century, desert culture of Islam. Muslims appear to be one thing to the U.S. public and something else to the rest of the world. Their allegiance, in addition to Islam, is to family and tribe; and immigrating to America, wearing blue jeans, eating pizza, and mouthing "cool" statements will not change them. Remember the old Arab proverb that is inculcated in every Arab that says, "My brother and I against our cousin, but my cousin and I against a stranger." You are a stranger, and you should remember that!

MONSTERS BUT NOT COWARDS

The Muslims who steered the planes into the Twin Towers and the Pentagon have often been called "cowards," but cowards don't study, work, and train for years to carry out an act that results in their deaths. These terrorists are highly motivated followers of their religion. It is not wise to mischaracterize an enemy nor is it necessary. If we make an enemy less than he is, then we cannot effectively deal with his desire to do us harm. Giving credit for a minor attribute does not condone his major activity. Why put ourselves at a disadvantage in this battle for our very lives? In fact, we need to look at their motives and grievances; after all, there could be **some** truth to them. However, sincere motives and grievances never justify killing innocent people, but knowing their complaints do help us understand the reasoning of the perpetrators.

I have sought for a descriptive word for the terrorists and "monster" seems very appropriate. There are many examples in America and the free world of such monstrous acts and attitudes following the September 11 attack. Notice the following vicious statements by leading Muslims:

"Ex-president of Iran backs nuking Israel"

"Terrorists shoot 18 during church service."

"U.S. Go to Hell!"

"Go To Hell America" and "Destroy America."

"Death to America, Death to Israel, Taliban, we salute you."

"America is the enemy of God."

"America is a great Satan."

"U.S. go to hell, Afghans will prevail."

"Down, down USA!"

"Yes to Sharia, no to Democracy."

They would really prefer going to democratic nations because it allows them to more easily take over control. They use free systems to take control of those systems, then change them. And most national leaders are blind to what is happening.

WHERE ARE THE MODERATES?

Salman Rushdie, a native of India but now a citizen of England, wrote a book considered critical of Islam. He, a former Muslim, bravely titled the book, *The Satanic Verses,* a subject I deal with in another chapter. The top Muslim in Iran put out a contract on his life! Ayatollah Khomeini of Iran said, "Even if Salman Rushdie repents and becomes the most pious man of all time, it is incumbent upon every Muslim to employ everything he has, his life and his wealth, to send him to hell." That was one of the leading "holy" men of Islam speaking!

My question: Where were all the "moderate" American Muslims at that time? Not **one** came to Rushdie's defense! Not one deplored the book burnings, riots, and killings that followed the publication of his book. It seems that many Muslims don't walk the talk of peace! To their credit, 127 Muslim international intellectuals (no Americans) came to Rushdie's defense in a signed protest statement.

One thing is sure: Muslims feel deeply about what they believe! Muslims killed both the men who translated Rushdie's book into Japanese and Italian! But then, murder is not unusual for dedicated Muslims. As I write, militant Muslims are training young Muslims to be dedicated terrorists to further their cause. All Muslims confess that world domination is their cause. Some have rejected terror, while many others have not. Many of those are hidden deep in America scheming against our nation which should concern everyone. They are concealed in the hordes rushing the border proclaiming refuge status.

FRENCH TERRORISTS

Terrorists have been reared for many years in the slums of Beirut, the hovels of the West Bank, Pakistan, Saudi Arabia, etc. They are being trained in London and Paris! The late Chuck Colson, who worked with U.S. prisoners, charged that al Qaeda training manuals specifically target black prisoners in the U.S. for Islamic conversion. Richard Reid, who tried to blow up an international flight with a shoe bomb, was converted to Islam while in a British prison.[1] Furthermore, we know that Abdullah al-Muhajir, alias Jose Padilla, the "dirty bomber," was converted to Islam in an American prison. In fact, more than 15 percent of the about 3 million-plus U.S. prison population is Muslim![2] It is much worse in France.

The Sante Prison, located on the Left Bank in Paris, is where many Muslim terrorists have been incarcerated for more than fifteen years. Inflammatory literature has been circulated throughout the prison, highlighting real and imaginary complaints of Muslims against Israel and the West. The prison is a recruiting station for Islamic terrorists.

In 2001, over half of France's prison inmates were Muslim according to Frank Viviano but in 2009 it was almost 70%! It is more than that in 2016. Viviano reports that extremists have built what amounts to an extensive and highly organized "terrorist university" behind bars, according to his sources in the prison guards' union. Smuggled tapes, books, and pamphlets preach the fiercely anti-Western and anti-Semitic gospel of al-Qaeda. Some inmates claim to have been offered instruction in the manufacture of homemade mines, bombs, detonators, and fuses. Prison officials, aware of the magnitude of the problem, have transferred the extremists to other prisons; however, that has only exacerbated the problem: the leaders are able to recruit new members with each move!

The Muslim prisoners are going after the other prisoners with a missionary zeal. (Would that the average Christian had their zeal.) But there is a major problem in an effort to dampen the Islamic terrorists' zeal: prison authorities are restricted by a law that guarantees each "detainee must be able to satisfy the demands of his religious, moral or spiritual life."[3] The inmates have taken over the asylum using French law to teach terrorism!

TERRORISTS IN LONDON

The city of London is being overrun with Muslims, and experts expect England to become the first European nation that falls into the Muslim community of nations! Think of that, in the land of John and Charles Wesley, Charles Spurgeon, etc. The English waited too long to do anything about their immigration invasion and now they are **fearful** of doing anything about it.

Gary North, Ph.D., quoted a London *Times* column about what is happening in the town of Luton:

> *There is a terrible, visceral rage among Luton's young Muslim brotherhood, a fury so powerful that already dozens of men, all British born and highly educated, have disappeared to fight for the Taleban. It has left parents terrified, the town's mosques full of loathing and yesterday, as The Times discovered first-hand, seen journalists and photographers physically attacked.... Within a minute of arriving outside the mosque, this Times reporter and cameraman were set upon by a Muslim man, who had rushed, enraged, from a halal butcher shop.*
>
> *"You insult Islam, you corrupt Islam!" he screamed, smashing the camera to the ground and grabbing another photographer by the throat. "You don't understand how angry we Muslims are!" Five other Muslim men joined him, surrounding us, as he demanded the other camera. Their sense of fury was frightening.*
>
> *"They want to die there," Mr. Abdullah said. "These are well-educated people. They have families. I knew Afzal. He loved his wife. But you must understand: all Muslims in Britain view supporting the jihad (holy war) as a religious duty. All of us are ready to sacrifice our lives for our beliefs. I am jealous of Afzal. He has reached paradise."*
>
> *He continued: "There are people leaving all the time. Not just in Luton, but all over Britain. We, as Muslims, don't perceive ourselves as British Muslims. We are Muslims who live in Britain. All we want to do is go to Afghanistan to defend the honour and sanctity of Islam."*[4]

These people drip with violence and hatred and are examples of the old saying that rage burns hottest in the weakest minds. These people are pursuing death. That isn't normal. We are born to seek life not death. Death comes sooner or later, and if you are a Muslim, it often comes sooner than later. However, we are not at war with all Muslims but with monsters that practice Islam. Moreover, we had better differentiate between them.

IDEOLOGICAL HATRED OF U.S.

Steve Emerson revealed to a Congressional hearing that the Muslims raised money for "suicide martyrs" in the Middle East and elsewhere, operated a military training camp in Arizona, and provided the money for a stream of terrorists to enter and leave the U.S. at will. In short, militant Islamic groups in America "experienced freedoms and maneuverability they never experienced in their native lands" while they used these freedoms to express their "ideological hatred for the United States."[5] Well, the Senators surely got an "ear full," but did little about it.

Emerson quoted Iran's Ayatollah Khomeini, saying, "The purest joy in Islam is to kill and be killed for Allah." Monsters like Khomeini are, without a doubt, within America's Trojan Horse, working, planning, and scheming while we sleep.

Mohammed and his followers slaughtered thousands in spreading Islam. Mohammed ordered Muslims, "Who relinquishes his faith, kill him." And "I have been ordered by Allah to fight with people till they testify there is no god but Allah and Mohammed is his messenger." Since Mohammed preached terror and violence, is it unusual that Muslims are responsible for most terrorism in the world today? All Muslims are not terrorists but **all** the September 11 killers were Muslims! Could there be some connection between terror and terrorist teaching? If not, then the educational foundation of the free world is based on a fallacy. Of course, there is a connection between what is taught and what is wrought.

Emerson quoted Fayiz Azzam in Brooklyn: "Blood must flow, there must be widows, orphans, [and] hands and limbs must be severed and limbs and blood must be spread everywhere in order that Allah's religion stand on its feet!"[6] Religion of peace?

In Kansas, another leader recruiting Islamic holy warriors against the United States exulted, "O, brothers! After Afghanistan [where Muslim 'freedom fighters,' aided by the CIA, drove out the Soviets and installed the brutal Taliban regime] nothing in the world is impossible for us anymore! There are no superpowers or mini-powers. What matters is will power that springs from our religious belief!"[7]

Some Muslim leaders reject the use of violence to advance Islam; however, every Muslim scholar knows that the Koran teaches that every single Muslim has an obligation to support conversion efforts until Islam has taken over the world. I write that with reluctance because it will turn some people off; however, reluctance will keep many people from hearing the truth. Still there is scheming taking place inside America by trained extremists who will do anything to advance their cause!

TRAINING CHILDREN TO HATE

What kind of monsters dedicate themselves to killing helpless, innocent civilians, even children? They are people who have been trained all their lives to do just that. A *WorldNetDaily* column reported that Palestinian children are taught to kill Jews through "Sesame Street"-type television shows![8] The column reported that "Palestinian children are taught to hate Jews, to glorify *jihad* (holy war), violence, death and child martyrdom almost from birth, as an essential part of their culture and destiny." The Israelis documented this proving the "Children's Club," along with puppets, songs, and other characters, promoted hate toward Jews. Kids were told of the perpetual *jihad* that would continue until the Israeli flag comes down from "Palestinian land" and the Palestinian flag is hoisted.

I have seen that video and it is shocking and nauseating as small children sing lustily about becoming suicide warriors! Groups of children are gathered shouting "*Jihad* against Israel." Others want to take a machine gun against the hated Israelis. A very little girl chants, "When I wander into Jerusalem, I will become a suicide bomber." Another boy is shown in class proclaiming, "We will settle our claims with stones and bullets." Now, is there any question why children throw stones at tanks when such monstrous men teach them?

Where Islam prevails, the Jews are persecuted and we are seeing that all over Europe. I don't want a resurgence of Jew-hatred in America as in Europe. In fact, it is epidemic wherever Muslims predominate according to a 2006 Pew Survey. Anti-Semitism is vocally expressed by 100% of Jordanians, 98% of Egyptians, 76% of Indonesians, 74% of Pakistanis and 60% of Turks![9] I remind you that when Muslims come to America they don't leave their anti-Semitism in their tents or in the saddle bags of their camels.

CHASING DEATH

It is impossible to understand how parents can promote death to their children. They are teaching small children that death, rather than life, is to be pursued! They not only risk death; they chase it! That is monstrous! Palestinians are told that the government will compensate their families if they give their lives for "the cause."

Gerald M. Steinberg, writing in the *Jerusalem Post,* provided details of statements made by Palestinians to reporters after their children had been killed in fighting. "Interviewed by journalists after [recent] tragedies, some of the parents of these young victims refer to their children as *shaheeds* (martyrs), whose lives were given willingly and proudly to the Palestinian cause in fighting the hated Zionist enemy," Steinberg said. There was a Palestinian man teaching children how to fire M-16 automatic assault rifles, and "In an unbelievably shocking scene, one mother boasted that she bore her son precisely for this purpose, and the father proudly claimed credit for providing the training."[10]

The *Whistleblower* magazine published an article titled, "The secret world of suicide bombers" that profiled the Hotari family as they prepared for a party to celebrate the killing of 21 Israelis earlier in the month by their son, a suicide bomber! The article reported, "Neighbors hang pictures on their trees of Saeed Hotari holding seven sticks of dynamite."[11] Kelley, a reporter for *USA Today* wrote, "They spray-paint graffiti reading '21 and counting' on their stone walls. And they arrange flowers in the shapes of a heart and a bomb to display on their front doors."

The boy's father, 54-year-old Hassan Hotari, reports Kelley, says he is "very happy and proud of what my son did and, frankly, am a bit jealous." His son was responsible for the terrorist bombing outside a disco in Tel Aviv. Mr. Hotari gushed, "I wish I had done it. My son has fulfilled the Prophet's (Mohammed's) wishes. He has become a hero! Tell me, what more could a father ask?" Now **there** is a legitimate case of child abuse where a father reared a monster.

"The secret world of suicide bombers" reports that in Hamas-run kindergartens, signs on the walls read: "The children of the kindergarten are the *shaheeds* (holy martyrs) of tomorrow." Furthermore, there is promotion of terror at the university level as well. The classroom signs at Al-Najah University in the West Bank and at Gaza's Islamic University say, "Israel has nuclear bombs, we have human bombs."[12]

HUMAN BOMBS

Hamas runs an Islamic school in Gaza City where 11-year-old Palestinian student Ahmed boasts, "I will make my body a bomb that will blast the flesh of Zionists, the sons of pigs and monkeys." Ahmed says, "I will tear their bodies into little pieces and cause them more pain than they will ever know." Ahmed's teacher shouts, "May the virgins give you pleasure," referring to one of the rewards waiting martyrs in Paradise. The principal smiles and nods his head in approval.[13] An empty head!

Muslims are taught to kill Americans and their allies, civilians, and military as an individual duty for every Muslim who can do it in any country in which it is possible to do it. It is noteworthy that all the homicidal bombers have been relatively young people. Where are the old dudes who push them into the grave? Some of the terrorist leaders praise the young killers, and they have talked of being a "martyr," but none have volunteered yet! Come on guys, step up to the line. Put your mark on the volunteer list to commit suicide.

I asked earlier what kind of people would train children to become assassins of innocent, helpless people, but there have always been dedicated people willing to give their lives for a cause. We saw that with the Japanese pilots during World War II who flew their explosive-loaded planes into allied ships. But it goes back into the distant past when young Shiite Muslims trained to be assassins under the influence of hashish. In fact, that is where the word "assassin" comes from.

OLD MAN OF THE MOUNTAIN

Muslim history reveals that in 1094 Hasan-i Sabbah, a native of Khurasan and supporter of the caliphate in Cairo until the caliph's death, refused to recognize the new caliph. Hasan and the Persian Muslims transferred their allegiance to the deceased caliph's deposed elder brother, Nizar. However, Nizar and his son were murdered in an Egyptian prison, but an infant grandson was smuggled out to Persia [Iran] and reared by Hasan to start a new line of Nizari imams.[14] Hasan and his followers adopted the concept of assassination as a "sacred religious duty." This group was known as the "Assassins" and they were promised Paradise if they died carrying out instructions.

Hasan became the first "Old Man of the Mountain," and all future leaders assumed the same title. He seized the castle of Alamut in an impregnable valley near Kazin in Iran. It had sheer sides about 600 feet high and accessed, by steps, one man at a time.

When an Assassin's mother heard that her son had been killed in carrying out his "religious" duties, she rejoiced and dressed in gay clothing, but if he returned alive, she wore mourning attire. The training of monsters goes back more than a thousand years.

When a visiting emissary visited the castle of Assassins, Hasan wished to display his power and ordered one young man to slit his own throat which he did to the horror of the emissary. Then a youngster was ordered to throw himself from the precipice, which he did without a moment's hesitation! And with a smile on his face! That was the kind of terrorists who steered the planes on September 11, attacked Paris in 2015, Brussels in 2016, and who have lit a burning fuse in America!

MARCO POLO AND TERRORIST TRAINING

How could human leaders instil bright, dedicated young men with a murderous instinct to train to be assassins and to give their lives for such a cause? Marco Polo (A.D. 1254-1324) had very enlightened information on the "Old Man of the Mountain" and his killing cadre in his bestselling book:

> *In a beautiful valley, he [the Old Man of the Mountain] formed a luxurious garden, stored with every delicious fruit and fragrant shrub. Palaces were erected in different parts of the grounds, ornamented with gold, paintings and furniture of rich silks. The inhabitants of these palaces were elegant and beautiful damsels, accomplished in the arts, especially those of dalliance and amorous allurement.*

> *The object which the chief had in forming a garden of this fascinating kind was this: that Mohammed having promised to those who should obey his will the enjoyments of Paradise, where every species of sensual gratification should be found, in the society of beautiful nymphs, he was desirous of it being understood by his followers that he was also a prophet and the compeer [peer, an equal] of Mohammed, and had the power of admitting to Paradise such as he should choose to favor.*

> *At his court, this chief entertained a number of youths, from the age of 12 to 20 years, selected from the inhabitants of the surrounding mountains, who showed a disposition for martial exercises and daring courage and at certain times he caused opium to be administered to 10 or a dozen of the youths; and when half dead with sleep he had them conveyed to the palaces in the garden. Upon awakening, their senses were struck with all the delightful objects that have been described and each believed himself assuredly in Paradise.*

> *When four or five days had thus been passed, they were thrown once more into a state of somnolency, and carried out of the garden. The chief thereupon addressing them, said: "We have the assurances of our prophet that he who defends his lord shall inherit*

Paradise, and if you show yourselves devoted to the obedience of my orders, that happy lot awaits you."

The consequence of this system was, that when any of the neighboring princes, or others, gave umbrage to this chief, they were put to death by these his disciplined assassins; none of whom felt terror at the risk of losing their own lives.[15]

Some have said that Marco Polo's account is fanciful if not fabricated, although there is no doubt that the group existed and the mountain fortress just northwest of modern Tehran was a reality. In recent years, scholars have confirmed the "solid core of historical and geographical information in the volume."[16]

CULTURE OF TERROR

Does the above training of Muslim assassins reveal Islam to be superior or even equal to Christianity? Can you even imagine Christians training to be killers? How can Islam be "superior" to Christianity when it is a violent and vindictive religion unlike Christ's teachings of love, peace, and forgiveness? **Professing** Christians have done horrible things, but never can the blame fall at the feet of the Savior who said in Matthew 5:44: "Love your enemies,…do good to them that hate you…."

The men who steered the planes into the Pentagon and the World Trade Center and others who killed in Paris, San Bernardino, etc., were doing what Muslims have been trained to do for centuries. And while some Muslims reject the actions of the fanatics, they don't reject the Koran, the Hadith, and Islamic doctrines that promote terror. Furthermore, many moderate Muslims decry the terrorist attacks but secretly raise money to train future terrorists and according to the Bush Doctrine that makes them terrorists! When those "moderates" in the U.S. and England start acting consistently, I'll believe them when they show disgust for terrorists.

The late Jerry Falwell called Mohammed a "terrorist" on CBS and the Muslims and the media went after his scalp. Ibrahim Hooper, communications director for the radical Council on American-Islamic Relations, said, "What concerns us the most is the complete failure of mainstream religious and political leaders to repudiate this kind of anti-Muslim hate speech." He added, "On the issue of bigotry, silence equals consent." No one asked, "Is Falwell's statement true?" Was Mohammed a terrorist? Of course he was. He instilled terror all over the Arabian Peninsula; however, truth is not as important as political correctness. In any war, truth is the first casualty–and be assured we are in a war. We are observing Muslim leaders rewriting history before our eyes. They are trying to sanitize their bloody religion.

I remind Mr. Hooper that "silence equals consent" on the issue of terror and is treason! I challenge Mr. Hooper to:

- demand religious freedom in Saudi Arabia and all Muslim nations.
- demand that Sudan stop its slavery and imprison all slavers–buyers and sellers.
- declare that the 19 terrorists on September 11 were murderous monsters who dropped into the lowest hell not into the arms of dark-eyed virgins in Paradise.
- declare that no one should give a dollar to any Islamic organization that supports any kind of terror.
- declare that bin Laden was a fool, a fanatic, and a fake.
- demand that airlines start profiling all passengers from the Middle East.
- declare that there is no such thing as a "good" terrorist. They are all bad.

Until Hooper is willing to do the above, I consider him a sanctimonious hypocrite and one who aids and abets terrorism. According to Bush, that makes Hooper a terrorist! Therefore, I challenge him to do the above then announce it on national television. I will be totally convinced of his sincerity and loyalty to America when he stands before the television cameras with an American flag in his right hand and a copy of the U.S. Constitution in his left hand held close to his heart as he sings all the verses of "It's a Grand Old Flag" and, while the cameras fade out, he whistles "Yankee Doodle Dandy" (or maybe, "Dixie!") Then he'll make me a believer in his sincerity.

American Muslims must take an unequivocal stand against monstrous acts done by their own, and we must not give them any wiggle room! The men who attacked the U.S. on September 11 and other attacks were monsters and those who sent them and financed them, gave them shelter and encouraged them are all monstrously evil men who must pay the price for their terror.

American and British politicians must realize that there is no total victory over "evil" and "terror" as long as evil men walk among us. We would be wiser and safer if we heed the admonition of Edmund Burke: "There is no safety for honest men except by believing all possible evil of evil men."[17] He was observing the total depravity of man. We are sentimental fools and slaves to multiculturalism if we don't recognize the culture of terror that accompanies Islamic immigration.

Islam has been training terrorists for this nefarious task for centuries. While we slept, the enemy lit the fuse and is patiently waiting for America to explode!

References:

1   *The American Sentinel*, Sept., 2002.

2   *Huffington Post,* March 7, 2013.

3   Hearst newspapers, Nov. 2, 2001.

4   *London Times,* Oct. 30, 2001.

5   Steven Emerson, *Jihad in America,* PBS Special, 1994.

6   Ibid.

7   Dave Hunt, *The Berean Call,* Oct. 1, 2001.

8   *WorldNetDaily,* Dec. 3, 2000.

9   Don Feder, *Whistleblower,* Dec. 2015.

10   *Jerusalem Post,* Oct. 27, 2001.

11   Jack Kelley, *Whistleblower,* Nov. 2001.

12   Ibid.

13   Ibid.

14   *Encyclopedia Britannica,* vol. 2, 1960, p. 553.

15   *The Travels of Marco Polo* and various web sites.

16   Charles Van Doren, *History of Knowledge*, New York, Random House, p. 170.

17   Edmund Burke, from his second speech on conciliation with America, March 22, 1775.

Chapter Five

When American Cities Are Burning!

In August of 1944, Hitler ordered his general, Dietrich von Choltitz, to blow up and burn Paris rather than have the city fall to Allied forces that were rapidly advancing in the suburbs. However, the German general wrestled with his conscience considering France's long history, its art, the Arch de Triomphe, the Eiffel Tower, Sorbonne University, Notre Dame, etc. As von Choltitz fled the room, he heard Hitler screaming into the abandoned phone, "Is Paris burning? Is Paris burning?" No, Paris did not burn because of a Nazi with a conscience!

Another maniac called to us from a cave in Afghanistan, "Is America burning? Is America burning?" That man was Osama bin Laden, a Muslim maniac with a mission to destroy America. America did not burn but the Twin Towers did and 3,000 Americans died from smoke, flames, and falling or jumping 100 floors above Manhattan. Osama's successors have much more ambitious plans for us.

WILL AMERICA BURN?

ISIS, ISIL, or IS (different terms for the same butchers) are monstrous Muslim maniacs with a mission–and without a conscience. Muslim terrorists take credit for the demise of the Soviet Union (rightly in my opinion) and have similar plans to destroy America. The humiliated Russians drove their tanks out of Afghanistan in 1989, and within two years the Soviet Empire was history! That historic success in humiliating the powerful Soviet Empire encouraged Muslim terrorists in their plan to destroy America, the "Great Satan."

It is said that Muslim terrorists have deployed small but powerful nuclear weapons into the U.S. and are ready to explode them any day! Many major U.S. cities could be in rubble and in flames any day with a Muslim terrorist shouting into a cell phone: "Yes! America is burning! America is burning! Praise Allah!"

The network news program "60 Minutes" reported an alarming story about claims made by the former Russian National Security Advisor, General Aleksander Labed. Labed revealed that the former Soviet Union had produced–then lost–about 100 "suitcase" nuclear bombs! Each bomb could be carried by one man and detonated by one person with 30 minutes notice yielding a blast equivalent to a thousand tons of TNT![1] General Labed was killed while riding in a Russian helicopter in 2002. Was that payback time?

CIA analyst, Michael Scheuer, author of *Imperial Hubris,* was in charge of "the Alec file," the CIA's file on bin Laden. Scheuer appeared on "60 Minutes" and warned the American people that a nuclear attack by al-Qaida "is pretty close to being inevitable."[2]

A Harvard professor, Graham Allison, in his *Nuclear Terrorism* revealed that after 9/11, the CIA told the President that Al Qaeda had smuggled a Russian-made 10-kiloton nuclear weapon into New York City![3] Moreover, the CIA had picked up surveillance chatter from Al Qaeda sources about an "American Hiroshima." President Bush, fearing that Washington might be a target, sent the Vice President to safety and sent bomb experts to New York City but did not tell Mayor Rudy Giuliani about the danger!

No bomb was discovered; however, the absence of evidence is not the evidence of absence. Osama bin Laden's top deputy, Ayman al-Zawahiri, bragged, "We sent our people to Moscow, to Tashkent, to other Central Asian states, and they negotiated, and we purchased some suitcase [nuclear] bombs."[4]

AMERICA'S HIROSHIMA

In 2004, Washington was abuzz about Osama bin Laden's "American Hiroshima," a plan whereby at least seven nuclear bombs were carried across the Mexican-U.S. border by Central American street-gang members. Those "suitcase" bombs were allegedly hidden in the U.S. and when detonated would kill at least four million Americans and millions more would die of radiation exposure. Ah, yes, a peaceful religion.

The New York Times reported in 2004 that if a nuclear bomb, smaller than the one that destroyed Hiroshima, were detonated in Times Square, it would destroy Madison Square Garden, the Empire State Building, Grand Central Terminal and Carnegie Hall, the UN and about 500,000 people would die if it were a weekday!

Will Muslim terrorists explode bombs simultaneously in various major cities or hit one city, then threaten to explode other bombs unless the American government surrenders to Islam and accepts Islamic rule? If Americans see a major city in rubble with thousands of charred bodies lying in the streets, would there be demands for surrender, or revenge? I suggest that every Muslim in America would have a target on his back and some Americans would consider any Middle Eastern person as fair game to be "taken out."

What do you think national politicians will do? They would probably recommend surrender! Ladies, how do you think you will like wearing a burka? While a burka will not permit your belly button or breasts to be revealed, it will reveal your eyes—only your eyes!

If major American cities were destroyed with millions dead, it would be the end of the greatest civilization of all time! Could that be the reason that the Bible does not refer to America whereas even very minor nations are mentioned in Scripture? I would think that a nation as impressive as America would be mentioned in Scripture, but not so.

You turn on your television set some morning to discover that a major city is in flames with hundreds of thousands dead and millions dying a slow death from radiation. Will you have a job after that? Will you even care about a job? Your first and major thought will be survival.

AMERICA BACK TO THE 1700S

Some are fearful that the followers of that "peaceful" religion of Islam will go high tech and set off an Electromagnetic Pulse (EMP) device resulting in wiping out all U.S. electronic devices but keeping our superstructure intact. Former CIA chief James Woolsey testified before a Congressional committee in 2005 that an EMP could have "devastating consequences."[5]

If all electronic devices and electronically powered equipment were terminated because of the effects of an EMP device, then the U.S. would quickly grind to a halt. It might be more devastating than a major nuclear bomb! Think what it would mean: no elevators to take people to the upper floors of apartment and office buildings; no air conditioning; no heat; no lights; no subways; no stop and go lights in any city; no telephones, no radio or television; no microphones; no computers, no cell phones, no air travel; automobiles would not start; water would not be pumped into your home; and many other problems. America would be back in the 1700s again!

Furthermore, no EMP would have a return address! So whom do we retaliate against? In addition, if all our electronic systems were down, how would we mount an effective response without planes, guidance systems for missiles, etc.? Maybe you are reading this book in the dark, and that is where our military might be at such an hour.

An EMP attack or nuclear bombing of only one U.S. city would impact the world economy and make the Great Depression look like a blip on the screen. Insurance companies would go into bankruptcy or into the courts to refuse claim payments and banks would be closed. You might try to call the toll-free number to sell your mutual funds only to hear a constant busy signal. You would talk to your broker only to find that both of you are broke.

The U.S. Government would be broke and would renege on its financial obligations. Tax payments to the IRS would plummet as the cost of rescue and recovery soar into the stratosphere. The Pension Benefit Guarantee Corporation, an agency that guarantees your pension, (already billions of dollars in the hole) would go belly up. So would Social Security. Everyone would be on his own.

AWAKE, AWARE, AND ALARMED

I hope you are not reading this book in a dark bomb shelter. It is not melodramatic to say that American streets could become dark, deserted, and dangerous places as anarchy reigns. I can almost hear the hoof beats of the four horsemen of the Apocalypse in the distance.

I suggest that U.S. politicians get serious about terror **today** and be honest about what is ahead of us. They should be telling us to prepare for disaster: food, water, bomb shelters, escape routes, etc. Peaceful Muslims must also get serious **today**, and report known terrorists to the Feds, vigorously condemn the killers, and wave the American flag as they sing, "I'm a Yankee Doodle Dandy."

But frankly, it is too late to close the barn door since the horses are galloping down the road. We have been soft rather than sensible; weak rather than wise; mild rather than militant; and relaxed rather than resolute. When the bombs explode, all bets are off. A reign of terror may ensue, and the America we know would be gone forever.

Talk show hosts have asked me if my message causes people to panic, and I always reply that I am trying to make people be awake and aware without being alarmed. However, at this time in the crisis, maybe it is time to be alarmed! No, not irresponsible, out-of-control panic. Just the everyday kind of alarm that makes your blood run hot, your adrenaline flow, your hands sweat profusely, and your mouth as dry as an oil well I invested in.

In a few days, or weeks, or months after an attack everyone who has not prepared for disaster will panic. I would like for you to realize that you may have already waited too long to properly prepare, and if you wait much longer, it will be too late to buy gold, guns, and groceries. Everyone will rush for the doors at the same time, and you and your family will be crushed. The name of the game will be survival, only survival. Forget the job since it will be gone. Your Social Security or pension check? Don't count on it. Protection from local authorities? Probably not. You will be on your own.

After the next major Muslim attack we will witness the demise of a once-great nation. Those with an understanding of history will also finally realize that we are in a Hundred Years' War between Muslims and the rest of the world. Muslims have known this was coming for decades.

HUNDRED YEARS' WAR WITH ISLAM

In Europe, the Hundred Years' War (1337–1453) and bubonic plague reduced the population more than 50 percent! France lost half its population during the Hundred Years' War and Paris lost two-thirds of its population. The population of England was reduced by up to 33 percent due to plague during the same period. The war seemed to be incessant as France and England (aided on both sides by various nations) fought for control of France. It became the most notable conflict of the Middle Ages. Ours will probably be far worse!

Europe would undergo changes that would never be reversed. Feudalism, which was the exchange of land for military service, was coming to an end. Peasants acquired more power since their labor was worth more because of the loss in the labor pool. Serfs moved to the growing towns and acquired skills in production of goods. The Pope lost his grip on the English as Henry booted him off the island in the 1500s. Yes, life was changing for everyone.

Europe was changed quickly in response to the War and the plague. Europeans knew that they had to look at life as it was, not as they wished it to be. They rejected what was not working, adjusted their thinking, started reading the new English Bibles (that transformed their lives), rearranged their economy, and moved into the Reformation and Renaissance. Nothing would ever be the same.

America and the free world are in a Hundred Years' War but many officials refuse to admit it! Some leaders can't even pronounce the name of our enemy that all sane people know! Some even allege that some major world leaders are even in collusion with the enemy for ideological reasons! Other leaders are simply spineless, in need of a spinal transplant! Whatever, the fact is we are at war with koranic Islam because they declared war against the world in the seventh century. However, those of us who firmly believe that fact are said to be guilty of *Islamophobia*.

The U.N. has defined *Islamophobia* as a "deep misunderstanding of Islam [that] is fueling anger, hatred, and fear about one of the world's great religions." I think I can help the U.N. and it won't require a U.N. conference or large consulting fees paid to me. *Islamophobia* is a non-word that was contrived to suggest that anyone concerned with the Muslim threat is somehow unreasonable, unfair, and maybe unstable. The U.S. media assumes that all sensitive, sane, and sensible people would recoil from Islamophobia like a mythical vampire recoils from sunlight. However, that is political correctness run amok.

We are urged not to judge all Muslims by the acts of a few extremists who target civilians. The U.N. rejects "widely held views that Islam is incompatible with democracy or irrevocably hostile to modernity and women's rights."

Of course everyone knows that Islam has always been incompatible with democracy. Muslims will cooperate and use democracy to further their cause of a world caliphate; but their minds are closed tighter than a miser's wallet where freedom is concerned.

As to women's rights, is there any doubt where koranic Muslims stand? You will note that American Muslims are not demanding a change in the treatment of women in Muslim nations. Female circumcision (read: sexual mutilation often performed on little girls with a dull blade and no anesthesia!) is common even in Germany, Austria, England, and Netherlands; women can't vote; then you have unfairness in inheritance laws; unequal treatment in courts; wife beating, etc.

The mistreatment of women comes directly from Mohammed's teachings: more women in hell than men; prayers are interrupted by a black dog, an ass, or a woman; if wife is difficult, withhold sex from her and then beat her if needed; he took his slave to bed; he took his son's wife as his own; he had a nine-year-old wife; etc. Sounds as if Mohammed was in fact "irrevocably hostile to modernity and women's rights." And if U.S. and U.N. officials were informed or honest they would know that Muslims worldwide are obligated to emulate the lifestyle of Mohammad as well as follow their two "holy" books.

The U.S. is not at war with terror, but with a religion/culture that has promoted terror from its beginning. We are involved with a clash of civilizations that may not end for a hundred years! In other words we are involved with a Hundred Years' War that will result in the destruction of some nations.

The media reported Osama bin Laden as saying, "In essence, this war is a religious war."[6] Osama was right and right is right no matter who says it and wrong is wrong if the U.N. and every media person in the world say it. Our "War on Terror" is a Religious War that may last a hundred years. The choice is not between war and no war but intermittent war and continual war. Plan on it!

Many will be disturbed by that statement but it is better to be disturbed by truth than deceived by lies. The free world will live with terror from now on, even more than a hundred years!

DREAMERS, DELUSIONAL, AND DENIERS

If U.S. officials are wrong and there is no danger from terrorists and Islam is a peaceful religion hijacked by a few terrorists then breathe a sigh of relief, thank God for His mercy, and continue with your life. However, if you are wrong (and U.S. officials are right), you and your family will be cold, hungry, and dependent on others to provide for your basic needs. Is it wise to take such an unnecessary risk?

Some people do not want to recognize the problem because they are dreamers, others are delusional, and still others are deniers! The dreamer does not want his life to be totally upset (who does?), so he blithely walks through life without looking at reality. Dreamers are so much happier in their dream world. After all, in dreamland they don't have any problems, don't have to make difficult decisions, and always feel warm and fuzzy. There is no confrontation, conflict, or combat. So why wake up? I would like this message to be a fire bell in the night to awaken them from their slumber.

The delusional cannot be helped. They will not even consider the possibility that the world is going to undergo an incredible change very soon. They think by not wanting something to happen, it will not happen. They are wrong. Furthermore, hand wringing won't do any good either!

Then there are the deniers. These people have made up their minds that God would never permit America to go down. We are so very special, so very strong, and so very supreme. So very stupid.

AMERICA MUST LEARN FROM OTHERS

All Americans have to do is to consider what Muslim immigration has done to other cities and nations. There are hundreds of zones in European cities where it is not safe for non-Muslims to enter. Steve Emerson made a similar statement on *Fox News* and Fox later apologized for his statement! Steve was right. No apology should have been made other than to satisfy political correctness. The reality is that there are hundreds of such zones in Europe. Europeans have seen their cities taken over by a foreign culture, religion, etc.

On Feb. 29, 2016, a television crew from *60 Minutes* in Australia went to Rinkeby, Sweden (populated by Muslim emigrates from Africa) to report on one such zone. Within seconds of entering the area, the crew was attacked by a gang of masked members of Islam, the religion of peace. The crew was punched in the face and had a jar thrown at them. The cameraman had his foot run over with a vehicle "on purpose." Journalist Liz Hayes reported that Sweden has 55 declared "no-go" zones because of Muslim immigration. Middle East foreign policy expert Daniel Pipes, has reported on France's 751 "Sensitive Urban Zones" which the state does not fully control.

SHOULD MUSLIM IMMIGRATION BE STOPPED?

Presidential candidate Donald Trump's declaration that, for now, all Muslims should be refused admittance into the U.S. has resulted in most of Washington's effete prissy politicians and media moguls getting their knickers in a knot–a tight knot. Note that he did not demand that all politicians tell the truth or go to jail–or worse, resign and go back to their backwater towns and live in obscurity. Nor did he demand personal accountability. Nor did he demand that each one take an oath of poverty or even an oath to be faithful to one's own wife. Nor to take a pay cut! He simply demanded that Muslim immigration be stopped until someone somewhere, somehow can determine what is going on in our population. To date, no American has stepped up to that plate.

One major Muslim leader stepped up to the plate and ridiculed the "religion of peace" mantra that know-nothings spout. ISIS caliph Abu Bakr al-Baghdadi said in an audio message: "Islam was never for a day the religion of peace. **Islam is the religion of war**. Do not think the war that we are waging is the Islamic State's war alone. Rather, it is the Muslims' war altogether. It is the war of every Muslim in every place, and the Islamic State is merely the spearhead in this war. It is but the war of the people of faith against the people of disbelief." So, a top Muslim says Islam is not peaceful! He knows the Koran better than you. He may be a bigot, barbarian, and butcher but he was honest about what Islam is. He is more believable than CAIR spokesmen!

What sane person interested in security, safety, and stability can disagree with Trump's demand? Muslims would not be rejected because of mere religion but all that goes with that religion. Islam is a political system, an economic system, and a legal system all totally adverse to freedom–our freedom!

It must be affirmed that no foreigner has a **right** to enter the U.S. It doesn't matter that he or she is highly intelligent, a freedom lover, hard worker, or needs asylum. All those circumstances should be considered; however, would he or she be a positive addition to our nation? If not, I don't want them, even if they were all Baptists.

Most Americans have been conned and conditioned by the entertainment industry, the public school system, higher education, etc., to react emotionally to every issue. Few will work at garnering the facts, then thinking the issue through, then making a decision–often a difficult decision. Islam wants no discussions, deliberations, or debates because that would prompt an international discussion of the distortion, destruction, and death that has pulsated through Islam since its beginning. Moreover, they are fearful that someone will point out the mistakes, misinformation, mishmash, and madness in their "holy" books.

So, there will be no discussions, no deliberations, no debates–because they can't defend their seventh century religion that refuses to conform to the 21st century. Instead, we have U.S. officials threatening those of us who tell the truth about Islam!

The following incontrovertible truths must be dealt with by everyone using the same facts. Each one can have his or her opinions but not his own facts. Some crucial facts:

- Islam permits lying! It's called *Al-taqiyya*. With America's future in view, we must keep this principle of Islam in mind whenever we deal with Muslims.

- It is a fact that Islam teaches that no one has a right to worship anyone but Allah. See Sura 9:29; 2:691; 47:4; etc. In fact, a Muslim is to be killed if he or she leaves Islam. See Hadith vol. 9, book 84, #64. Will some national official ask moderate Muslims to repudiate that teaching?

- It is a fact that *jihad* is considered the "sixth pillar" of Islam, and while *jihad* can mean inner struggle, etc., it has always meant, "holy fighting in the cause of Islam."[7] My official Koran published in Saudi Arabia reveals this truth, as do *New Encyclopedia Britannica* and the *Dictionary of Islam*.

- It is a fact that Muslims true to the Koran (and Hadith) are not moderate. The terrorists are carrying out the commands of Mohammed, and those terrorists are targeting true moderates (who would be considered the equivalent of modernists in Christian circles) with death.

- Koranic Islam (historic Islam) is America's enemy that has clearly proclaimed ambitions to conquer or destroy America. If our leaders do not recognize that fact and act accordingly, they are like a man wading waist-deep through a snake and alligator infested Everglade swamp. They are going to get bit!

What should U.S. authorities do to escape planned Islamic terror? First, recognize that our enemy is koranic Islamists (not genuine moderates) because the first principle of war is to identify your enemy. Second, apprehend and arrest every person associated with terrorist groups. Third, freeze all terrorist funds in the U.S. and free world with cooperation of our European allies. Fourth, thoroughly investigate all Muslims in the military and academia, and then arrest those having terrorist connections. Fifth, stop playing games at the airports. Realize few Americans are terrorists and spend time on those who are more likely to cause harm. Sixth, stop **all** immigration for five years. Build the wall then patrol the wall with high tech equipment. Seventh, fine astronomically the first time then arrest the second time any American businessman who hires an illegal alien.

Put this book aside, for I guarantee that when the first U.S. city is bombed and burned, the above suggestions will be implemented–but too late.

I have been called a "hater" because I have reported the historical facts about Islam, Mohammed, and the Koran. I am not a hater, but a lover. It must be remembered that love without truth is not love. I am interested in truth–not political correctness, unity, diversity, pluralism, multiculturalism, ecumenism, or making Muslims feel warm and fuzzy with their 7th century religion. Truth and honesty are still important.

In America, there is no guarantee that one will not be offended or embarrassed. Catholics don't have to like Jews, Jews don't have to like Baptists, and God knows some Baptists don't like religions that don't start with B.

If Americans do not wake up, we will go the same way many European nations are going. A recent survey of **Muslims in America** shows exactly where we are headed. The Center for Security Policy reported:

"A majority (51%) agreed that 'Muslims in America should have the choice of being governed according to shariah.' Even more troubling is the fact that nearly a **quarter** of the Muslims polled believed that, 'It is legitimate to use violence to punish those who give offense to Islam by, for example, portraying the prophet Mohammed.' Nearly **one-fifth** of Muslim respondents said that the use of violence in the United States is justified in order to make sharia the law of the land in this country." Better read that again!

Peaceful religion hijacked by extremists? For an American to vote for unlimited Muslim immigration is like a chicken voting for Col. Sanders.

Any politician who does not know or believe the above facts should run, not walk, to hand in his or her resignation. Then get a real job where they can't do irreparable harm to future generations of Americans.

PREPARING FOR DISASTER

So I have some practical suggestions for the approaching disaster. The power may be off for long periods of time so you may not have lights, heat, or refrigeration. Water may not be pumped into your home, and phones may not work, even cell phones, since the towers may be destroyed. Elevators may not work; same with trains, subways, and traffic lights. Banks will fold as will insurance companies and major corporations. Don't count on your job being there or your investments, even **guaranteed** investments. When governments teeter on the edge of collapse, there are no guarantees. Well, you get the idea that you won't have a nice day!

While no one on the face of the earth can say for sure how bad it is going to be, it will be bad, and Proverbs tells us that the prudent man looks ahead, sees the danger, and plans for it. The fool goes on and must suffer for his folly. So pray and hope for the best and prepare for the worst. After all, you don't have to **believe** the worst is going to happen to prepare for it! Your fire insurance policy is an example of that. You don't **really** expect a fire but you have insurance, don't you?

I don't want to be melodramatic; but knowing that politicians have a tendency to over-react, I see ominous days ahead. If our cities are in flames, jobs are gone, people are hungry, hospitals are full, funeral homes are open 24 hours, banks are closed, major corporations are bankrupt, government checks are no longer being mailed, citizens are angry, hungry, and scared, then we can expect officials to continue to do stupid things. Martial law may be the norm in disaster areas. We have never heard the chilling march of highly polished jackboots on deserted and darken streets; moreover, the Constitution may be put in a velvet box for the duration, and America may only be a goose-step away from goon squads.

References:

1 "60 Minutes," Sept. 7, 1997.
2 "60 Minutes," Nov. 14, 2004.
3 *The New York Times,* August 11, 2004.
4 *USA Today,* March 21, 2004.
5 WorldNetDaily, May 2, 2005.
6 *USA Today,* Nov. 3, 2001.
7 Koran footnote, p. 39.

Chapter Six

Immigration Will Destroy America!

Immigration during bad times is dumb; and non-vetted Muslim immigration anytime is dumb, dangerous, and deadly as seen in a recent federal report. There are **officially** about 5.7 million illegals in America at this time although many conservatives and border watch groups suggest the number to be about 35 million! Almost half of the 12 million are Mexicans. Others are from Iran, Iraq, Yemen, Egypt, Syria, etc., and are identified as Other Than Mexicans (OTMs). More than 6,000 OTMs are apprehended each month so how many came undetected?[1]

The U.S. President wants to bring 10,000 more Syrians to America but there is rebellion on the reservations! A new Bloomberg Politics Poll found that 53% of Americans don't want to accept any more Syrian refuges. About 11% more would accept only Christian Syrians.[2] Also, about half of the governors have promised to refuse to have them settled in their states.

In 2014, for the first time, more OTMs were apprehended at the southern border rather than Mexicans! Furthermore, Border Patrol agents "seized 1,920,411 pounds of marijuana, 4,443 pounds of cocaine, 9,205 pounds of heroin, and 3,772 pounds of methamphetamine. They also seized $7,351,640 in currency, 475 firearms, and 63,493 rounds of ammunition."[3] I want to know what was brought across the border by the hundreds of OTMs that cross each day undetected.

CATCH AND RELEASE

When Mexicans are caught at the border they are supposed to be deported; however OTMs must be held for a deportation hearing. The problem is compounded by packed detention centers so they are given a summons to appear in court in 30 days. However, 85% refuse to show for their hearing. Some may live near you. And yes, some may have jobs while others are making bombs. According to the Border Patrol, some 465,000 OTMs have taken advantage of this "catch and release" policy to settle here in the U.S.[4]

On March 14, 2016, the U.S. Immigration and Customs Enforcement (ICE) revealed that 124 illegal immigrant criminals who were released from jail by the Obama administration since 2010 have been subsequently charged with murder! "[These] criminal aliens released by ICE in these years—who had already been convicted of thousands of crimes—are responsible for a significant crime spree in American communities, including 124 new homicides. Inexplicably, ICE is choosing to release some criminal aliens multiple times," said the report written by Center for Immigration Studies' (CIS) respected director of policy studies, Jessica M. Vaughan.[5] That is insane!

In 2015, *The Washington Times* (4/27/16) reported that Homeland Security released into the community nearly 20,000 immigrants last year who had already been convicted of crimes— including hundreds charges with sexual assault, kidnapping, or homicide — according to figures sent to Congress this week!

The illegal aliens had committed a "total of 64,000 crimes, including 12,307 drunken driving convictions, 1,728 cases of assault, 216 kidnappings and more than 200 homicide or manslaughter convictions, U.S. Immigration and Customs Enforcement (ICE) told the House Committee on Oversight and Government Reform ahead of a hearing Thursday."

IMMIGRATION IS KILLING LIBERALISM

Unrestricted immigration is destroying Europe as I write and the continent is no longer seething but boiling in resentment, anger, even hatred. Their open door policy whereby anyone is free to travel to any European nation was the lethal weapon used by "refugees" from Muslim nations in the Middle East and North Africa. To make matters far worse, there have been thousands of sexual assaults in Germany, Switzerland, Austria,

Sweden, Norway, and Finland resulting in demands for the borders to be sealed. France, Germany, Austria, Sweden, and Denmark have at least required identification at the borders. The liberals' dream of a borderless Europe has become a nightmare.

Muslim men are taught that they are superior and have a right to have sex with any non-Muslim female. Emulating Mohammed, that includes sex with children. Muslims ran a child sex ring in Rotterdam, England that involved 1400 British girls some young as eleven. That was the fifth such sex abuse ring run by Muslims discovered and shut down in England.

In March of 2016, a small Swedish town had ten sexual assaults in eight days, all perpetrated by Muslim men. One out of four women in Sweden will be raped. 77% of the rapes are done by Muslim men who make up 2% of the population. Gang rape is not uncommon nor is child rape. Norway and Sweden officials tell women not to go out at night alone and Norway is now paying Muslims to leave the country!

Many gang rapes by Muslim "refugees" in the U.S. are so depraved I will not go into detail. One example took place in 2014 in Colorado Springs but they are happening worldwide.

This crisis has killed liberalism in Europe which is the only positive thing to be said on this subject. The Prime Minister of Slovakia opined, "The idea of multicultural Europe has failed." Hundreds of women were molested and raped in various European cities that have never had such crimes in such numbers. Cologne had over 170 women assaulted on New Year's Eve of 2015 alone.

It seems many Americans want to follow Europeans off the cliff! Not I.

IMMIGRANTS WILL CHANGE OUR CULTURE

The media reported that the European Union predicts that another 3 million immigrants will invade the continent in 2016! "Only" 700,000 arrived last year.[6] Sweden has accepted more immigrants than any other European nation but now realize they were stupid to do so. However, it is too late. The horse is galloping down the road.

When thousands of immigrants rush into a European city, the city is totally transformed immediately. It is not an exaggeration to say that Europe is no longer Europe and America is rushing into that maelstrom because of legal and illegal immigration.

There are now more than 80,000 illegal aliens from terror-friendly or terror-supporting nations hiding in the U.S.! *CNSNews* reported in 2015 that the Department of Homeland Security's Customs and Border Protection revealed that in 2014 their agents apprehended 1,191 persons from 12 of the 14 nations that DHS and the State Department consider nations that have problems with terrorism. Pro-immigration spokesmen declare that only a **few** non-Hispanics cross the border illegally so there is little to fear from terrorists. However, in 2014 out of 486,651 apprehensions, 257,473 were from countries "other than Mexico."[7]

The above horror-tale was reinforced by Texas Gov. Rick Perry declaring that undocumented immigration along the U.S.-Mexico border constitutes a significant terrorist threat. Speaking on *CNN's* "State of the Union," Perry said the United States is at "historic record highs with individuals being apprehended" from countries "that have substantial terrorist ties," such as Pakistan, Afghanistan and Syria. They are not interested in picking tomatoes!

OUR BEST INTERESTS

It is obvious that U.S. immigration policies should be in the interest of U.S. citizens! It is insane to think there is any validity in the arguments used by liberals/progressives in this debate. Social policy is not a main interest. Relieving social and economic problems of another nation is not relevant. Nor is it desirable or in our best interest to placate and serve an elite group of U.S. business people. Nor do we make policy decisions to make whiners feel good. What is best for our nation must be the criterion.

The Jordan Commission said it best in its 1995 call to Congress: "Credibility in immigration policy can be summed up in one sentence: those who should get in, get in; those who should be kept out, are kept out; and those who should not be here will be required to leave." Can any honest, sane person disagree with that?

As of 2016, we are accepting a million **legal** immigrates each year; a number that should be cut to zero for a five year period. If migrant workers are needed then temporary worker cards can be awarded with strict supervision. When the time has expired, each case can be evaluated and if workers are still needed then the cards can be renewed. Everyone wins since the necessary laborers are found; poor foreign workers have temporary jobs; money is sent home; etc.

We must admit that if large numbers of immigrants, legal or illegal, enter the U.S. it will relieve some of the other nations' social and economic problems, but what will it do to America's problems? By what twisted logic are U.S. citizens expected to forfeit their hard-earned money to provide for foreigners, especially those foreigners who are criminals? Remember that the Boston terrorists were on welfare. We are financing our own destruction!

COSTS

Should U.S. taxpayers be expected to finance millions of uneducated, unskilled, and often un-American illegal immigrants? I can defend the position that we should not finance **legal** immigrants? With the administration's legalization of at least five million illegal aliens, it will destroy a once-great nation.

While many of the aliens are decent, hardworking people, many are not. I think this tragic immigration policy will create political, financial, and cultural anarchy. For sure, it is changing America.

In times past, most immigrants melted into the pot but not today. They have no desire to assimilate and become Americans. Harvard immigration expert George J. Borjas declared, "In fact, the evidence suggests that there has not been any economic assimilation for the cohorts that entered the country in the 1990s."[8]

The current very negative consequences of immigration are largely because more recent groups aren't learning English at the same rates as their predecessors. Borjas suggests that "it's not very costly anymore" for new immigrants if they don't learn English because so many of them have formed communities that insulate them from other Americans. Therefore, they don't need to learn English since they can function with each other. Illegal aliens get lost in a huge group of their own kind and don't need to melt into the pot. They sit, soak, and sour in the salad bowl.

We are told that the U.S. economy depends upon foreign workers; however, Borjas reveals that legal and illegal immigrants in the labor market produce $1.6 trillion per year; however 97.8% of that money goes to the illegal workers and only "2.2% accrues to native-born Americans."[9] Borjas suggests that there is more cost to America than financial benefit. The net benefits to American workers from illegal immigrates is 0.06% of our Gross National Product. Studies indicate that immigration reduced the income of native-born high school dropouts up to 5%.

HELPFUL WORKERS

The pro-immigration people tell us that immigrants don't take jobs, they make jobs and pay taxes. However, while that is true in some individual cases, it is not true in the aggregate. Borjas estimates that the immigrants' cash welfare benefits alone cost about $1 billion **more** than is paid by them in taxes each year.

Illegal immigrants take jobs at **lower** wages thereby subsidizing the American businesses that hire them illegally. If laws were enforced against hiring illegals then Americans would be the source from which businesses hire their workers–paying them the going wage and benefits. High-paid American workers "willing to work hard" are often laid off, because illegal immigrants are willing to work just as hard, but for much less money. Who do you think a business owner is going to hire under those conditions?

We are told that immigrants are needed as agricultural workers, work that Americans will not do, but a more correct statement is that they take jobs that Americans refuse to take at greatly reduced wages! Furthermore, when an American gets a job he must be paid the minimum wage with all required benefits. No wonder businessmen prefer to hire illegal aliens. When times get tough, Americans will work at any job to put food on the table. Don't you feel good knowing that foreigners are working at very low wages to make more profit for those agribusinesses?

FREE RIDE

According to the *Los Angeles Times*, 2% of illegals are picking crops (while the rest are picking our pockets). Fact is, for every 100 illegal aliens who get a job, 60 Americans will lose their job.

It is a fact that **well-educated** immigrants usually pay taxes that exceed the benefits they receive. The school system, fire protection, police protection, etc., generate vast expenses that are paid by the taxpayers but poorly educated immigrants, legal or illegal, do not pay their share. They are tax consumers getting in services far more than they pay in taxes. That means other taxpayers must "carry" the non-payers on their backs.

The cost of government to provide education and police and fire protection is far larger than many people imagine. The average U.S. household in 2010, received $31,584 in government benefits and services. If families pay less in taxes than what government services cost to provide then obviously such expense cannot be sustained indefinitely.[10]

America has immigration laws and illegal immigrants break those laws to come here. The fact that many are hard workers and sincerely want to better themselves is irrelevant. The fact that family members are U.S. citizens is not the issue. The issue is that "the lifeboat is full" and it won't hold anymore without sinking the boat and drowning everyone.

WELFARE

The typical poorly educated illegal immigrant is limited in what he or she can contribute to America. Such people can succeed as farm workers, household help, laborers, lawn workers, etc., but their limited education will lock them into the lower income group where they will stay.

Some say that these people don't use much welfare but that is a myth. Furthermore, it is a fact that legal immigrants and U.S. born families with little education "receive far more in government benefits than they pay in taxes."[11] The bottom line is that education produces higher income and lower education results in less income and dependence on taxpayer-funded welfare.

Another fact is that illegal immigration makes it more difficult for the least advantaged U.S. citizens to participate in the American dream. That is insane because American public policy should support the interests of those who have a legal right to be here, not the law breakers.

Illegal immigrants (at this time) do not receive Social Security or Medicare but that does not mean they don't receive free benefits and services. Their children receive free education and medical care, and when they have children born in the U.S. they get the full list of freebies. Additionally, they receive police and fire protection, free library services, use of roads and bridges without helping financing them. When police and firemen need to be hired and roads and bridges need to be repaired, the legitimate taxpayers are sent the bill. Illegal aliens only pay taxes on what they purchase.

The fact is that the average illegal immigrant family receives in benefits more than twice what they pay in taxes. And if or when they get amnesty they will have access to more than 80 means-tested welfare programs. That means your tax bill will soar into the stratosphere unless the progressives have repealed basic math. What few people are discussing is what happens when the amnesty-given individuals reach retirement! You think Social Security is in trouble now!

When immigrants work for less money, the restaurants, hotels, etc., that use their labor realize benefits. Those benefits can be passed on to other Americans by lower prices. So we pay less for food, lodging, etc., but is it worth the cost?

NEGATIVES

The Heritage Foundation reported: "In 2010, the average unlawful immigrant household received around $24,721 in government benefits and services while paying some $10,334 in taxes. This generated an average annual fiscal deficit (benefits received minus taxes paid) of around $14,387 per household. This cost had to be borne by U.S. taxpayers.... Under current law, all unlawful immigrant households together have an aggregate annual deficit of around $54.5 billion."[12] So, it is untrue to state that illegal immigrations do not cost America.

There are many negative results from illegal immigration: bankrupt hospitals, burgeoning schools, welfare funds, soaring crimes; lower wages; fewer jobs for legal Americans; and invasion of violent gangs even into northern cities.[13]

It is said that there are about 35 million illegal aliens in the U.S. that do not speak English, have no plans or desire to speak English and do not give a flip for American culture.[14] They ridicule the notion of American being a "melting pot" and consider it more of a "salad bowl."

One tax expert suggests that legal taxpaying Americans will hand over $380 billion per year to fund the illegal aliens living here; and that's after accounting for the sales taxes and any other taxes they might pay. The cost of police and fire protection, parks, sanitation, health inspections, food safety, etc., is additional. Forget that, if you can, and consider what a massive influx of uneducated, unmotivated, and often uncouth aliens will do when they have the right to vote. Do you think they will vote for freedom, responsibility, and accountability? Your vote will be worthless. This mass movement of people will produce a huge lower class and a shrinking middle class with all the attendant problems.

NATION OF PARASITES

As the population expands, the cost of services must expand. More police, firefighters, health inspectors, schools, and teachers. If immigrants don't pay their share, then legitimate taxpayers must pay the bill. Of course, adding new non-producing families does not always add cost to all government programs such as national defense, scientific research, spending on veterans, etc. Such costs are not impacted by any number of illegal immigrants; however, that would not be the case for fire and police protection and school teachers.

If a citizen receives a benefit for which he or she has not financed through taxes then someone else has had to pay that share. I caused a stir on national television hosted by Sally Jesse Raphael when I stated that "If I get money I did not earn then someone earned money they did not receive. That's thievery." I added fuel to the fire by adding, "This nation of producers has become a nation of parasites." Amazingly, thousands of people stood to their feet and cheered! Most people expect to pay their own way and consider it poor character if they don't.

A few years ago, I was told by a post office official in San Luis, Arizona their office has 11,200 post office boxes in a town of about 3,000 people because people living across the border in Mexico use them as a permanent American address to collect public benefits. Courtesy of YOU. Don't you feel warm and fuzzy knowing that you go to work each day to support parasites across the border?

FBI REPORT

Since people from Middle East nations, Mexico, and South America often have lower skills, they are more likely to request public assistance, gorge the public school system, overwhelm the health care industry, and spike the crime reports. Bigotry? Not at all. Just the facts. Did you know that 15% of California students are illegal aliens and they cost California citizens over 11 billion dollars per year for health, education, and incarceration! No wonder, the state is bankrupt! Moreover, 25% of inmates in federal prisons are criminal aliens and are not in prison for being gate-crashers but for committing crimes in the U.S.! Furthermore, about 300,000 of all state and local prisoners are illegal aliens![15] You are funding them! Moreover, 75% of those on the most wanted list in L.A. are illegals. The following stats from the FBI should sober any pro-immigration zealot:

- 83% of warrants for murder in Phoenix are for illegal aliens.
- 75% of those on the most wanted list in Los Angeles, Phoenix and Albuquerque are illegal aliens.
- 24.9% of all inmates in California detention centers are Mexican nationals.

- 40.1% of all inmates in Arizona detention centers are Mexican nationals.

- 48.2% of all inmates in New Mexico detention centers are Mexican nationals.

- According to the Government Accountability Office, 25% of prisoners in Federal prisons are illegal aliens who have been arrested an average of seven times!

- 53% plus of all investigated burglaries reported in California, New Mexico, Nevada, Arizona and Texas are perpetrated by illegal aliens.

- 50% plus of all gang members in Los Angeles are illegal aliens.

- 71% plus of all apprehended cars stolen in 2005 in Texas, New Mexico, Arizona, Nevada and California were stolen by illegal aliens or "transport coyotes."

- 47% of cited/stopped drivers in California have no license, no insurance, and no registration for the vehicle. 92% of that 47% are illegal aliens.

- 63% of cited/stopped drivers in Arizona have no license, no insurance, and no registration for the vehicle. 97% of that 63% are illegal aliens.

- 66% of cited/stopped drivers in New Mexico have no license, no insurance, and no registration for the vehicle. 98% of that 66% are illegal aliens.

CRIMINALS AMONG US

Information in the FBI's 79-page National Gang Report published in 2013, proves to any reasonable person that illegal immigrants are a major threat to all Americans especially, but not exclusively, along the southern border.

FoxNews.com reported that federal statistics reveal that "the estimated 11.7 million illegal immigrants in the U.S. account for 13.6 percent of all offenders sentenced for crimes committed in the U.S. Twelve percent of murder sentences, 20 percent of kidnapping sentences and 16 percent of drug trafficking sentences are meted out to illegal immigrants."[16] Those numbers even shock me!

But it gets worse! Foxnews.com continued to report that there are about 2.1 million "legal or illegal immigrants with criminal convictions living free or behind bars in the U.S., according to ICE's Secure Communities office! Each year, about 900,000 legal and illegal immigrants are arrested, and 700,000 are released from jail, prison, or probation. ICE estimates that there are more than 1.2 million criminal aliens at large in the U.S." Sleep well tonight, friends.

According to the FBI, criminal gangs are wreaking havoc in the U.S., with 65 jurisdictions nationwide reporting gang-related offenses committed with firearms account for at least 95 percent of crime in those areas. Gangs are responsible for an average of 48 percent of violent crime in most jurisdictions and up to 90 percent in several others, according to National Gang Intelligence Center analysis.

The report further documented gangs in Southwestern border regions consisting of up to 80 percent illegal aliens were committing a multitude of crimes in America, "including drug-related crimes, weapons trafficking, alien smuggling, human trafficking, prostitution, extortion, robbery, auto theft, assault, homicide, racketeering, and money laundering."

U. S. gangs consist of several types of groups, including street gangs, prison gangs, motorcycle gangs, and ethnic and organized crime gangs. Approximately 1.4 million people were part of gangs as of 2011, and more than 33,000 gangs were active in the United States.[17]

Furthermore, criminal street gangs—mostly comprised of illegal immigrants—are responsible for the majority of violent crimes in the United States and are the primary distributors of most illicit drugs.[18]

Now there are reports that a large part of Arizona is literally controlled by Mexican drug lords! May I humbly suggest that we do what we have done for two hundred years and "call out the marines"? It might take 24 hours to clean out the drug lords, but it can be done and should be done.

LEGAL AND ILLEGAL

It is time to take charge of our borders, keep out illegal aliens, apprehend those now living in the U.S. illegally, and demand that our "friends" south of the border stop playing the hypocrite and enforce their laws. It's past time to get started.

We should be concerned about illegal and legal immigration since there are 35 million immigrants in the U.S. Harvard economist George Borjas affirmed that "the United States has been granting entry visas to persons who have relatives in the United States, with no regard to their skills or economic potential." He said that, "Immigrants today are less skilled than their predecessors, more likely to require public assistance, and far more likely to have children who remain in poor, segregated communities."[19]

POVERTY AND DISEASE

Immigration expert Borjas says immigration is positively bad news for America's poor. The wages of America's high school dropouts have fallen 10% since the 1980s relative to the wages of more educated workers. Borjas declares that about a third of that decline is because of immigration. About half of the immigrants now living in this country are of Mexican origin.

The empirical evidence suggests that immigration is exacerbating this problem of poverty according to Professor Borjas. Surely all thinking people would agree that any immigration policy should not be detrimental to the present legal population. A policy that increases poverty is suicidal.

In recent years most American's income slowed while immigration did not. It is suicide to continue on the path of disaster we are traveling. If we don't take action now we will see dozens of "Detroits" across the nation.

Mexican, Salvadorians, Ecuadorians, etc., illegals have already proved to be diseased, disruptive, divisive, even dangerous, for many Americans but Muslim legal and illegal immigrants will prove to be a disaster. All illegals must be dealt with in a lawful, even gentle (if possible; rough if necessary) and methodical way. The longer we delay in handling Muslim and other immigrants the more costly it will be for everyone.

This is incredible, indefensible, and insane yet our politicians and fuzzy Christian leaders seem to think it is acceptable and admirable instead of abhorrent and abominable. Furthermore, illegal aliens kill about 10,000 Americans each year–when they are not "picking tomatoes."

Each year about 500,000 illegal aliens cross into the U.S. with many carrying drugs, disease, and destructive plans for our nation. In recent days Border Patrol agents have contracted various diseases, lice and scabies. Many illegals want to pick tomatoes; however if tomato pickers can slip in, so can terrorists. Yet, we have major politicians who are so unconcerned they want to give amnesty to the illegal gate-crashers already here!

OPEN BORDERS

Even in normal times, it is insane for a nation to have unrestricted immigration, and during wars, national pestilences, or terror it is doubly insane to have porous borders! That's about where the U.S. is today.

Open border fanatics tell us that "The U.S. had open borders from its inception until 1882. It makes one wonder what the Founding Fathers would think of us today!" However, that is not the whole story because in those days there was much of America unexplored, uninhabited, and undeveloped. We needed the people–farmers, carpenters, smiths, merchants, salesmen, trappers, and cobblers who came and fell in love with their new nation, learned English, and melted into the pot. But the pot is not melting today. It is now a salad bowl where many different peoples do their own thing and have no interest in the general welfare.

American citizens will hold elected officials responsible for terrorism resulting from their inaction, ineptitude, or incompetence relating to border security. As the numbers grow, the crimes accelerate, and the costs escalate there will be devastating results. America's seething volcano is going to erupt!

HARD DECISIONS

Should U.S. taxpayers be expected to finance illegal immigrants? I can defend the position that we should not finance legal immigrants. "Thanks" to Republicans and Democrats, with amnesty just around the corner, immigrants will get on the welfare rolls and most will stay there. Have the loonies taken over the asylum? There are non-thinkers, even "evangelical" Christians, who defend illegal aliens getting all kinds of welfare benefits! Such gullible people would qualify as Lenin's "useful idiots."

It is time for some hard decisions: Is it reasonable to know who is entering our nation? Is there not a limit as to the number who come? Shouldn't we have some requirements as to education and ability so they can contribute to America? Is it unreasonable to expect people to be in good health and be free of contagious diseases? Should we not expect arrivals to have some kind of retirement plan or funds to sustain them? Should arrivals be expected to learn our language and accept our culture? Is it unreasonable to demand that immigrants obey our laws? Is it reasonable to expect hospitals to treat people without cost even if it means bankruptcy for the hospitals?

The basic premise is that every nation has an obligation to have distinct borders and defend those borders. However, the globalists have always demanded open borders in every nation! The U.S. Secretary of State, John, Kerry expressed the globalist position when he told graduates at Northeastern University in Boston on May 6, 2016 that they ought to realize a "borderless" world was something they couldn't stop, and should instead accept.[20] That would mean that nations would cease to exist and people could go wherever they wanted without any restrictions.

I ask those who want unlimited immigration if they will invite anyone and everyone to come to America? Are there not some limits? If so, then what are the limits? It is almost too late to implement policies to save America from being totally destroyed by immigrants with alien customs, alien skills, alien language and an alien religion.

With the knowledge of the massive catastrophic results there are still major political, religious, academic, and other leaders demanding that all those who crashed our gates should be given legal status! Amnesty for all! That is insane.

The illegal alien invasion of America has resulted in a dangerous, dark, decaying, and dying nation, and I see no hope for the future even if there were a return to genuine Christianity. And there is no hope for sure if we refuse to restrict immigration and grant amnesty to lawbreakers already here.

The bleeding at the borders must be stopped while other immigration matters are decided. If we don't stop the bleeding, more Americans will bleed.

References:

1   Sara Carter, *The Blaze*, Oct. 10, 2014.

2   Pew Research, Nov. 19, 2015.

3   Breitbart News, Jan. 2, 2015.

4   *Christian Science Monitor*, July 26, 2005.

5   *Washington Examiner*, March 14, 2016.

6   *Newsmax* magazine, Jan., 2015.

7   Penny Starr, *CNSNews*, Jan. 6, 2015.

8   George J. Borjas, "The Slowdown in the Economic Assimilation of Immigrants: Aging and Cohort Effects Revisited Again." March, 2014.

9   George Borjas, "Immigration and the American Worker," April 2013.

10   Robert Rector and Jason Richwine, "The Fiscal Cost of Unlawful Immigrants and Amnesty to the U.S. Taxpayer," Heritage Foundation, May 6, 2013, pp. v-vii.

11   Ibid.

12   Ibid.

13   Jim Gilchrist, "The Crushing Economic Burden of Illegal Immigration"; FrontPageMagazine.com, Oct. 10, 2005.

14   Ibid.

15   FAIR, "Criminal Aliens," (Updated 2015).

16   Malia Zimmerman, FoxNews.com, Sept. 16, 2015.

17   U.S. National Gang Intelligence Center, "National Gang Threat Assessment, Emerging Trends," 2011, p. 9.

18   Judicial Watch, "Illegal Immigrant Gangs Commit Most U.S. Crime," Jan. 30, 2009.

19   George J. Borjas, *National Review,* June 16, 1997.

20   Katie Reilly, *Time* magazine, May 6, 2016.

Chapter Seven

Amnesty is Destructive, Dangerous, and Deadly!

R ecent headlines blared, "Illegals now flooding U.S. Border" and some just-arrived illegal aliens asked, "Where do we go to get our amnesty?" Many of the illegals are unaccompanied children some of whom are delivered to relatives who themselves are illegal aliens and authorities do not ask their status! And the ACLU filed a suit demanding each and every illegal alien must have a lawyer and YOU will pay the bill. The message sent to every person: sincere refugee, thief, terrorist, or thug is, "If you get here, you can stay" so they come by the trainloads. And when they come they will be handed a bag of freebies: education, medical care, welfare payments, legal advice, etc.

PRO-AMNESTY DEMANDS

Hispanic extremists continue to raise the ante to get as much as they can, after all, we "owe" it to them. One sign demanded, "Give us FREE Health care, Jobs–no taxes, House, Food - You OWE us America! We will shoot more police in Arizona until we get FREE!" Has anyone but me asked why that person did not go to jail? Another sign demanded, "Citizenship for 11 million." And "citizenship" means "Democrat" voters–to be sure they get all the freebies. And Republicans are too stupid or cowardly to resist it.

The pro-amnesty zealots have written what they call a "Bill of Rights for Undocumented Americans" in which they make their demands to U.S.

officials. They assume or presume that if a person is present in the U.S. (even illegally) they have certain rights that must be recognized. They contend that since they are human, they have certain rights and of course that is true but one of those rights is not U.S. citizenship. U. S. citizenship is a privilege not a right.

Here's an appropriate analogy: You have worked hard, saved, and finally built a nice home, not a palace, but a nice home. One evening a man walks in your unlocked door and asks for food and water. You are surprised and offended but kindly provide his request. As he eats at your table, he starts to watch television and moves to your favorite chair. You think he is being pushy but you want to be a thoughtful host. He stays all evening and when you suggest that it is time for you to go to bed, he asks where he can sleep. You don't have a spare bedroom but he decides that he will take yours. After all, it's a matter of humanity.

The next day he informs you that he likes the area and has decided to stay; however, you tell him that is impossible. You have your own life to live but he demands that you accommodate him, even build an additional room for him. You are incensed but you do as he demands.

Later that day he informs you that his religion requires special foods and would like to have it prepared for the evening meal. He specifies no pork or shrimp and any beef or lamb must be prepared to exacting standards.

He settles down in the new room you built at your expense but he tells you that he has some health problems and needs for you to get him a doctor–at your expense.

Next, he is concerned about his future so he wants you to provide him a retirement program.

He observes your frustration, anger, and resentment and with a sinister smile he suggests "You should have stopped me at your front door."

IMMIGRANTS' BILL OF RIGHTS

Only a fool would acquiesce to such free-loading tyrants. But that's where the U.S. is with illegal aliens. They are here and they are demanding their "rights." It is called their "Bill of Rights," but it is only a start! They want any talk of building a wall stopped as well as talk about airline security since it is "chest-thumping rhetoric." They arrogantly demand that everything is "on the table." That means legal residency–citizenship.

The first demand is "Acknowledgment that we are already here, that we are human beings with a right to be, that our mere presence cannot be deemed illegal or our existence alien." Well, just because they are humans does not justify legal existence in the U.S.

Another demand is, "Affirmation that we are to be treated with dignity and respect, not just because of who we are, but who you are." Who I am determines how I react to freeloaders who don't display much dignity, humility, or gratefulness.

Another demand is the "right to be presented with a path to citizenship… combined with interim deferment of all law-abiding Undocumented Americans against detention and deportation." But there are problems in that criminals cannot become U.S. citizens. Plus, there are procedures that must be followed and requirements met. It is rather asinine for them to use the term *law-abiding*.

Still another demand is a "Guarantee of wage equality with a legal right to petition for wage theft or workplace mistreatment without jeopardizing our immigration status." Maybe when pigs learn to fly in formation over the White House!

And another demand is "Assurance of humanitarian treatment, including medical care." That just broke the bank.

It is my humble opinion that anyone who agrees with the above is incompetent, inconsiderate, or insane. It is like a lifeboat full of survivors floating in the frigid Atlantic. The boat is just above water and a 300 pound man swims along and demands to be pulled aboard. Of course, everyone is compassionate, concerned, and contrite about his plight but they also know that if he is pulled on board, everyone drowns.

SERIOUS COSTS

In 1986 Congress tried to fix the immigration problem but made it worse with their amnesty plan. Moreover, to give amnesty to lawbreakers in 2016 is unfair to those who obeyed the law and did it the right way albeit the difficult and time-consuming way. One of our daughters-in-law came as a legal immigrant. I remember when she finally finished the paperwork and she became a citizen. She said, "I'm so glad it's over. The waiting, standing in line. The paperwork. The cost. It's finally over." She could have procured a student visa and dropped out of sight as thousands of

Muslims have done. If illegal aliens get amnesty, she will appear to be a fool to have done it the right way.

However, granting amnesty to the illegal alien population would come at a serious cost. First and foremost, it would be costly to American workers in job opportunities since jobs would be taken by illegals who work for less. It would also result in depressed wages as amnesty recipients gained the opportunity to compete for legal jobs.

But even those Americans whose jobs and wages are not immediately affected by a massive amnesty would pay a significant price. Amnesty would impose enormous burdens on American taxpayers as illegal aliens became eligible for medical and welfare benefits. And amnesty would be costly to current and future workers by undermining the already vulnerable Social Security system.[1]

Pro-amnesty advocates respond that the opposite is true since illegal immigrants have payments taken from their salary for Social Security yet cannot legally receive them so they are funding your mother's retirement. This was articulated by Greg Schell: "They almost certainly will never get back the money they are paying, and so they are helping keep Social Security solvent."[2]

But Greg was wrong: there is no such Social Security Fund; and only about half of illegal workers are working above ground with payments taken from their salary.[3] Moreover, most of those illegal workers are using a fake Social Security number and when amnesty comes, they could receive new numbers and their past deductions could be added to their retirement using the new valid numbers. Depending on Congress, there could be a period of time when past illegal "contributions" could be credited. However, any money taken from their salaries they more than get back in freebies.

IMMIGRATION AND SOCIAL SECURITY

Furthermore if illegal workers became legal and started claiming benefits that had accrued, the whole Social Security program would have to be recalculated "leading to a greater possibility of the fund drying up."[4]

Those beating the drums for amnesty tell us that it along with more legal immigration would really save Social Security by increasing the contributions. However, Stephen C. Goss, Chief Actuary of the Social Security Administration told the Senate's Homeland Security and Governmental

Affairs Committee on February 4, 2015 that Obama granting legal status to five million illegal aliens would only result in Social Security being "improved slightly." Amnesty would not save Social Security and even if true, the deleterious results would be far worse than the trivial benefits.

The other half of illegal workers are in the underground economy and pay no Social Security taxes, Federal income tax, or state income tax. Of necessity they pay sales tax. If amnesty were given then both legal and illegal immigrants would receive Social Security numbers and enter the system for all benefits.

Social Security is already in trouble and rushing toward bankruptcy. Since 2010 the benefits exceeded taxes paid and are expected to do that into eternity! The difference is now 10% and is expected to be 20% by 2030.[5]

IS AMNESTY CHRISTIAN?

A report in the *Washington Post* revealed that illegal aliens in the United States cost the federal government more than $10 billion a year and that amount would almost triple if they were given amnesty.[6]

Amnesty is a program pushed by pathetic progressives to legalize millions of illegal aliens giving them citizenship. Many of the migrants are diseased, deranged, and dangerous as thousands of Americans have discovered. With this vast number of people from other cultures, languages, and religions we will see a massive shift in American culture not seen in our history.

My critics declare that I am unkind, unreasonable, and even unchristian for opposing amnesty and sanctuary cities; however, their charge is not based on solid reasoning or the Scripture. They twist the Scripture like a pretzel to make it fit their unreasonable, unconstitutional, and unbiblical demands.

We are told that the illegal immigrants are trying to escape Islamic tyranny, gangs, and poverty so America should make room for them since we are a Christian nation. Well, first of all, only people can become Christians; however, a nation can become Christianized or influenced by the Bible. Secondly, almost all my critics and supporters of amnesty and unlimited immigration confuse what a person should do with what a nation should do. All people who interpret ancient literature know one of the first questions that must be answered is, "To whom was this written."

Pro-amnesty evangelicals are not asking that question.

Exodus 23:9 is usually used by the Bible-twisters to support their cause; however they use a flawed hermeneutic to build their case. "Also thou shalt not oppress a stranger: for ye know the heart of a stranger, seeing ye were strangers in the land of Egypt." That chapter is dealing with a person's obligation not national obligations. Of course, those religious leaders who use that verse know that but are being deceitful to establish a very shaky principle.

It is easy to prove my contention about this being a personal obligation. Verse 3 of that chapter warns the ancient Jews (and us today) that "Neither shalt thou countenance (give approval) a poor man in his cause." Moses was warning us about showing favor to a person because of his condition, whether rich or poor. We are not to be swayed by our emotions but by justice. The ancient maxim is, "Let justice be done, though the heavens should be dissolved." I heard one of the great evangelists of the last generation say, "Do right though the stars fall from Heaven."

The illegal immigrants have not done right. They resolutely broke our laws and crashed our gates and forced themselves in front of others who have followed our laws and procedures. There are four million people who are waiting in line legally. The illegal aliens refused to wait.

JIM WALLIS OF SOJOURNERS

Jim Wallis, president of Sojourners (a leftwing religious outfit), said that "Evangelicals finally realize that how we treat the stranger, these 11 million undocumented people, is how we treat Christ himself." Jim must have been sleeping during his hermeneutics class in seminary because he did not get that from the Bible. Of course, Christians are to be kind, gracious, helpful, but that does not translate into being suckers, softies, and sycophants. We could really show how kind, gracious, helpful as well as stupid we are by emptying all our prisons! And the most hard core could move into Jim's neighborhood.

Wallis went on to say that the leadership of the Evangelical Immigration Table (EIT which includes the National Association of Evangelicals, and the Ethics and Religious Liberty Convention of the Southern Baptist Convention), and the evangelical community has "never been more united on an issue." Jim has one of two problems: he is disingenuous or uninformed because the vast majority of evangelicals want illegal immigrants to go home. A 2014 Pulse Opinion poll revealed that 78 percent of evangelicals surveyed believed that the biblical command to "love the stranger" means "to treat the stranger humanely while applying the rule of law."

TWISTING OF SCRIPTURE

The pro-amnesty preachers tell us that all people should be treated with dignity and thereby win some to Christ, but you can arrest someone and still show him or her some dignity. Amnesty has nothing to do with personal dignity. Evangelical leaders would be wiser to listen to their members rather than rush to the microphones and cameras to speak **for** them. As for helping the poor and evangelizing them why couldn't that be done in their home nations? If amnesty happens the wall would not be built and tighter controls would be even looser. It's like the hole in the dike. Then it is too late to fix our problem.

We are told that amnesty and even more immigration would be an incredible opportunity to win people to Christ without the cost of sending missionaries. However, Christ commanded us to go into all the world and win them, not have some government send them to us thereby destroying our own nation. If we win them in their culture, it will change their culture but then radical leftists think that is wrong, even a kind of genocide! But they think it is right to change and destroy our culture!

When John Geddie went to the New Hebrides as a missionary he found constant violence, murder, thievery and cannibalism. When he left they established a plaque in his honor: "In memory of John Geddie....When he landed in 1848, there were no Christians here, and when he left in 1872, there were no heathen."[7] The Gospel changes people and a culture. Islam also changes a culture.

Leviticus 19:33 is also used wrongly: "And if a stranger sojourn with thee in your land, ye shall not vex him." Again, the preceding verses prove that God was giving instructions for personal conduct by warning them not to consume blood, not to get tattoos or pierce their flesh, not to prostitute their daughters, not to break the Sabbath days, and not to be involved with sorcery, fortune telling, etc. Then He warned them not to vex a stranger living among them. In fact Moses went on to say that "thou shalt love him as thyself."

Jews were to be kind to strangers because it is the right thing to do and it could be good for the strangers and good for the nation. Many visiting strangers came to visit Israel, were impressed by their faith, freedom, and fairness and converted to Judaism. New Testament Christians are commanded by Christ to treat others the way we want to be treated.

Let's return to Exodus 23:9: "Also thou shalt not oppress a stranger: for ye know the heart of a stranger, seeing ye were strangers in the land of Egypt." But that has nothing to do with illegal aliens. Fuzzy preachers neglect to tell their congregations that the Jews were in Egypt by invitation and were not trespassers. In fact, they were special guests as long as Joseph was alive and a friendly Pharaoh reigned. They had not entered the land illegally as do modern invaders. The Jews were strangers in Egypt but not illegal aliens even though they ended up as slaves.

These verses do not apply to the immigration issue even slightly. Illegal aliens purposefully chose to break our laws, even arrogantly demanding entrance into our nation expecting to be cared for upon their arrival. They are not sojourners or strangers but scoundrels and are encouraged to break our laws by many leftwing religious groups, even some Evangelicals.

LEFT WINGERS DEMAND AMNESTY

The international money speculator George Soros is sugar daddy to the Evangelical Immigration Table (EIT), a leftist group of Christian leaders that never saw a socialist scheme they didn't like. Soros' agenda, in addition to making money, is to promote every leftwing program–especially transplanting Muslims into Europe and America. He is funding various religious non-profits to accomplish that task. EIT gets a substantial portion of its funding from groups backed by George Soros.[8]

Soros also demanded that the European Union provide $16,800 per asylum-seeker for two years to help cover housing, health care, and education costs! Well, that should break the bank!

In December of 2015, the EIT asked Congress to authorize **more** Syrians into the U.S. and many professing Christian leaders stood up and yelled, "Bring them on, even more to our shores."

The U.S. government is shoveling the cash into religious non-profit groups whose purpose is to deliver more immigrants into your neighborhood. This is part of a one billion dollar annual refugee resettlement budget.

Among other requests, the EIT wants Congress to not exclude any specific religious group or nationality from the massive resettlement program. In recent years the group has brought in about 2,000 Syrians to the U.S.

and 97% are Muslim. Obama plans to bring in another 10,000 "refugees" in 2016 although more than half the governors have refused to cooperate with him. Note that no one insists that maybe Christians should be at the top of the list.

Let me see if I understand this situation. American Evangelical leaders are pressuring Congress to bring in people who know nothing about democracy, have no concept of freedom, speak a foreign language, worship a pagan god, will immediately become a financial leach on the face of America, and have peed into a hole in the floor all their lives! Now, I think it is wonderful that they want to upgrade their living standards and culture (as well as their sanitary procedures); however, it doesn't seem wise to change the face of America to accomplish that. Future Americans will rise up and call our present leaders of both parties, traitors.

Moreover, why are Evangelicals receiving barrels of money from the federal government anyway? If they are so concerned about "refugees" then let them pass the collection plate the way our church does when people have a need. Of course they should help people but don't expect taxpayers to pay the bill. May I suggest that there exists no constitutional provision for such a program. But then, there is no constitutional provision for abortion, same-sex "marriage," farm subsidies, student loans, etc., but that doesn't bother our esteemed officials.

EVANGELICAL LEADERS WANT AMNESTY

Admittedly, most of the immigrants will not be extremists and relish beheading "infidels" but they will delight in others doing the same. A May 2015 poll showed that 51 percent of **U.S. Muslims** prefer *sharia* courts to American courts! Make no mistake; America is being transformed in front of your eyes. Europe is lost, gone, hopeless, destroyed, wrecked, smashed and America is following the exact path. Only a fool, fanatic, or falsifier says otherwise. We are like the frog in the slowly heating pot of water.

Note that these Evangelical leaders are not responding to their constituency because the rank and file has already spoken. A Pew Research Poll revealed that white Evangelical Christians were opposed to the Syrian refugee resettlement program by a two to one margin but the leaders plow on since they know what's best. After all, what do the *hoi polloi* know about such matters?

Mike Philips senior pastor of Immanuel Fellowship Church in Frisco,

Colorado declared that he and his liberal friends are "bothered by the rhetoric" from critics. I suppose he means those of us who suggest that we can't afford to lose more jobs, lower wages, confusing, compromising, and corrupting the culture, lack of vetting, etc. Mike declared, "I realize that some are genuinely concerned about the vetting process. Personally, I've looked at it; I think it's a very tight, very good process." No, he is wrong; the FBI director said that they could not vet so many immigrants with their resources.

Galen Carey works for the National Association of Evangelicals (NAE) and declared "How safe it is," speaking of the resettlement program. Well, then I suppose he would be the first to invite the "refugees" to move into his neighborhood. But then, we have an "obligation" to accept these people after all the senior pastor of Mosaic Church in Memphis said, "We were once the same kind of refugees. Our families come from similar situations." No, these modern "refugees" chose to break the law and come unvetted and unwanted to America.

BIBLE AND AMNESTY

I remind these "do gooders" (as opposed to those who do good) that the Bible often speaks of borders, borders that should be respected. All the major cities in the Ancient Middle East had massive walls, not to keep people in but to keep gate-crashers from coming in uninvited.

These compromising evangelical leaders are trying to drive a square peg into a round hole with a sledge hammer, but it simply won't fit. The President of the National Hispanic Christian Leadership Conference, Samuel Rodriquez opined, "It's about our Christian faith. It's about Matthew 25 and Leviticus 19. It's about finding a way where we can reconcile Romans 13, 'respecting the rule of law.'" No, Sam, like many Evangelicals, has to twist the Scripture like a pretzel to make it mean what it was never meant to mean. That is dangerous.

Matthew 25 deals with the Judgment of the Nations and in verse 35 Christ said, "For I was an hungred, and ye gave me meat: I was thirsty, and ye gave me drink: I was a stranger, and ye took me in." No, that has no relevancy to the immigration issue. Christ is judging the nations as to their treatment of the Jews during the Great Tribulation. I ask Evangelical leaders who use this verse out of context: "Have you no shame?"

Open border and amnesty people should read and understand Acts 17:26: "And hath made of one blood all nations of men for to dwell on all the face of the earth, and hath determined the times before appointed, and the bounds of their habitation." That verse teaches that while all mankind are of the same blood, i.e., the human race, there are some bounds of their habitation. Since all men have the same source, there is no valid reason to think one is better than another although each should be loyal to and proud of his roots. The Athenians had a foolish notion that they were self-produced, and were the aboriginals of mankind. They said that the first men sprung up in Attica, like radishes! Well, that's about what evolutionists believe. Science has come a long way baby.

All the pro-amnesty preachers use the same verses to support their unsupportable position. They are defending a castle in ruins. Some perspective follows that soft Evangelicals do not provide.

GOD ESTABLISHED BORDERS

God respects borders, after all, He set them! *Border* is used 129 times in the Bible and *borders* is used 49 times. Only a few times does the word refer to the border of a piece of clothing, the rest has to do with tribal or national boundaries. *Border* is first used in Gen. 10:19 when He set the borders of the Canaanites. From scriptural evidence, God does not believe in open borders. He set firm borders as recorded in Deut. 32:8: "When the most High divided to the nations their inheritance, when he separated the sons of Adam, he set the bounds of the people according to the number of the children of Israel." This refers to Noah's sons, Shem, Ham, and Japheth and the areas of the world their posterity would populate and control.

I remind you that God scattered and separated the people into nations and languages at the Tower of Babel where they were trying to build a tower to reach Heaven. Some say they were building a tower so that they would have a refuge if another global flood happened. Probably, it was a plan to thwart God's will since He had told them to scatter across the face of the earth and multiply. They wanted to make a name for themselves and stay where they were. That was the first attempt to produce a global society. Progressives are still at it today telling us that nationalism is narrow and bigoted.

The Tower of Babel and the confusion of tongues are often ridiculed by sceptics as allegorical but the sceptics are usually uninformed God haters. Historian Herodotus (born 485 B.C.) visited the tower and described it in his writings as did Eupolemus and Abydenus. These two were not an ancient vaudeville team but respected Jewish and Greek historians who lived about 200 B.C.

The *Targums* were vocal explanations and expansions of the Hebrew Scripture by Jewish rabbis and they provide insight about the Tower of Babel. During a *Targum*, a rabbi would read the Word then paraphrase it in the common language to the congregation. This practice became a necessity just before the birth of Christ since the Hebrew language was in disuse and the common people spoke Aramaic. Hebrew was used by the scholars. The *Targums* declare that the tower was used for pagan worship with the intent of placing an image at the top with a sword to protect against their enemies. There is no doubt that Nebuchadnezzar repaired the tower and it was dedicated to Bel. Mankind has drifted far from the message that God gave: He scattered mankind and separated them into various nations within firm borders.

God gave Israel the land of Canaan and divided the land giving specific portions to each tribe except for the tribe of Levi. God clearly provided the boundaries of each tribe as when Joshua declared in Joshua 15:1, "This then was the lot of the tribe of the children of Judah by their families; even to the border of Edom the wilderness of Zin southward was the uttermost part of the south coast." God gave Judah–the largest and most important tribe from which the kings and the Messiah would come–the southernmost part of the land. Their portion was from the Dead Sea southward and west to the Mediterranean Sea. God cared about boundaries and so should we. People who don't respect borders don't respect law, order, tradition, freedom, property rights, civil rights, etc.

Open borders are anti-biblical, totally contrary to God's plan for man's survival. Europe has had open borders for many years. The citizens of the 28-country European Union may travel freely among any of the member states except Bulgaria, Cyprus, Ireland, Romania, and the United Kingdom that require travelers from other European Union states to present a passport or ID card at the border. You can see the folly of open borders in the daily newspapers as thousands of migrants have been trampling through Greece, Bulgaria, Romania, Hungry, Slovakia, the Czech Republic and into Germany. Now that it is too late some European nations are reinstating border controls; however, the horse is galloping down the road.

SANCTUARY CITIES

Amnesty and sanctuary cities are destructive, dangerous, disastrous, even deadly. It is time for Congress to put on their big-boy pants and stop Obama's "Get Out of Jail Card" and "Pass Go, Collect Welfare" schemes.

While progressives are beating the drums for amnesty, the reality is that during the 1980s various cities implemented amnesty by designating themselves as *sanctuary* cities.

The policy was begun in 1979 in Los Angeles to prevent police from inquiring about the immigration status of those arrested for other offences! So local officials thumbed their noses at federal laws put in place to protect all of us! How asinine, audacious, and arrogant! It gives illegal immigrants a "get out of jail free" card while taxpayers pay.

There are more than 300 sanctuary cities in the U.S. that flaunt federal laws to the determent of everyone. Case in point is the shooting death of 32-year-old Kathryn Steinle in San Francisco (a sanctuary city) by an illegal immigrant who had been deported five times! Federal authorities had asked the city to hold him for deportation hearings but city officials refused! The city fathers put their leftist ideology above the safety of its citizens and federal law (that required his deportation).

The socialist, leftist, bleating hearts have declared that they will not enforce federal law and will not inquire into the immigration status of any person within their city. The officials spouting such nonsense think they are being gracious, forgiving, and kind but they are turning those cities into third world slime pits.

CITIES OF REFUGE

Historically, sanctuary cities were necessary and legitimate in ancient days but modern counterparts are a distortion of the original purpose. In the early days of Hebrew society, six Cities of Refuge were established throughout Israel to protect people guilty of accidental murder from being slain by a blood relative of the victim. It must be remembered that cities in ancient Israel did not have a police force, nor did they have prisons, nor an elaborate judicial system. God had given them the Ten Commandments that provided a safe society; but for those who disobeyed, there were problems. The murderer was to be put to death even if the victim's family was willing to forgive and accept a "blood payment."

God is the giver of life and to take a life was to pollute the land, and the land could only be redeemed by blood: the manslayer was to have his life taken. Such action was also a legitimate step in preservation of society.

Cities of Refuge among the Hebrews were necessary because patriarchal law fittingly, in that day, required the nearest relative to avenge the death of his relation by slaying the murderer. Cities of Refuge were established to prevent hasty executions of this law and prevent injustice and the Cities of Refuge were judged proper for this purpose. There is no record of this system being inefficient or being abused.

Human nature, being what it is, often was the cause of injustice because of sudden heated vengeance taken by a victim's relative. A sanctuary city permitted a manslayer to run to that city giving him time to prove his crime was not premeditated and did not require the death penalty. Moreover, it also permitted a "cooling off" period for the aggrieved relatives. This was the humane and equitable end contemplated in the institution of Cities of Refuge.

GOD'S PLAN

God told Moses in Num. 35:14 to provide "three cities on this side Jordan, and three cities shall ye give in the land of Canaan, which shall be Cities of Refuge." The six cities were located all over the land to provide easy access for any Jew or even any stranger in the land. No Jew was ever far from a City of Refuge since everyone lived within a day's journey of a designated city. Also, the roads to the cities were far better than the other roads in the land.

If a manslayer fled to a City of Refuge, the city officials inquired into his crime as to whether or not he planned to slay the victim. If found guilty, he was to die but if the killing was not premeditated, he was permitted to live in that city until the death of the high priest. Getting to a city was not enough since the killer had to present his case and defend himself "in the ears of the elders of that city" (Joshua 20:4) to the satisfaction of the city officials.

While the offender preferred to return to his home, he was required to stay in the city until the death of the high priest, after all, he **had** killed another person. So, he did not get away with his offence. Justice was served. After the death of the high priest he could return to his home and possessions. However, if he left the city before the death of the high priest, he could rightly be killed by the aggrieved relative.

The Cities of Refuge protected the innocent and helped diffuse family feuds that often resulted in whole families being killed. God's gracious provision was not an "eye for an eye" but "no **more** than an eye for an eye" and "**only** an eye for an eye." But then wimps don't desire any repercussions for crime. Too judgmental, you know.

The purpose of the cities was not to harbor killers but to ascertain guilt and provide justice. That is the opposite of present day sanctuary cities where the whole idea is to give sanctuary to the guilty. This is a producer of further crime because it does not hold the guilty accountable. Such city officials are promoters of wickedness, injustice, crime, and hatred.

GOD'S PURPOSE

The City of Refuge represents Christ since "The Lord also will be a refuge for the oppressed, a refuge in times of trouble" (Psalm 9:9). The manslayer had to confess his transgression and his mistake. A fake repentance for a premeditated murder did not gain the slayer any safety whatsoever. Getting to the city was not the answer. He still had to have his case adjudicated by the town fathers. If guilty, he was punished.

The Cities of Refuge typify the relief which the gospel provides for poor, penitent sinners. Their protection from the curse of the law and the wrath of God is found in Christ to whom desperate offenders flee for refuge.

God's interest was to punish and prevent crime whereby sanctuary cities promote and protect crime. It's time for city officials to be held accountable for their criminality. By protecting criminals, city officials become partakers in their guilt and expose themselves to share in their punishment. It is time for awakened, alarmed, and angry citizens to recall the mayor and city council members responsible for any Sanctuary City.

The big differences in Cities of Refuge and Sanctuary Cities are:

- In one the innocent offender is protected and in the other the guilty is protected.
- In one the offender must give an account and in the other the guilty is protected without remorse, repentance, or restitution.
- In one the offender goes home to a productive life after the death of the chief priest and in the other the offender never goes home and can be supported by American taxpayers for his lifetime.
- In one the basis is law and the other the basis is lawlessness.

- In one the offender has committed one offense and in the other there are often many offences.

- In one the offender was a legal citizen and in the other the offender is an illegal alien with no constitutional rights.

- In one the offender must prove his innocence and in the other the offender has to prove nothing.

City and county officials must be reminded that their mandate is not social experiments but the operation of the city (or nation) for the benefit of legal citizens who elected them. It is obvious that illegal aliens, especially those of a backward, brutal, and bloody culture will destroy our nation. We are observing this in many European nations as I write and such destruction will be a reality if our laws are not implemented immediately.

Otherwise, there may be a Muslim caliphate in our future.

References:

1   "Amnesty: Breaking the Social Security Bank," The Federation for American Immigration Reform, July 2015.

2   "Illegal immigrants pay Social Security tax, won't benefit," *Seattle Times*, December 28, 2011.

3   Randolph Capps, et al., "A profile of the low-wage immigrant workforce," Urban Institute, October 27, 2003.

4   Martin H. Bosworth, "The Earnings Suspense File: Social Security's 'Secret Stash,'" *Consumer Affairs*, Feb. 22, 2006.

5   Samuelson, Robert J., "Who's not bargaining in good faith," The *Washington Post*, December 3, 2012.

6   *Washington Post*, Aug 26, 2004.

7   Wikipedia, "John Geddie," accessed April 15, 2016.

8   *National Review*, Oct. 24, 2013.

Chapter Eight

Mohammed: Prophet, Patriot, or Pedophile?

Since Islam is one of the largest movements in the world and the fastest growing, we must look closely at what it is, **not** what some people claim it is. I interviewed three Muslim leaders in Indianapolis, one of their main centers in the U.S. In that interview, I asked, "Are you willing to characterize the suicidal bombers as homicidal bombers?" I thought I might get such an admission; however, I got much more than I expected. One of their most respected leaders calmly asserted that such terrorists "were freedom fighters." He confirmed this statement a few weeks later by telephone. "They are freedom fighters." That is proof that some "moderate" Muslims are supportive of terrorism. It further substantiates the fact that U.S. leaders are uninformed or are dancing around the issue when they say, "extremists have hijacked a peaceful religion."

U. S. OFFICIALS WRONG

President Bush told Muslims at a Washington area mosque: "The face of terror is not the true face of Islam," and he told a Joint Session of Congress: "Its teachings are good and peaceful, and those who commit evil in the name of Allah blaspheme the name of Allah." Is that true or not? If it is **not** true, then Christians are obligated to reprove, rebuke, and rectify the error, even error coming from the President! After all, he was only the President of the United States, not a member of the Trinity! (Don't tell that to fanatic Republicans who think the GOP is the fount from which all blessings flow.)

At a White House press briefing, spokesman Ari Fleischer said, "This attack had nothing to do with Islam. This attack was a perversion of Islam...." Bush and Fleischer were not served well by their fact checkers and speechwriters.

Attorney General John Ashcroft, referring to a four-page document belonging to one of the terrorists, said the "references were a stark reminder of how these hijackers grossly perverted the Islamic faith to justify their terroristic acts...." Ashcroft was wrong. The terrorists were simply carrying out many injunctions found in the Koran, the holy book of **all** Muslims.

Most U.S. Government leaders are fearful of giving the impression that we are fighting a "religious" war. They cannot admit the terrorists are true Muslims because if they did, the U.S. would be perceived as anti-Muslim, and the U.S. would then be declaring a war against a religion! Of course, politics must be considered, but it is not helpful to dance around the truth: the U.S. did not start this war. It was declared by a bunch of Muslim terrorists following a seventh century camel driver.

Our national leaders, like the Clintons, Obama, and establishment Republicans will not admit that we are involved in a clash of cultures and a religious war that could last a hundred years! It is not a war of our making. When the next major terrorist attack happens you will notice that Clinton, Obama, Biden, and Company's unwisely and hastily adopted sympathy and pandering to all things Muslim will be discarded as quickly as long underwear in a Texas heat wave.

CHRISTIANS ARE NOT TERRORISTS

Authorities get very uneasy around committed Christians who declare that there is one genuine, authentic, reliable religion that is totally different from all other religions. That is breaking the first rule of multiculturalism and authorities don't really want us to admit the possibility of one religion being superior. Moreover, it is a fact that our government is much more fearful of Muslims than they are of Christians. For once, they have made a correct assessment. Christians are not flying planes into buildings! Many are just sipping a cold drink as they watch "Gilligan's Island" for the 24th time!

The message that the world is getting from our politicians, preachers, professors, performers, and pundits is that there are many religions and each one is as good as any other. All are equal. Of course, that is heresy and nonsense. All religions fall into one of two categories: the religion of Abel or the religion of Cain. Abel offered a God-required sacrifice while his brother offered the crops he had produced. Abel's offering was accepted and Cain's was rejected. On one side, you have salvation becoming reality through repentance and faith, only through the meritorious work of Christ in dying for man's sins. Personal salvation comes through regeneration, not reformation or rehabilitation or religion. On the other side, you have all the other religions of the world: religions of works.

In America, (an America that was founded upon the fact of Christ's finished work!), it is almost a hate crime to assert that one religion is true and all others are false. I would further remind you that following the terrorist attacks, almost no one has mentioned Jesus Christ, but always some unknown god out there somewhere. We are seeing government, at all levels, trying to placate the non-thinking public by calling upon an unknown, ambiguous god to support their policies. Everyone is saying, "God bless America," but we must ask, "Whose God?" The God of the Bible, I trust. One thing is sure: we cannot expect the blessings of God if we are fearful and reticent to proclaim Christ as the only hope for this nation and world!

Christians must not give anyone a reason to mistreat others. We are obligated to truth, not error. Moreover, Americans can discuss, debate, and disagree on any issue without fear. While there are some Muslims who are embarrassed and horrified at the terrorism that took place in America, Paris, Brussels, etc., we must not permit them to distort facts, the facts about the Koran, to make themselves more comfortable. Here are documented facts as to the real face of Islam and the real Mohammed.

THE REAL MOHAMMED

We need to examine some facts about Mohammed, the founder of Islam. Mohammed, with its various spellings, is the most common name in the world![1] He was born in Mecca (Saudi Arabia) in 570 of the Quraysh tribe to Abdullah (Abd-Allah) and Aminah. He was distantly related to the royal family; however, his parents were poor. After the death of his parents, Mohammed was passed among different wealthy relatives and was finally reared by a poor uncle.

Mohammed had visions even as a youngster and some historians think they involved epileptic seizures. Muslims get indignant when this is suggested, but he had the symptoms of epilepsy: he fell to the ground, foaming at the mouth, throwing his head from side-to-side, his eyes rolling back in his head, his heart thumping wildly, and his body jerking and perspiring heavily. Sometimes, he heard bells. I'm not sure what he had, but I sure don't want it, and it sounds like epilepsy to me.

During those episodes, Mohammed received his visions. McClintock and Strong reveal: "Muhammad, as we gather from the oldest and most trust-worthy narratives, was an epileptic, and as such, was considered to be possessed of evil spirits."[2] Historian Norman Cantor also says Mohammed was given to epileptic fits. Muslims have a right to disagree with such an assessment, but are obligated to explain his seizures that no one denies.

Mohammed's problem, as suggested above, may have been demon possession. Vol. 4, book 53, number 400 and vol. 4, book 54, number 490 of the Hadith (one of Islam's holy books) reveals that he was bewitched, at times seeing things under satanic inspiration. In fact, at one point, that's what Mohammed thought his problem was, and he decided to commit suicide after his next seizure. His family convinced him that he was not possessed because he was such a "good" person; however, we do know that his mother claimed to be visited by spirits, had visions, and was involved in the occult arts.

Mohammed could have been epileptic or demon possessed! On the other hand, it could have been both! If I had my choice, I would rather be an epileptic than demon-possessed. I mean no disrespect to sincere Muslims, but I am not going to "waltz around the issue" just to make them more comfortable with their religion. Just as I will stand with Christ and His preaching, His person, and His program of world evangelism, the Muslims must stand with Mohammed's deception, demonism, debauchery, and depravity.

HIS EARLY YEARS

The facts of his life are really not disputed: When he was age 25 he married Khadija, a rich widow 15 years his senior who had hired him to manage her caravan trade. They had two sons who died young and four daughters. At age 40 he received his calling as an *apostle* or *prophet*. He wanted to appeal to Christians and Jews as his first converts (after his family of course), so he thought apostle and prophet would open doors for him. He was wrong. The Jews and Christians could see that he was a charlatan.

Allah couldn't get his facts straight as to Mohammed's calling! In sura (chapter) 53:2-18 and 81:19-24, Mohammed had a personal appearance from Allah. Then we are told in sura 16:102 and sura 26:192-194 that his call came from Gabriel. Again, in sura 2:97 it was the angel Gabriel who gave him his call and provided him with the perfect Koran right from the throne of Allah. According to Muslims there was no human author of the Koran and it was handed down to mankind from Allah through the angel Gabriel.

Mohammed won a few members of his family to Islam but only received ridicule, resentment, and rejection from the Mecca community. The leaders of Mecca were fearful that this new religion would hurt their business at the Kaaba where the worship of 360 pagan gods brought many rich caravans and pilgrims to the city. The financial success of the city, especially Mohammed's Quraysh tribe (who controlled Mecca), depended on the caravans that planned their route to go through Mecca so the caravan workers could stop and worship their god at the Kaaba. (And throw a few rocks at the devil. More about that exciting event later.)

The followers of Islam react angrily when we speak of Islam's pagan origins but Arab scholar Nazar-Ali commented, "Islam retained many aspects of pagan religion."[3] Professor of Arabic Alfred Guillaume admitted, "The customs of heathenism have left an indelible mark on Islam, notably in the rites of the pilgrimage."[4]

RELIGIOUS DESPOT

Mohammed left town in a hurry for Ta-if but was no more successful there than he was at Mecca. In fact, they ridiculed him and pelted him with stones. He returned to Mecca and found that the anger had not abated but had intensified, so in 622 he went to Medina (250 miles north) where he found some success by uniting two Arab clans and neutralizing various Jewish tribes. Rulers in Medina had invited Mohammed and his followers to that city because they needed to restore order. Mohammed agreed to move if they accepted him as prophet. His move to Medina is known as the *hijra*.

It is believed that in Medina Mohammed was a sincere (although misguided) seeker of religion, but that was lost quickly with the acquisition of power, position, and popularity. That should not be unexpected since he was, like others of the Arabian Peninsula, deprived of education and culture and driven by his instincts. Add to that his twisted, fragmented ideas of Judaism and Christianity, along with his visions and vivid imagination, and it is not surprising that he changed from a religious devotee to radical despot. It is no surprise that he could not differentiate right from wrong or truth from falsehood. Mohammed could justify every assassination, every beheading, every robbery, every truce breaking, and every act of adultery with the help of his personal heavenly emissary, Gabriel.

PREACHING AND PLUNDERING

With every new convert, Mohammed grew more hostile and led three unsuccessful attacks upon Meccan caravans as they were going to or returning from Syria. In his Nakhla Raid, he attacked a caravan and a man was killed. His followers split the loot (and Mohammed took his 20%), and the plunder brought him more converts. (Well, if preaching won't do it, plunder will.) Wonder why a prophet who gets direct messages from heaven has to fund his new religion with plunder? Is Allah in Chapter 11 bankruptcy? Is he broke? Doesn't he own even a few cattle on a few hundred hills and maybe a copper mine someplace?

Mohammed led the next raid known as the Battle of Badr where 49 Meccans were killed and about that number were taken prisoner and his plunder pile grew. He had hit the jackpot. Religion **was** paying off. At the conclusion of the battle, the bloody head of Mohammed's enemy was hurled at his feet, and Mohammed cried out, "It is more acceptable to me than the choicest camel in all Arabia." To justify his blood thirst, Mohammed said, "I have been ordered by Allah to fight with people till they testify there is no god but Allah and Mohammed is his messenger." Therefore, it wasn't the devil who made him do it, but Allah! Compare that with Christ who said in Matthew 5:44, "Love your enemies, bless them that curse you, do good to them that hate you...."

MOHAMMED THE ASSASSIN

Mohammed was bursting with power, and he exercised it by taking vengeance against his enemies. One was a young poet who had accused him of using her dead father's writings in the Koran. One night, Mohammed's designated assassin crept into her home and found her sleeping, surrounded by her children, one at her breast. He removed the suckling baby and plunged a sword into the poet.

The next morning the assassin went to morning prayers where Mohammed asked if he had slain her. Mohammed was pleased to hear the positive news. The assassin asked, "Is there a cause for apprehension?" Mohammed assured him that all was well and said, "A couple of goats will hardly knock their heads together for it." Later, Mohammed had another poet, a man over 100 years old, killed as he slept. Seems he, too, had written some poems that offended the prophet. I've read some of their poetry and while it wasn't very good, it didn't require the death penalty!

Mohammed was very disappointed when the Jews refused his convoluted message and ridiculed his calling of a prophet. He tried to placate the Jews by insisting all Muslims pray toward Jerusalem; preaching that there was only one god (Allah); observing the Jewish Sabbath; and even adopting some Jewish dietary laws. Sounds as if he was pandering to the Jews, but the pandering didn't pay. They rejected him so he changed his beliefs! No, don't observe Saturday but observe Friday as the day of worship. No, don't pray toward Jerusalem but pray toward Mecca. Moreover, he was now killing individual Jews who had offended him.

A Jewish poet named Kab, who had also written poems condemning the Muslims' killing at the Battle of Badr, was lured to a waterfall and murdered. Every Jew now feared for his life. The Jews had not responded to Mohammed's office of "prophet," so now the prophet would have his way with them. Kab's death was ordered by Mohammed according to the Hadith.

The morning after Kab's murder, Mohammed said, "Kill any Jew who falls into your power," so Muhayyisa b. Masud killed Ibn Sunayna, a Jew with whom he and his family had had some commercial relations. When Muhayyisa's brother Huwayyisa badgered him about killing the Jew, Mkuhayyisa told him that if Mohammed had told him to kill him (his brother) then he would do so. Then Huwayyisa, not yet a Muslim, said, "Any religion that can bring you to this is indeed wonderful!" Wonderful? How about wicked?

OVER 800 JEWS BEHEADED

As he built his army, Mohammed discovered that Jewish towns were an easy and rich target, so he and his holy robbers started attacking their settlements, especially those that specialized in gold and silver. Mohammed continued to raid Meccan caravans with sporadic success. Back at Mohammed's hometown of Mecca there was concern that he was "getting too big for his britches," so they attacked him. During the battle,

Mohammed was hit in the mouth with a sword (Gibbon says, a javelin). Historians cannot explain why the Meccans did not pursue the battle and devastate their opponents, but they did not. Of course, Mohammed still had influential family members in Mecca who did not recognize his new religion but probably did not wish him dead.

The Meccans began a two-week siege on Medina in 627, known as the Battle of the Trench; some Jews helped in defense of the city, but most were neutral. Mohammed questioned their loyalty, and after the battle, he had all the Jews in the crosshairs. He said that the judgment of God was "the Jews shall be killed." During the night, ditches sufficient to contain the dead bodies of the Jews were dug across the market place of the city. In the morning, Mohammed ordered the male captives to be brought forth in companies of five or six at a time. Each company was forced to sit in a row on the edge of the trench (mass grave) and were there beheaded. The bodies were cast in the trench. Some of the women were given to his troops and others sold into slavery.

The butchery lasted all day and into the night with the killing of about 800 men. After the killing spree was over, Mohammed relieved his stress by sleeping with Rihana whose husband and all male relatives had just been beheaded! War is so stressful! And civilization marches on.

Of course, the above massacre (admitted by Muslim and Western historians) was very profitable. After Mohammed squirreled away his normal 20% of the booty, the rest was divided among his followers. And he got **more** followers. After all, there were ladies, loot, and land available for the taking, and they took.

The above massacre is denied by uninformed or dishonest Muslims, but it is a fact of history recorded in the *New Encyclopedia Britannica*: "Some of the evidence against him such as his connivance at assassinations and his approval of the execution of the men of a Jewish clan, are historical matters that cannot be denied."[5]

MOHAMMED TAKES MECCA

With every month, Mohammed grew stronger as more converts showed up at his tent. (Ladies, loot, and land will do that.) Now was the time to take Mecca for good. A treaty was made between the leaders of Mecca and Mohammed whereby he and his followers could make the pilgrimage to the Kaaba; Mohammed could "preach some revivals" but could not engage in any forced conversions. However, true to his lack of character,

Mohammed broke the treaty within a year, since he believed it was legitimate to fake a peace when you are weak so that you can smash your enemy when you are eventually strong. Muslims call that *takiya*. Principled people call it "deception."

His impressive army forced the leadership of Mecca to capitulate. Mohammed was back home as the "top honcho" religiously and politically with the necessary troops to have his way. Moreover, his way was to destroy the idols at the Kaaba and institute one true god–Allah and Mohammed as his prophet.

CHRISTIANS AND JEWS GO TO HELL

Nevertheless, we are told Mohammed was a man of peace! Yes, he brought peace (of the grave) to thousands of people; his followers have brought "peace" to millions. Mohammed, like Hitler, Stalin, and Mao, made clear his intentions, and his followers have been carrying out his instructions since his death. He said that Muslims are to "Fight against those who believe not in Allah...(Jews and Christians), until they pay *Jizyah* [tribute] with willing submission and feel themselves subdued" (sura 9:29).

Moderate Muslims want us to believe that Mohammed was supportive of Christians, but that was only in the early days when he thought he could get their allegiance. Later, he considered them unbelievers and consigned to hell:

> *Verily, whosoever sets up partners (in worship) with Allah, then Allah has forbidden Paradise to him, and the Fire will be his abode....Surely, disbelievers are those who said: "Allah is the third of the three (in a Trinity)"....And, if they cease not from what they say, verily, a painful torment will befall on the disbelievers among them. (Sura 5:72-73.)*

When you hear Muslims speak about tolerance and building bridges between Islam and Christianity, remember that Mohammed forbade Muslims to make friends of Christians and Jews. In fact, he taught that Christians and Jews were going to Hell.

Koran-believing and Hadith-believing Muslims believe that only Muslims are going to Heaven. Everyone else is going to Hell. Don't believe them if they tell you otherwise. Mohammed cursed Christians in his dying breath: Bukhari vol. 1, book 8, number 427:

> *Narrated 'Aisha and 'Abdullah bin 'Abbas: When the last moment*

of the life of Allah's Apostle came he started putting his "Khamisa" on his face and when he felt hot and short of breath he took it off his face and said, "May Allah curse the Jews and Christians for they built the places of worship at the graves of their Prophets."

FRAUD AND DECEPTION

Mohammed commanded: "Fight those of the disbelievers who are close to you, and let them find harshness in you" (sura 9:123). In fact, Muslims are told in sura 8:39 to, "Fight them until there is no more (disbelief and polytheism, i.e. worshipping others besides Allah) and the religion (worship) will all be for Allah Alone [in the whole of the world]." Peaceful religion? I think not.

Gibbon, in his *Decline and Fall of the Roman Empire* supports my contention: "The use of fraud and perfidy, of cruelty and injustice, were often subservient to the propagation of the faith; and Mahomet commanded or approved the assassination of the Jews and idolaters who had escaped from the field of battle."[6]

Will Durant in his *History of Civilization* was a little kinder to Mohammed and Islam but quoted Mohammed's successor as saying: "'Compel the rest of mankind to become Moslems or pay us tribute. If they refuse these terms, slay them.' The choice given the enemy was not Islam or the sword; it was Islam or tribute or the sword."[7] Many non-Muslims converted to Islam to save a buck!

Non-Muslims must not be confused and deceived by statements of Muslim leaders that seem to contradict some of the above quotes. The Koran, while the most influential book written by one man, is not without error nor is it balanced. It is not a cohesive, systematic treatise on what Mohammed believed. The Koran has contradictory statements that Muslims can use to soften their violent image. It was written on scraps of paper, palm leaves, leather, bones, etc., that were collected by others after Mohammed's death. Obviously, it did not come from Heaven!

MOHAMMED: CHILD MOLESTER

Mohammed was betrothed to Aisha, a six-year-old girl (still playing with dolls!), but he managed (we are told) to constrain his ardor until she was nine! (See Hadith, vol. 7, book 62, number 64.) One politically correct historian was disingenuous when he mentioned the marriage to Aisha but added, "who lived with her parents until she came of age."[8] Has a nine-year-old come of age, even on the Arabian desert? Even the liberal *Encyclopedia Britannica* reports that she "had scarcely passed the period of infancy."[9]

I believe all civilized people would consider that child molestation, right? I was told by a Muslim cleric that on the Arabian Peninsula it was not uncommon to take a child bride. It was common. Oh, all right. That means that child molestation was common in Arabia, doesn't it? And can any sane, sensitive, person believe otherwise, whatever his religious belief? The above Muslim leader told me that Mohammed did not "take her as his wife" until she was eleven years old; however, no other source reports that to my knowledge. Besides, does that make a difference? What it means is that in Arabia during that time, the male sexual appetite was to be satisfied without confining notions of morality.

The rights of women and children were not considered. However, even in that desert "culture," Mohammed got flack for his marriage to Aisha; but surprise, surprise, surprise, he had another vision from Gabriel who said that Mohammed's pedophilia was acceptable to Allah! Allah endorsed sexual perversion, but Christ said that if we even thought about unlawful sexual activity it was adultery! Yet we are to believe that Islam is superior to Christianity!

Muslims have great difficulty in a civilized culture with Mohammed's marriage to Aisha, and there has been a great amount of dissimulation, but let me nail it down. One of their own "holy" books could not be any clearer that the marriage was a fact. In Hadith vol. 7, book 62, number 65:

> *Narrated 'Aisha: that the Prophet married her when she was six years old and he consummated his marriage when she was nine years old. Hisham said: "I have been informed that 'Aisha remained with the Prophet for nine years (i.e. till his death)."*

Again, in vol. 7, book 62, number 88:

> *Narrated 'Ursa: The Prophet wrote the (marriage contract) with 'Aisha while she was six years old and consummated his marriage with her while she was nine years old and she remained with him for nine years (i.e. till his death).*

Let Aisha speak again in vol. 5, book 58, number 234:

> *Narrated Aisha: The Prophet engaged me when I was a girl of six (years). We went to Median and stayed at the home of Bani-al-Harith bin Khazraj. Then I got ill and my hair fell down. Later*

on my hair grew (again) and my mother, Um Ruman, came to me while I was playing in a swing with some of my girl friends. She called me, and I went to her, not knowing what she wanted to do to me. She caught me by the hand and made me stand at the door of the house. I was breathless then, and when my breathing became Allright, she took some water and rubbed my face and head with it. Then she took me into the house. There in the house I saw some Ansari women who said, "Best wishes and Allah's Blessing and a good luck." Then she entrusted me to them and they prepared me (for the marriage). Unexpectedly Allah's Apostle came to me in the forenoon and my mother handed me over to him, and at that time I was a girl of nine years of age.

The greatest historian of Islam was Tabari (839-923), a physician, philosopher, astronomer, and mathematician who wrote a 39 volume history that dealt from the time of creation to A.D. 915. He wrote in volume 7, page 7 quoting Aisha: "My marriage (to Mohammed) was consummated when I was nine…." On page 131 of volume 9 he quoted Aisha: "then the men and women got up and left. The Messenger of God (Mohammed) consummated his marriage with me in my house when I was nine years old."

The above information should be sufficient but I will add two more authorities: The *Encyclopedia of Islam* informs us under "Aisha": "Aisha went to live in an apartment in Muhammad's house, later the mosque of Median. She cannot have been more than ten years old at the time and took her toys to her new home." Then from a Muslim book, *Women in Islam* published by Islamic Publications in Pakistan: "She (Aisha) was the youngest of his wives. It is said that she was nine years of age when he married her." Therefore, there is no doubt except in the minds of fanatics that Mohammed married a six-year-old girl and consummated the marriage when she was nine. That is child molestation and has no defense!

MOHAMMED'S SEXUAL APPETITE

Gibbon was right when he said that Mohammed "indulged the appetites of a man, and abused the claims of a prophet."[10] It seems that whenever he was caught in an embarrassing situation, the angel Gabriel paid him a visit to extricate him from his problem. Example: when Mohammed wanted Zaynab, his adopted son's wife, he took her (with his son, Zaid's approval). It caused a stir since it was considered incestuous because an adopted son had the same standing as a natural born son. But not to fear because Gabriel was near. Mohammed went into one of his famous swoons, fits, visions, or whatever and when he came out of it he said, "Who will go and congratulate Zaynab (his new bride) and say that the Lord has joined her to me in marriage?" Sura 33:36-38 is his justification for taking his son's wife.

Aisha had an interesting retort to Mohammed following the above "vision." She said, "Truly your God seems to have been very quick in fulfilling your prayers." Sarcasm is not called for, Aisha, but preparing fresh poison mushrooms for his dinner might be acceptable?

Mohammed's sexual life was the talk of the desert since it was claimed he had sexual relations with **each** wife every day–before prayers! He had the stamina of 30 men and needed it since he had more than 16 women including his concubines and slaves in his harem!

Narrated Qatada: Anas bin Malik said, "The Prophet used to visit all his wives in a round, during the day and the night and they were eleven in number." I asked Anas, "Had the Prophet strength for it?" Anas replied, "We used to say that the Prophet was given the strength of thirty (men)" (vol. 1, book 5, number 268). Aisha said, "I scented Allah's prophet and he went round (had sexual relation with) all his wives" (vol. 1, book 5, number 270 and 267).

The above ridiculous and immature boast that Mohammed was capable of being with each of his wives every day was only wishful thinking. The Hadith vol. 7, book 71, number 660, tells us magic was working on Allah's Apostle so that he used to think he had had sexual relations with his wives while he actually had not.

IT GETS WORSE

Mohammed spent each night with a different wife but when it was Hafsa's turn she was visiting her father, so what's a man to do? Mohammed took Mary his Egyptian slave to bed, but Hafsa returned early to find Mary in her bed with her husband. Fireworks in old Arabia! Hafsa agreed not to tell anyone but decided to tell Aisha, and soon all Mohammed's wives were in rebellion. Mohammed promised to stay away from Mary if the harem would calm down; however, he had another fit and Gabriel gave him special revelations to change the rules. Sex with a slave was acceptable. Rank hath its privileges–and in spades for the Prophet!

Sura 66 is the message that Allah gave to Mohammed that solved his marriage mess: "O Prophet! Why do you forbid (for yourself) that which

Allah has allowed to you [i.e., Mary], seeking to please your wives?... Allah has already ordained for you the absolution from your oaths....when the Prophet disclosed a matter in confidence to one of his wives then she told it (to another i.e. Aisha) And Allah made it known to him....It may be if he divorced you (all) that his Lord will give him instead of you, wives better than you...." Principled Muslims have gagged on that sura for centuries.

It gets worse, if possible. Mohammed conjured up the temporary contractual marriage (see book 8, number 3243) whereby a man was permitted to "marry" a woman for 15 minutes for the purpose of sex! This fact is endorsed by one of Islam's top leaders, Al Baydaivi, who wrote, "The purpose of the contractual marriage is the mere pleasure of intercourse with a woman...."[11] Mohammed later forbade the practice since it was even too obnoxious for him.

ILLITERATE BARBARIAN

Mohammed had some strange habits especially for a desert Arab. He wore a veil, dyed his hair a reddish orange color and painted his eyes each night. While the red dye colored his graying hair, it did not get rid of the lice that lived there. (See Hadith vol. 1, book 4, number 167; vol. 9, book 87, number 130.)

Gibbon characterized him correctly as being "an illiterate barbarian" who united "the professions of a merchant and a robber."[12] Mohammed also permitted, in his presence, the torture of a tribal chief to discover his hidden treasure. He accepted slavery as a law of nature, but mitigated it somewhat by saying that families should not be separated at the time of sale! While he did unify numerous Bedouin tribes and made significant improvements in the social welfare of the people (those he didn't kill), he left a legacy of hatred, treachery, slavery, and forced submission.

References:

1   Asma Gull Hasan, *American Muslims,* Continuum, New York, 2000, p. 9.
2   John McClintock and James Strong, *Cyclopedia of Biblical, Theological, and Ecclesiastical Literature,* Grand Rapids, Baker Book House, 1981 reprint), 6:406.
3   Michael Nazar-Ali, *Islam: A Christian Perspective,* Philadelphia: Westminster Press, 1983, p. 21.

4   Alfred Guillaume, *Islam* London: Penguin Books, 1954, p. 6.

5   *New Encyclopedia Britannica*, Edition 15, vol. 22, p. 4.

6   Edward Gibbon, *The Decline and Fall of the Roman Empire*, D. M. Low, ed., 1960, p. 690.

7   Will Durant, *The Story of Civilization*, Book 4, 1950, p. 188.

8   Bruno Leone, ex. ed., *The Spread of Islam*, Greenhaven Press, San Diego, CA, 1999, p. 19.

9   *Encyclopedia Britannica*, vol. 15, 1960, p. 648.

10 Gibbon, op. cit. p. 691.

11 *Voice of the Martyrs*, April, 2002.

12 Gibbon, op. cit. p. 663 and 679.

Chapter Nine

Islam Requires Submission!

Muslims try to put a good face on an ugly fact: it is a religion based on violence. Islam means "submission." Its original meaning was "defiance of death; heroism; to die in battle." It requires every person on earth to submit to the teachings of the Koran. While there are many sects of Islam, they all teach obedience to the Koran. Everyone must bow toward Mecca–or else.

Mohammed seldom taught about the love of God or man's love for God, but he sure spent a huge amount of time talking about judgment, hell, death, and war. Muslims get very uneasy when we speak of their easy acceptance of violence. They tell us that all Muslims are not terrorists but Muslim terrorists have been killing innocent people with bullets, bombs and beheadings almost weekly! When *jihad* is discussed, Muslims get as uncomfortable as a dog in hot ashes, but it is a major part of Islam.

A cursory reading of the Koran and the Hadith easily proves Islam's propensity toward violence and complete submission. Vol. 1, book 2, number 25 tells us: "Allah's apostle was asked, 'What is the best deed?' He replied, 'To believe in Allah and his Apostle.' The questioner then asked, 'What is the next (in goodness)?' He replied. 'To participate in *Jihad* (religious fighting) in Allah's cause.'" The Hadith, vol. 1, book 2, number 35; vol. 4, book 53, number 386 assures any Muslim killed in a *jihad* that he will go straight to Paradise and experience incredible sexual pleasures for eternity.

Every Muslim has a lifetime obligation to fight for the faith, expanding Islam to every nation on earth. "Moderate" Muslims are disingenuous or dishonest when they deny that Islam requires all Muslims to spread their religion through speech, sperm, and the sword.

JIHAD, JIHAD, JIHAD

The first example of *jihad* is found in Sura 2:191 and my Koran, published in Medina, has an explanatory footnote to make sure even the dullest Muslim understands what the passage means. The passage commands every Muslim to fight (*jihad*): "*Al-Jihad* (holy fighting)...is given the utmost importance in Islam and is one of its pillars (on which it stands). By *Jihad* Islam is established...*Jihad* is an obligatory duty in Islam on every Muslim." Muslim theologians wanted to emphasize that message in a footnote **so** that should end the argument as to *jihad* or holy war.

The Koran declares in *Sura 2:191 and 193:*

> "*Kill them wherever you find them....*" And "*fight them until there is no more disbelief and worshipping of others....*" Sura 2:216 tells all faithful Muslims, "*Holy fighting in Allah's cause is ordained for you....*" Muslims are promised rewards if they die for their cause: "*And if you are killed or die in the Way of Allah, forgiveness and mercy from Allah are far better than all that they amass (of worldly wealths)*" (sura 3:157).

> Sura 47:4: "*So, when you meet those who disbelieve, smite (their) necks till when you have killed and wounded many of them, then bind a bond firmly (on them, i.e. take them as captives).*" Sura 9:5-6 says, "*Kill those who join other gods with God wherever you may find them.*"

> Sura 17:16: "*When We decide to destroy a town (population), We (first) send a definite order (to obey Allah and be righteous)...Then we destroy it with complete destruction.*"

> "*Believers, take neither Jews nor Christians for your friends*" (sura 5:51).

> "*Fight and slay the pagans [unbelievers] wherever ye find them, and seize them, beleaguer them, and lie in wait for them in every stratagem of war*" (sura 9:5).

Egyptian judge Kamal Aboulmagd is quoted as saying: "In Islam and in Islamic literature there is no such thing as 'a holy war.'"[1] The confused judge added, "This is [a] Western invention that was attributed to us, I don't know how and why and when." Well, let's check out whether that is an accurate statement. Anyone who reads the papers or watches television knows that Muslim clerics in Pakistan, Saudi Arabia, Iraq, Iran, etc., are convinced that "holy war" is a reality. *Jihad* was not "attributed" to Muslims by wicked, hateful Americans. It is **a** core teaching of the Koran and Hadith and no matter if Muslim leaders say otherwise, that wouldn't make it so. U.S. media people who declare *jihad* as being benign are little more than pathetic prostitutes.

You might ask the people in Paris, Brussels and Orlando if they think holy war is a reality.

John Esposito, a major cheerleader for Islam said. "The message at the end of the day is clear, the message is simple–Islam is not the enemy, religious extremism is."[2] John is wrong. At the beginning of the day, at the end of the day, Islam is the enemy! No, all Muslims do not follow the Koran so they are decent, law abiding Americans; but koranic Islam is the enemy.

Islam always killed pagans who refused to convert but would often permit Christians and Jews to pay the *jizya*, a very heavy tax that seemed to lead to many "conversions." In paying that tax, they were to be humiliated as a common and expected procedure. The *jizya* tax means literally *punishment*. It was so important that in many Islamic lands, such as the once vast Ottoman Empire, non-Muslims were required always to carry a receipt as proof that they had paid the *jizya* or face imprisonment. The Koran in sura 9:29 mandates that non-believers should pay the *jizya* **and be subdued.**

MUSLIMS SEEK RESPECT BY HUMILIATING OTHERS

The Guinness Book of World Records declares that the University of Al Karaouine in Fez, Morocco was the oldest degree-granting university in the world with its founding in 859. Baghdad was the greatest city in the world. During Islam's Golden Age it passed on to Europeans classical Greek civilization through their translation of many classical books. Islam "invented windmills, trigonometry, lateen sails and made major advances in metallurgy, mechanical and chemical engineering and irrigation methods. In the middle-ages the flow of technology was overwhelmingly from Islam to Europe rather from Europe to Islam."[3] But things had been changing for many years. Islam was on the way down, way down.

Then Mohammad's dream became a nightmare. Muslim armies started losing and they lost their grip on their world. Europeans began building massive cathedrals, universities, hospitals, highways, cities, and industries, as Muslims seemed to be relegated to third class status in their world. Printing and other inventions were developed and Europe became the leader of the pack while Muslims sat in disintegrating hovels and licked their wounds as they relished their glorious past.

Today, Muslims are told of their illustrious past and realize they are losers. But they realize they are hated, feared, and ridiculed for their backward, brutal, and bloody culture with no hope for improvement, so they humiliate "infidels" when they have the chance. For hundreds of years, Muslims have used the tactic of browbeating, bluster, and braggadocio to keep non-Muslims in their place and subdued.

JIZYA WAS TO HUMILIATE NON-MUSLIMS

London resident Islamist leader Abu Waleed (a major welfare recipient) tells his video audience "The kaffir [non-believer], when he walks down the street, he has to wear a red belt around his neck, and he has to have his forehead shaved, and he has to wear two shoes that are different from one another. He [the non-believer] is not allowed to walk on the pavement, he has to walk in the middle of the road, and he has to ride a mule."[4] He is kind to say that churches will be permitted but they will not be permitted to ring church bells. He continues: "We are the ones who want to work for the sake of Allah, to establish the manifestation of Islam, and make sure David Cameron [Prime Minister of the UK] comes on his hands and knees, and gives us the jiziya." He added that the Queen and Kate will be forced to wear veils when *shira* is enforced.

Islamists like Waleed teach that Islam is incompatible with the UN Declaration on Human Rights because Islam cannot treat all people as equal. Any Muslim is superior to the most educated, qualified non-Muslim! A non-Muslim living in a Muslim nation is known as a *dhimmi*. They are forced to follow the above rules and pay the excessive tax but the main purpose is not to collect a tax but to humiliate non-Muslims to provoke them to convert. And it works.

Historians point to the first appearance of the *dhimmi* under Mohammed and the agreement he reached with the Jewish population of Khaybar, an oasis near Medina, in modern Saudi Arabia. Rather than fight and be slaughtered, the Jews of Khaybar surrendered to Mohammed after a brief siege. In return, Mohammed granted them the right to remain in Khaybar provided they pay the Muslims one half of their annual produce!

The treatment of non-Muslims has been and is different in various nations and in different times but the following are examples of the Muslims desire to humiliate and subdue all non-Muslims.

When a Jew or Christian pays the *jizya*, he must drop his head as the Muslim official grabs his beard and hits the non-Muslim beneath his ear. Christians cannot ring church bells or if that is permitted, they must not ring them loudly. Their churches must not be elaborate with stained glass, high steeples, and their homes must never be higher or nicer than Muslims. The Jew or Christian may not ride an elegant horse or mule; he may ride a donkey only if the saddle is constructed of wood. He may not walk on the best part of the road or walkway. He or she must wear an identifying badge that tells everyone that they are inferior to all Muslims. Moreover, a non-Muslim can never testify in court against a Muslim but only against another non-Muslim.

A non-Muslim could not be buried near Muslims nor could a non-Muslim raise a pig next to a Muslim neighbor. If a Muslim wished to sit, a non-Muslim had to rise from his seat and let the Muslim take his place. A non-Muslim was forbidden to comb his hair sideways as the Muslim custom, and Christians had to wear blue belts or turbans and Jews had to wear yellow belts or turbans. Non-Muslims had to host a Muslim traveler for at least 3 days and feed him whatever the circumstances. Homes of non-Muslims had to be low so that each time that they would enter or exit their houses they would have to bend in a way that it would remind them of their low status in the world.

Depending on the time in history, the sect of Muslims, and the state, non-Muslims were not permitted to build new churches, temples, or synagogues; they were allowed to renovate old churches and synagogues (those prior to the Islamic conquests) so long as there were no new additions.

In 2016, no churches, synagogues, sacred texts, or Bibles are permitted in Saudi Arabia. In Egypt no new churches can be built and to improve or repair old ones requires a permit–that is very difficult to get. In some nations non-Muslims are not allowed to sell or distribute Bibles or Christian literature in public places. They are not allowed to read their sacred texts out loud, even in their homes. Crosses cannot be displayed in houses or places of worship nor can Christians gather and walk to their church on Christian festival days.

All non-Muslims are considered second class citizens where Islam prevails.

NON-MUSLIMS ARE SECOND-CLASS CITIZENS

American Muslims strive diligently to project a false image and have used excuses such as the following author wrote to deny the obvious:

> *Islam does not permit discrimination in the treatment of other human beings on the basis of religion or any other criteria....it emphasizes neighborliness and respect for the ties of relationship with non-Muslims...within this human family, Jews and Christians, who share many beliefs and values with Muslims, constitute what Islam terms Ahl al-Kitab, that is, People of the Scripture, and hence Muslims have a special relationship to them as fellow "Scriptuaries."*[5]

One must remember that the above writer was trying to impress the free world (as opposed to the real world behind the black curtain of Islam). If the nation were an Islamic nation ruled by Muslim clerics, he would write something else. He would tell you that you are a second-class citizen, that you cannot have a public worship service, that you will be arrested if gospel singing is heard from your home, and that in court a Muslim always will be believed before you are. Muslim countries are totalitarian and the people are slaves to Islam. The only concession I make to them is that they really believe what they believe.

Women are always second class as during the war in Afghanistan when U.S. female soldiers had to wear a head scarf when they were off their base! Furthermore, they had to sit in the back of cars, and be escorted by a male soldier! When President Bush the First was in Saudi Arabia during the Gulf War, he was told by Saudi officials not to say grace during the Thanksgiving Day meal with American troops! American soldiers were there to keep them from being invaded by their Muslim pal in Iraq, and they gave our President orders about praying before a meal! Bush had dinner on a ship in international waters. I think he should have prayed anyway, loudly, and in the name of Jesus of Nazareth who died and rose again on the third day. But then, Bush the First always did need a spinal transplant!

ISLAM AND WOMEN

Non-Muslims are turned off when they discover the Islamic attitude toward women. Paradise seems to be filled with dark-eyed virgins that are available to the men who arrive there. Sura 55:52-66 promises Muslim men: "Shall the reward of goodness be anything but good?...Dark-eyed virgins sheltered in their tents....They shall recline on green cushions and fine carpets...Blessed be the name of your Lord...." Thinking female Muslims should want to know what awaits **them** in Paradise. Mohammed didn't say.

If that's not clear enough, sura 78:31-33 promises: "But for the God-fearing is a blissful abode, enclosed gardens and vineyards; and damsels with swelling breasts for companions; and a full cup." Translation: plenty of sex and wine. Sura 55:70-74: "In these gardens will be chaste and beautiful virgins....nymphs, cloistered in their tents....which neither man nor demon will have touched before them."

CONVERTS FROM ISLAM

What happens if one wants to leave this religious movement? Mohammed made that very clear. Kill him! Bukhari vol. 9, book 84, number 64: Narrated 'Ali:

> Whenever I tell you a narration from Allah's Apostle, by Allah, I would rather fall down from the sky than ascribe a false statement to him, but if I tell you something between me and you (not a Hadith) then it was indeed a trick (i.e., I may say things just to cheat my enemy). No doubt I heard Allah's Apostle saying, "During the last days there will appear some young foolish people who will say the best words but their faith will not go beyond their throats (i.e., they will have no faith) and will go out from (leave) their religion as an arrow goes out of the game. So, where-ever you find them, kill them, for who-ever kills them shall have reward on the day of resurrection."

Most thinking people will agree that the above clearly commands all followers of Islam to kill those who leave the religion.

ISLAM DOES NOT MEAN PEACE

Muslims are working full time to convince us that Islam means peace. It does not. It means "submission." Non-Muslims should spend time looking at Islam, its teachings and practices. Any honest Muslim will confess that Islam is the only true religion. Their mission is to convert the world. Similarly, Christians are commanded to preach the Gospel to the whole world. We should do it more effectively, I might add. Islam seeks to conquer with error while Christians seek to convince with truth. (What did you expect me to say? I'm a born-again Christian!)

Islam is a religion that soaked the Middle East, India, North Africa, and Europe in blood. To deny that is to deny history. Will Durant, who smacks Islam and Mohammed with a soft hand (whereas Gibbon does so with a mailed fist), asserts that the Muslim "conquest of India is probably the bloodiest story in history."[6] Wherever they conquered, there were ladies, land, and loot for the taking. Not a good foundation for a world religion! But it worked!

Folks, the barbarians are not at the gates; they are **inside** the gates while U.S. politicians and religious leaders stand around sucking their thumbs, as a strange wooden horse is pulled even deeper inside our national walls.

And if they get control you would have to submit to them and be humiliated.

References:

1   Radio Free Europe, "World: UN Forum Explores Ways to Fight "Islam-ophobia," December 10, 2004.

2   Ibid.

3   Jared Diamond, *Guns, Germs, and Steel - The Fates of Human Societies, Guns, Germs, and Steel - The Fates of Human Societies*, New York, W. W. Norton & Co., 1999, p. 253.

4   *Daily Mail*, June 28, 2014.

5   Suzanne Haneef, *What Everyone Should Know About Islam and Muslims*, Kazi Publications, Lahore, 1979, p. 173.

6   Will Durant, *Story of Civilization*, Book 1, p. 459.

Chapter Ten

The Real Face of Islam!

Civilization has come a long way driven by Christianity, but Muslims would drag us kicking and screaming back to a seventh-century, desert culture where passions ruled over principles. I demand that Muslim leaders who talk like moderates tell the truth about the historical truth of what Islam was, is, and is going to be.

Muslims insist that Allah is the God of the Bible. Not so. Allah was just one of 360 pagan gods that was worshipped by desert pagans at the Kaaba in ancient Mecca. Religious zealots of the day ran seven times counter-clock-wise around the cube-shaped Kaaba (temple), kissed the black stone, then sometimes ran about a mile to a dry riverbed and threw stones at the devil! (Before Mohammed, the zealots were naked!) That sounds more exciting than a revival meeting but it will never catch on. Too much work for so little pleasure.

Muslims believe that the Kaaba was first constructed in heaven and Adam built it on earth; however, the Flood swept it away. They believe that Abraham was instructed to rebuild it and did so with the help of Ishmael. However, Abraham was never in southern Arabia, but adding Abraham gives the tale a little credibility. They need some credibility since some scholars say that the Arabs have no connection to Abraham and his descendants! But then, Josephus informs us that the Arabs **are** descendants of Ishmael. Muslims believe that Gabriel gave Abraham a completely white stone that was used in the building but has since turned solid black by the sins of those who touched it.

133

Running around temples was not uncommon to pagans of the era, but throwing rocks at the devil was not as common. Mohammed institutionalized the rock throwing by teaching that Satan allegedly appeared to Abraham, Hagar, and Ishmael and they each threw seven rocks at the devil. Moreover, at that place (where the incident did **not** happen) Muslim pilgrims throw rocks at the same devil today. The rock-throwing could be an attempt to dispose of a dangerous spirit or to throw away personal evil in the stones. Or, they may **really** be throwing rocks at Satan.

ALLAH: PAGAN GOD

Any good resource book will reveal that Allah was the male, pagan moon deity who married the sun and had daughters as a consequence of that celestial union–the stars! And all those heavenly bodies are gods! Temples to the moon god have been uncovered all over the Middle East. Not unusual since it was the most prevalent religion. Some think that Allah was the leading god of the 360 gods in the Kaaba. It is also a fact that the crescent moon, found in numerous archeological digs in the Middle East, was the symbol of the moon god, and it is also the symbol of every Muslim on earth.

The *Encyclopedia of Religion* agrees about Islam's origin: "Allah is a pre-Islamic name....corresponding to the Babylonian Bel."[1] Scholar Henry P. Smith of Harvard stated: "Allah was already known by name to the Arabs."[2] Middle East scholar E. M. Wherry stated that "Allah worship and the worship of Ba-al involved the worship of the sun, moon and stars."[3] So Mohammed did not get knowledge of Allah from heaven, but from the pagan Kaaba temple. A good question for Muslims: how could Mohammed have received the Allah revelation from Heaven when his own father was named "Abd-**Allah**"? Allah was a common name for a pagan god long before Mohammed walked the Arabian Desert. Mohammed only cleaned the Kaaba of all **other** pagan gods.

HEART OF ISLAM

Mohammed did not preach a new revelation to his desert buddies. They were all familiar with Allah and the "buffet of gods" at the Kaaba, so it was much easier for them to accept Mohammed's pagan religion than if it had been a new revelation as claimed. Islam was simply a new twist on the old religion familiar to everyone.

Mohammed provided five pillars of Islam for every Muslim:

- They must confess, "Allah is God and Mohammed is his prophet."
- Muslims must pray five times a day toward Mecca.
- They must give 2 to 10% of their income to the poor.
- They must fast during Ramadan.
- They must make a pilgrimage to Mecca once in their lifetime.

Cantor and other historians report that "holy war" is the sixth pillar of Islam.[4] Most moderate Muslims disagree, but history supports those historians, and Koran footnotes support Cantor. My official Koran without a doubt supports the fact that *jihad* or holy fighting in the cause of Islam is their sixth pillar.

EMISSARIES OF ISLAM

Blerime Topalli, a Muslim, wrote a column criticizing Muslim terrorists and called them "enemies of Islam." However, the terrorists were not enemies of Islam but **emissaries** of Islam. They were doing what Islamist extremists demand. About the Koran, Topalli falsely said, "It is a book of faith and a way of life, not a weapon with which to manipulate people." No, that is exactly what it is. She closed by requesting "firmly" that American flags "be raised at each mosque so that the communities that surround us can view our solidarity with them as Americans."[5]

I appreciate, applaud, and approve her condemnation of terrorists, and I think she is sincere; however, Islam will never be respected by an informed, civilized society unless leading Muslims repudiate the oppression and hate as taught in the Koran and the Hadith! But that would dismantle Islam which they will not do. People like Topelli are decent, law-abiding Americans as loyal as I; however, there are numerous Muslims in America who would never be terrorists but apparently approve of their attacks!

Moreover, they do plan to change our nation, make no mistake about that. Their plan is literally to conquer the world, nation by nation. The first Muslim missionaries who came to America in the 1920s bluntly boasted, "Our plan is to conquer America." And they are doing it, even as I write.

We must get below the rhetoric to the reality. What are they really saying? What do they really intend to accomplish? Pass over their public comments and listen to what they say to their own people. We saw this when the late Yasser Arafat tried to keep the Israelis from blowing him into Paradise. He talked in English like a pacifist with doves flying around his head, but a few days later he was breathing out fire and thunder in Arabic to his extremist followers.

MUSLIM FANATICS

Daniel Pipes reports that Ahmad Nawfal, a leader of the Jordanian Muslim Brethren and frequent speaker to U.S. Muslims, said the United States has "no thought, no values, and no ideals." If militant Muslims "stand up, with the ideology that we possess, it will be very easy for us to preside over this world."[6] If you think these people are not serious, you are living in a state of denial, and denial is dangerous and deadly.

Another Islamic fanatic is Shamim A. Siddiqi who wrote a book about the need to convert Americans to Islam. He said that all Muslims in America must be involved in this great missionary effort to win America to Mohammed using "all of their energies, talents, and resources." He said that every Muslim will face consequences on the Day of Judgment about how energetic they were in their missionary efforts. He wrote: "Every Muslim living in the West will stand in the witness box in the mightiest court of Allah ... in *Akhirah* [the last day] and give evidence that he fulfilled his responsibility ... that he left no stone unturned to bring the message of the Qur'an to every nook and corner of the country."[7]

Islamic dominance in America will completely change it. Is that what you want? Muslims want students in public schools to be permitted (then later required) to recite "In the name of God, the Merciful, the Compassionate" each day. They want to broadcast the calls to prayer five times each day. They demand that affirmative action for Muslims be established (as we try to dismantle all affirmative actions for others). They want laws that would restrict any criticism of Islam and Mohammed! They would institute the chopping off of hands and feet for minor crimes, beheading for adultery (Saudi Arabia beheaded 84 people during 2015!), no radio, no television or record sales, etc. Some of the above is now a reality in U.S. cities!

MULLAH IN THE CATBIRD SEAT

America would not be America with a Muslim mullah in the catbird seat. Since the Muslim attacks on America, California public school districts are teaching a required, three-week course on Islam! Children memorize verses from the Koran, adopt a Muslim name, wear Muslim robes, study the tenets of Islam, learn about their main leaders, and form their own *jihad*! Children are taught to pray "in the name of Allah, the Compassionate, the Merciful" and are instructed to chant, "Praise to Allah, Lord of Creation."[8] The textbook used always presents Christianity in a negative light highlighting the Salem witch trials, the Inquisition, etc., in bold type while Islam is broadly presented in a very positive light with no mention of the oceans of blood shed to spread its culture/religion! (And some people still defend public education!)

Well, surely the ACLU and other Protectors of the Oppressed such as Americans United for the Separation of Church and State (who recently held their national meeting in a New Jersey phone booth) and People for the American Way all had a collective fit. No, not a word. Not a fax. Not a news conference. Can you imagine if those schools were teaching **Bible** verses, and the tenets of Christianity, and teaching kids to pray in the name of Jesus Christ? This further proves that liberals are the biggest hypocrites in the world.

FEMALE CIRCUMCISION

Muslims in control would legislate the way we dress, eat, rear our children, shop, what we purchase, how and where we worship, and how we treat our daughters and wives. Muslims are not female friendly! Muslims show their hatred of women by their angry, aggressive, and abusive practice of female circumcision. It must be understood that the Koran never commands circumcision of males, much less females; additionally, most people have never heard of female circumcision.

FrontPageMagazine.com had a chilling article titled "Islam's Hatred of the Clitoris" that dealt with female circumcision. It said that it is "about obliterating the clitoris, or the entire outer vagina. It is the barbarity that exists where misogyny festers most: in the Muslim and African world."[9] The article reveals that 97% of women in Egypt have been circumcised, meaning their clitorises have been amputated. Moreover, in places like Sudan, **all** of a woman's external genital organs are removed!

How is the mutilation accomplished? Women commonly hold down a girl as young as one month but usually about seven or eight years, and the "surgery" is always done without anesthetics! The "surgery" is often done with broken glass! As I think about the possibility of my daughters and granddaughters going through such barbaric mutilation, I would like to get my hands on those "surgeons"! What kind of culture or religion would permit something like that to flourish? Note that this practice is common. In fact, if a female has not had this "surgery," she is considered unclean and only the surgery can make her clean!

Many times the victim dies after going through the torture; others suffer from chronic infections for a lifetime. But possibly worse than the suffering is that the surgery makes them less than God intended them to be. God gave females the clitoris to permit them to have sexual pleasure within the confines of marriage. It is not an exaggeration to say that about 75% of women do not achieve orgasm without clitoral stimulation. The clitoris has nothing to do with child bearing, only sexual pleasure. However, warped Muslims apparently believe women should have no sexual pleasure, so they try to undo what God did. On the other hand, there are eternal rewards for Muslim men who commit homicidal killings–unlimited sexual pleasure! Many of those unfortunate women are traumatized for a lifetime with sexual, emotional, and mental repercussions.

In Somalia and some other parts of the Arab and African world, the entire vaginal area is sewed up around a hollow reed to permit urination and menstrual flow to take place. On the wedding night, the husband beats his wife with a whip, then after this bit of "foreplay," he cuts the vagina open with a razor to permit penetration. For the following week, they have frequent intercourse to prevent the vagina from closing again. Following the "honeymoon," the husband takes his bloody razor or knife to all the local hangouts to show his buddies the proof of his wife's virginity.[10]

DARK SIDE OF DIVERSITY

Female sexual mutilation is the dark side of diversity and a curtain of silence has been pulled to cover it. I have had Muslims even deny that it is a common practice in the Islamic world. They say that it is only a local African custom, and "maybe a few Muslims" practice it. They are dishonest or uninformed.

Can any person, Muslim or non-Muslim, defend such a barbaric practice? A British daily reported, "Local authorities and social workers have turned a 'blind eye' to the genital mutilation of young girls among African and other third world communities in Britain for fear of being labeled racist."[11] Female circumcision has been illegal in Britain since 1985! Medical and social service staffs are "nervous" about reporting female circumcision, no, call it what it is, female mutilation. Why? Because it may be racist! One health official, quoted in the previous article, said, "There continues to be confusion as to what is legitimate in culture, which should be respected, and what is human rights abuse."

Incredible, but understandable! When a nation is set adrift without a compass, it is no wonder people make such stupid statements. England was not only adrift years ago, but their ship also went down. They forbid the spanking of children but wink at female mutilation! Hypocrites!

DESPOTIC RELIGION

When the Taliban controlled Afghanistan, they prohibited all music, photographs, clean-shaved men, and women in high heels. Men could go to soccer games but they could not enjoy them **too** much! If people yelled too loudly, a member of the Vice and Virtue Squad whipped them where they sat! (As shown on an *MSNBC* special.) In addition, you may remember that halftime was very special. City officials executed men and women by shooting and hanging them at center field. We are told that such officials are Muslim extremists or fundamentalist Muslims, but they indicate they are simply carrying on the culture and religion of hundreds of years. The word is control, total control of a populace. When Islam takes control, they control every facet of life.

If Muslims are successful in America as they have been in Michigan, Minnesota, and other places, then your life will be changed. A good example has already happened. Her name is Rifqa Bary who grew up in Sri Lanka. At age 6 her older brother threw a small toy at her and blinded her in one eye. The family sought medical help but the result was she was blind for life. From the day they got that news, she was considered blemished. All members of her family mistreated her from that day. Her family fled their homeland because of their "shame" and moved to Ohio. She experienced increasingly worse abuse and finally escaped to Florida after trusting Christ as Savior. Her family was not punished. She lives in fear for her life.

Terrorists are following Mohammed and the dictates of the Koran. For moderate Muslims to deplore the actions of the fundamentalists is simply an attempt to make themselves more comfortable in a radical, undemocratic, despotic religion. Moderate Muslims must not only condemn terror, they must repudiate the violence in the Koran and stop funding terror while they condemn it! Until they take that stand, I refuse to believe their sobbing sentiments and will insist they are a danger to all honest people, Muslims and non-Muslims.

HONEST MUSLIMS

Kateb Yacine, who died in 1989, was an Algerian writer whose assessment of Islam is brilliantly insightful. In a famous radio interview he said, "Islam does not develop with sweets and roses, it develops with tears and blood. It grows by crushing, by violence, by contempt, by hatred, by the worst humiliation a people can support. We can see the result."[12]

Muhammad Hisham Kabbani is head of the Islamic Supreme Council of America and reported on his visits to U.S. mosques. He claimed at a January 1999 State Department that 80 percent of U.S. mosques teach "extremist ideology."[13] Kabbani seems to be a reasonable, sincere, and capable man who is willing to risk his life to take a stand for the truth. I know few Muslims like him.

Truly, Islam is on the march around the world–the world they really expect to conquer. The former Director of the Islamic Cultural Centre of London, Dr. Zaki Badawi, declared: "A proselytizing religion cannot stand still. It can either expand or contract. Islam endeavors to expand in Britain. Islam is a universal religion. It aims at bringing its message to all corners of the earth. It hopes that one day the whole of humanity will be one Muslim community, the Umma."[14] If that happens, how will it affect our American way of life? Is there some way we can predict the results of an Islamic America? Just look at the past.

In the fourteenth-century, Ibn Khaldun lived in Tunis and observed that the Arabs created the deserts in which they lived. He wrote that civilization "always collapsed in places the Arabs took over and conquered." He reported that settlements became depopulated "and the very earth there turned into something that was no longer earth."[15]

I have traveled through Muslim countries and even their major cities are dirty, the food in the best hotels is miserable, and thievery abounds. You see a different world if you travel from Rome to Athens to Jerusalem then to Damascus or Amman or Cairo. Beirut used to be an exception and was a lovely city but now it is dominated by Muslims. I have had some delightful days in Beirut but those days are gone forever.

MUSLIM CONTROL OF U.S.

Don't be deceived–Muslims plan to control America someday. Do you want to live in a Muslim-controlled society? They may not be successful, but there is no doubt that they are sincere. Look at Britain where Muslims are taking over. Patrick Sookhdoe is a former Muslim who said in a speech recently: "I think we face a much greater threat from Muslim communities within our own countries than we realize….In Britain today, where Islam controls the inner cities, we have major social exclusion and the development of *sharia* (enforcement of Koran law). We have had churches burned, Christians attacked, and a mission center destroyed. The media has deliberately kept everything off the air. This plays into the hands of Muslims ultimately."[16] And now London has a Muslim mayor!

So, why did American officials skirt the Muslim issue and pander to them? They did not want to antagonize Islamic governments and give cause for a Muslim uprising, especially in the "moderate" nations such as Egypt and Jordan. So, they kissed the extremists while they kicked the moderates. The fact is that **all** Muslims, if they believe what they profess, would climb into bed with the terrorists. If not, they should renounce their "holy" book.

Why haven't you heard Obama, Biden, Clinton and Company demand accountability from Islamic states that persecute Christians? If we are to have foreign aid (state welfare), how can it be justified when practically **all** Muslim states permit persecution of Christians? A simple statement could be sent to each Muslim government: "No more trade between our nations and no more welfare checks will be sent until we have guarantees that all persecution of Christians has stopped. The slave trade in Sudan must stop now, and all slavers must be brought to justice." Don't hold your breath.

FUTURE PRESIDENTS WILL BE MUCH HARDER ON TERRORISTS

How can any world leader sit down with Muslim terrorists whose hands drip with the blood of innocent Jews and Arabs? How could sane people award Arafat the Nobel Peace Prize? Of course, one doesn't **have** to be a socialist, totalitarian, or one-worlder to qualify for the Prize, but it seems to help! After all, other socialists, communists, and one-worlders such as Nelson Mandela, Martin Luther King, and Kofi Annan of the U. N. are prizewinners.

The politicians who pander to Muslim terrorists are wrong, and while I commiserate with their sensitive positions, I refuse to commend their policy. I wonder if we will ever see U.S. government officials commiserating with Bible-believing Christians as they do with Muslims. Don't hold your breath unless you like the color blue.

Bush, Blair, and Company put together a coalition of many countries to fight the Iraqi War, including some from the Islamic world, but they never understood that the Muslim kings and dictators don't sleep well at night. Uneasy rests the head of the kings and dictators because they know that Muslim terrorists can get to them rather easily. Therefore, while Islamic leaders are impressed with our gun power, our money, and influence, they are more fearful of fellow Muslims. Those leaders must walk a very thin line–or else.

It is long past time for moderate American, English, and French Muslims to take a stand with the U.S. against their buddies in Baghdad and other Islamic states. Moreover, informed citizens should hold politicians' feet to the fire and declare that Muslims (true to the Koran) are the enemies of free people everywhere.

You can count on future U.S. Presidents to be much harder on Muslim terrorists when terrorism is a weekly affair. Politicians always see the light when they feel the heat and Muslims are applying plenty of heat.

References:

1   *Encyclopedia of Religion*, eds, Paul Meagher and Thomas O'Brian, Consuela Aherne, Washington D.C., Corpus Pub., 1979, 1:117.

2   Henry P. Smith, *The Bible and Islam: or, The Influence of the Old and New Testament on the Religion of Mohammed*, New York, Charles Scribner's & Sons, 1897, p. 102.

3   E. M. Wherry, *A Comprehensive Commentary on the Quran*, Osnabaruck, Otto Zeller Veriag, 1973, p. 36.

4   Norman Cantor, *The Civilization of the Middle Ages*, HarperCollins Publishers, 1993, p. 134.

5   Belerime Topalli, column on *Heal the World* web site, Crescentlife.com, Oct. 5, 2001.

6   Daniel Pipes on Daniel Pipes.org, Nov., 2001.

7   Shamim A. Siddiqi, *New York Post*, Oct. 12, 2001.

8   *WorldNetDaily*, "Islamic studies required in California district," Jan. 11, 2002.

9   Jamie Glazov, *FrontPageMagazine,* Oct. 19, 2001.

10   Ibid.

11   *Independent,* July 7, 1992.

12   Interview on Radio *BEUR,* 4-20-94, quoted in *Why I am not a Muslim,* p. 352.

13   Speech at an Open Forum at U.S. State Department in January, 1999 from The Root and Branch Ass'n Ltd., website.

14   Cited in *Why I Am Not a Muslim,* p. 352.

15   Tom Bethell, *The American Spectator,* Nov./Dec. 2001.

16   *Christian News,* Jan. 28, 2002.

Chapter Eleven

Mistakes, Mishmash, and Madness!

Muslims claim that the Koran is a holy book sent from Allah to Mohammed through various visions. They claim that it has been preserved **exactly** as it was revealed to the prophet with no corrections, additions, or subtractions, and that it is pure Arabic. If so, I demand to know how the Arabic in the Koran is the vocabulary and dialect of a member of the Quraysh tribe living in or near Mecca during the seventh century![1] Is it unkind to suggest that the Koran came from Mohammed's fevered mind, not the mind of an all-powerful, all-knowing God? The "holy" books of Islam are filled with mistakes, mishmash, and madness and have numerous contradictions with the Bible.

THE HADITH

The Hadith is a collection of Mohammed's sayings, speeches, actions, etc., as attested by various relatives and followers. There is a big debate in Muslim circles whether or not the Hadith is inspired. Muslims can't agree on the issue. It is my opinion that thinking Muslims know the Hadith can't be defended to the satisfaction of sane, honest people. Those who defend the Hadith are defending a castle in ruins.

Many Muslims consider the Hadith (traditions) as "holy" yet scholars such as Schacht, Goldziher, and others have concluded that most or maybe all of the traditions were forgeries put into circulation a few hundred years after Mohommed![2] Following Mohammed's death, Islam split as

145

Muslims opposed Muslims. The unauthorized splits managed to "find" other hadiths to support their particular doctrine! (Could that be the rationale behind the many Bible versions we have today?)

Muslims consider Sahih Bukhari (also Bukhary) the best translator of the Hadith. He considered 600,000 traditions out of which he accepted only 7,295. Since the same tradition is often repeated more than once in different chapters, the number of distinct hadiths is reduced to 2,762. All right, we have fewer than 3,000 hadiths that scholars consider authentic, while the others are unacceptable because they are unreliable or repetitious. Question: why are there so many unreliable statements of Mohammed floating around out there? For the same simple reason that there are many spurious writings of the early church leaders in Christianity. A sect arises and it needs validation for its aberrational teachings, so a "Gospel of Paul" or a "Gospel of Barnabas" is written that "substantiates" the false doctrine.

The above process is a reasonable phenomenon when you understand the wicked heart of man. Islam started splitting immediately following the death of Mohammed; consequently, various hadiths were produced to support each faction, but there was no Koranic support for those splits. However, Muslims are told that they can accept weak hadiths if it is for a good purpose!

HADITH BACKGROUND

Rashad Khalifa revealed on his pro-Muslim website how the hadiths came to be written: "It is well known that the first book of Hadith is that of Bukhary, who was born more than 200 years after the death of Muhammad. When Bukhary wrote his book of Hadiths, he used to visit the people whom he knew as sources. After verifying that his source is 'truthful,' and known as a man or woman of righteousness, Bukhary would ask, 'Do you know a Hadith?' The person would answer, 'Yes,' then proceed to narrate the 'Hadith' as follows: 'I heard my father, may God bless his soul, say that he heard his older brother, may God bless his soul, say that he was sitting with his grandmother, may God bless her soul, and she told him that she was having dinner one day with her great uncle, may God bless his soul, when he stated that his maternal grandfather knew Imam Ahmad ibn Muhammad alAmawy, who mentioned that his grandfather heard from his oldest uncle that he met the great companion of the Prophet Omar ibn Khaled AlYamany, and he told him that the Prophet, peace be upon him, said, ...'" Is it any wonder that honest, thinking Muslims reject the Hadith?

I interviewed three clerics at the Indianapolis mosque, and the top hon-cho (an Indianapolis physician) later responded to my e-mail regarding the Hadith as follows: "There is not much split on Hadith but the fact is hadith or sayings of prophet do not have same weight as Quran which we believe is word of God. Hadith were not guaranteed protection by God. Some hadith we call authentic or agreed upon as they are mentioned in all the collections. While some other, if mentioned by only one chain of narrator we call weak hadith. To those who do not consider Quran to be inspired, what difference it makes if certain hadith is inspired or not?"

The above notwithstanding, there seems to be a serious split in Islamic thinking as seen in the following statement (from his website) by Muslim Rashad Khalifa: "Since the socalled (sic) hadith & sunna of the Prophet have been vastly corrupted, they can never meet the criterion of divine revelation. It is an acknowledged fact that the vast majority of Hadiths are false fabrications." He also added that saying the above was like telling Christians that Christ was not the Son of God.

Khalifa gained great popularity in Islamic circles when he scientifically "proved" the Koran was without error but his life was threatened when he made his critical assessments of the Hadith. So there is a major split in Muslim circles as to whether the Hadith is a "holy" book or not.

Furthermore, the Muslim clerics in Indianapolis gave me a copy of the Koran published by the King Fahd Complex in Saudi Arabia and almost every page has one or more hadiths to help explain the confusing, con-voluted, and contradictory verses in the Koran. So the official Muslim position is apparently that the Hadith is a "holy" book of Islam. Why then are American Muslims trying to distance themselves from it? Because it is impossible to defend to the satisfaction of sane, sensible people.

The Koran is insufficient in support of Islam since it does not even men-tion praying five times a day, circumcision, Jerusalem, etc.? No, Muslims must have the Hadith to bring Islam full circle and make an attempt to be consistent. The Koran without the Hadith is like a car without an engine? And even with both, the "car" still doesn't run! And it sure won't take you where you want to go!

WHICH KORAN?

If the Koran is from God, then it must be perfect, without contradictions. A Muslim booklet, *The Amazing Quran* challenges readers to show any mistakes and contradictions. I accept that challenge with gusto! Now, we must admit that there is a difference in confusion and contradictions. So I will try to be fair, honest, and candid dealing with mistakes in the Koran, the Hadith (their second holy book) and Islam in general.

Most Muslims are uninformed, as are most Christians, as to their "holy" books. What the average Muslim knows about their "holy" books would fit into the navel of a flea. They don't know that the Hadith says that Uthman got the Koran compiled and sent copies to various places. Wait a minute; I thought Mohammed received a perfect text from heaven during his fits, swoons, seizures, etc.!

It is a fact that there was no definitive Koran text even as late as the ninth century.[3] The sayings of Mohammed had not been collected and put in a volume. Many Muslims began to collect Mohammed's sayings and soon there were many "Korans." The third caliph after Mohammed, Caliph Uthman, tried to bring order to the disorder and clearness to the confusion by putting his stamp of approval on what was called the "Medinan Codex." He then sent copies to all the major Muslim cities with orders to destroy all other variations of the Koran. Dr. Robert Morey asks four penetrating questions about the work done by Caliph Uthman:[4]

- Why did he have to standardize a common text if there was already a standardized text available?

- Why did he try to destroy all the other manuscripts if there were no other conflicting manuscripts? Vol. 6, book 61, number 510 reveals that Uthman tried to destroy all conflicting copies.

- Why did he use death threats to force acceptance of his text if that were the only available text?

- Why did many people reject his text in favor of the one they already had?

SCHOLARS ASSESS THE KORAN

A major **supporter** of Islam was Thomas Carlyle, yet he assessed the Koran as "A wearisome confused jumble, crude, incondite [unpolished, crude]; endless iterations, long-windedness, entanglement; most crude incondite–insupportable stupidity, in short! Nothing but a sense of duty could carry any European through the Koran."[5] That was written by a big supporter of Islam!

About A.D. 830, al-Kindi analyzed the Koran deciding that its "histories are all jumbled together and intermingled; an evidence that many different hands have been at work therein, and caused discrepancies, adding or cutting out whatever they like or disliked. Are such, now, the conditions of a revelation sent down from heaven?"[6] Great question!

Mohammed was not well acquainted with the Bible as his many errors proved. Obermann speaks of "gross discrepancies, inaccuracies and delusions he exhibits," whenever he makes observations about the Old Testament and often about the New Testament.[7] Numerous scholars agree.

Islamic scholar Ali Dashti assessed the Koran as "not fully intelligible without the aid of commentaries; foreign words, unfamiliar Arabic words, and words used with other than the normal meaning; adjectives and verbs inflected without observance of the concords of gender and number; illogically and ungrammatically applied pronouns which sometimes have no referent; and predicates which in rhymed passages are often remote from the subjects."[8] Translation: It's a mess!

The German scholar Salomon Reinach wrote: "From the literary point of view, the Koran has little merit…It is humiliating to the human intellect to think that this mediocre literature has been the subject of innumerable commentaries, and that millions of men are still wasting time in absorbing it."[9]

The Koran is incoherent without any logical order of thought and an Islamic reference work refers to the "disjointed and irregular character" of the Koran.[10] Ali Dashti wrote: "To sum up, more than one hundred Qur'anic aberrations from the normal rules and structures of Arabia have been noted."[11] In fact, there are more than 100 non-Arabic words in the Koran![12] I suppose it is good that Allah is multi-lingual! Middle East scholar Canon Sell revealed that there are many foreign words.[13] Many verses have been lost and even Shiite Muslims admit that 25 percent of the original verses in the Koran were left out for political reasons.[14] When you consider the mishmash in the Koran, it makes one wonder what was left out!

Mohammed used a juvenile device, although somewhat innovative, to promote the alleged miraculous nature of the Koran. Many suras (chapters) start with letters that have absolutely no meaning! One example is sura 50: "Qaf. [These letters (Qaf, etc.) are one of the miracles of the Qur'an, and none but Allah (Alone) knows their meanings]. By the Glorious Qur'an." I can just hear Mohammed say, "Now, how about **that?**" Gibberish disguised as a miracle, and to think that some people are impressed!

TREASURE OR TRASH

The above characterizations of the Koran are understandable when one discovers that it was written on pieces of papyrus, flat stones, palm leaves, shoulder blades and ribs of animals, pieces of leather, wooden boards, etc.[15] The 114 suras (chapters) were collected long after Mohammed's death and were not in any logical order. They are arranged from the longest to the shortest suras. Muslims tell us that Allah is always speaking directly to Mohammed; however, that is not true. It is obvious that, at times, Mohammed is speaking. (Of course, Mohammed is **always** speaking.)

The first English translation of the Koran by a non-Muslim scholar in the West was in 1734 by George Sale. Many others were to follow, although Muslims tell us that the Koran **cannot** be translated; however, they tell us that in the **very** translation they have done! Notwithstanding, there are many translations available.

There is general agreement among scholars that the Meccan suras were written during Mohammed's early life and the later suras were written during his days in Medina. When in Mecca during his early years, he was persecuted and rejected, but in Medina, he was in the seat of power. During those early days, he spoke of tolerance because he **wanted** tolerance. When he came to power, the early suras were abrogated (cancelled) in favor of later ones that demanded persecution of Islam's enemies. It seems Mohammed was an unprincipled opportunist. And, if the Koran came from Allah, then why didn't an all-powerful, all-knowing God get it correct the first time? Dashti rightly wrote, "Evidently even the simple, uneducated Hejazi Arabs could understand that Almighty God, being aware of what is best for His servants, would prescribe the best in the first place and would not have changes of mind in the same way as His imperfect creatures."[16]

Some Muslims angrily deny the abrogation doctrine; however, some of their scholars say otherwise. In his book, *How to Perfect the Science of the Quran* (Al-Itqan), Mr. Al-Syoti, writes in volume 2, page 37; "The verse of the sword has abrogated (annulled, cancelled) one hundred and twenty four Quranic verses and all what came in the Quran on matters of forgiving and ignoring, unbelievers have been replaced (Mansookha), by the verse of the sword." The **most famous** interpreters of the Koran also confirm this. For further evidence refer to the following: Kitab Al-Nasekh Wal-mansookh, Al-Hafeth Ibnu Katheer Ibin Abas. Al-Tasheel Lulum Al-Tanzeel, Al-Husain Ibn Fadl, Abu Abdullah Muhammad Ibn

Hazm, Al-Muhaqiq Abu Al-Qasim Hibatullah Ibn Salameh, Al-Sudy Wa-AlDahak, and Muhammad Abdulsalam Faraj.

Most scholars have concluded that to leave the Bible for the Koran is to go from a greater to a lesser.[17] They are correct. It is going from a Treasure to trash, from the real to the ridiculous, from reality to rubbish.

MOHAMMED'S FOUL-UPS

Mohammed had a scribe named abd Allah b. Sa'd Abi Sarh, and "On a number of occasions he had, with the Prophet's consent, changed the closing words of verses. When the Prophet had said 'And God is mighty and wise,' Abd Allah suggested writing down 'knowing and wise' and the Prophet answered that there was no objection. Having observed a succession of changes of this type, Abd Allah renounced Islam on the ground that the revelations, if from God, could not be changed at the prompting of a scribe such as himself. After his apostasy he went to Mecca and joined the Qorayshites." Eventually, Mohammed had him assassinated when he took Mecca.[18]

Mohammed really fouled his nest, so much so that it stinks to this day. The problem arises with the famous "satanic verses," made famous in recent years by Rushdie's book by that title. The "stink" arose following one of Mohammed's visions. It seems he was courting the folks at Mecca, but they weren't responding, so he decided to "give a little" to get some consideration for his new religion. He, of course, received a revelation: It would be acceptable to Allah for the Meccans to worship their favorite gods, the three daughters of the moon. Prayers to them might impress Allah to answer their requests! Wow! That was an incredible concession for the "prophet" to make. However, it didn't last long. He received a later revelation that told him Satan had given him permission to use al-Lat, al-Uzza, and Manat as divine intercessors. It was all a dirty trick of Satan. So the early revelation was abrogated. Well, if Satan deceived Mohammed at that time, is it not possible that he was deceived many times? **All the time?**

IS THE KORAN RELIABLE?

The "Abrogation" (cancellation) doctrine is essential for Islam to hold together because of the contradictions. Mohammed revealed in sura 2:106: "Whatever a Verse (revelation) do We abrogate or cause to be forgotten, We bring a better one or similar to it." It is believed by scholars that there could be up to 500 such verses. Sane people want to know how an all-knowing God can revise his plans so often and why he couldn't do it right the first time![19] So how can a Muslim, with a straight face, say the Koran is totally reliable when much of it is obsolete?

Muslims affirm that Islam is a religion of peace, not violence, and they expect us to wipe out 1400 years of history to make them comfortable in a "civilized" era. They point to sura 2:256 that teaches, "There is no compulsion in religion," but sura 9:5 commands them to "Kill the idolaters wherever you find them." So sura 9:5 abrogates all the "tolerate" verses.

In my copy of the Koran, given to me by Muslim clerics in Indianapolis, there are numerous examples of abrogation. The first one is sura 2:109 where Mohammed tells his followers to forgive the Christians and Jews who try to turn Muslims away from Islam. The footnote on page 21 clearly commands Muslims, "The provision of this verse has been abrogated by the (V. 9:29)." That verse commands Muslims to "fight against" the Christians and Jews. Abrogation is a kind of damage control.

It is very important to note that the early verses that preach tolerance are considered to be the Meccan passages and those that advocate decapitating, maiming and general killing are Medinan. Why? Because in the early days, Mohammed and his few followers were ridiculed and persecuted, so of course, he preached toleration; but when he was the top honcho and ruled like an Arabian despot, toleration was a sign of weakness and aggression was a sign of strength. Mohammed changed his tactics and preaching depending upon his circumstances. After all, he may have been a liar, thief, killer, child molester, and desert despot, but he wasn't a fool.

After reading all of the Koran many times and studying many of the hadiths, I have found numerous errors of historical fact, scientific fact, and scriptural fact. It must be remembered that sura locations may vary with each translation. The desired verse may be a few verses before or after the given location.

DID MOHAMMED PERFORM MIRACLES?

We are told that Mohammed did no miracles in sura 17:90-93 and 29:50 as the latter reveals: "The signs are only with Allah, and I am only a plain warner." While Mohammed did not perform miracles according to the Koran, we know that Christ did according to the New Testament and according to sura 2:253: "And to Jesus the son of Mary We gave clear proofs and evidences...."

Herein is a contradiction because while the Koran tells us Mohammed **did not** perform miracles, the Hadith reveals many of his miracles: healing the sick, feeding a thousand people with one kid, etc. Which is it? Did he or did he not perform miracles? A few hundred years after Mohammed died, his followers were faced by Christians who spoke of Christ's miracles. So Muslims replied, "Well, Mohammed **also** performed miracles." Then they proceeded to write hadiths that revealed miracles performed by Mohammed!

Following are some of the miracles allegedly performed by Mohammed: Vol. 4, book 56, number 779 tells that as Mohammed ate food, the food shouted praises to Allah and the Prophet! When he multiplied the bread, he had the people come in groups of ten. (Sound familiar? Christ, in Luke 9 had the crowd sit down in groups of fifty.) Mohammed healed a man with eye trouble by spitting in his eyes according to vol. 4, book 52, number 192 and vol. 5, book 57, number 51; vol.7, book 71, number 641 and 642, reveal that Mohammed could heal all kinds of diseases with his spit. Holy spit! In fact, vol. 4, book 56, number 777 and vol. 5, book 59 numbers 471 and 472 reveal that Mohammed spat a mouthful of water into a well and satisfied 1400 men and their camels! The Hadith tells us that Mohammed's spit, his quoting the Koran, and waving his hand over a wound healed all kinds of illnesses including scorpion stings and snakebites. There is power in spit!

Mohammed cursed the tribes of Mudar because they rejected him, and within a year they were eating hides and dead animals. Another time he prayed for rain, and it rained! How about **that**!

When Mohammed was asked to perform a miracle to prove he was a true prophet, he pulled his sword and cut the moon in half according to Hadith vol. 4, book 56, numbers 830-832; vol. 5, book 58, numbers 208-211; and vol. 6, book 60, numbers 387-390. Desert Arabs thought the moon and sun were about the size of a basketball! When Muslims needed water, Mohammed rode to the rescue. He called for a bowl and water flowed from his fingertips into the bowl until each person could perform his ablution (vol. 1, book 4, numbers 170, 194; vol. 4, book 56, numbers 773-779). How many people were satisfied? Well, it depends on which hadith you read! Number 774 says it was 70; number 775 gives 80, then number 772 says it was 300, but number 776 and vol. 5, book 59, number 473 give 1500. Most people expect a holy book to be **exact** in every respect.

WHAT THE KORAN TEACHES

In sura 4:106; 40:55; and 47:19 we discover that Mohammed was a sinner. Of course, that is no surprise because all men are born sinners. Informed people are aware that he kept slaves, killed people, tortured people, etc., and most people would agree that he was a sinner. However, we know that Christ was sinless but became sin for us according to II Corinthians. 5:21: "For he hath made him to be sin for us, who knew no sin; that we might be made the righteousness of God in him." I Peter 2:22 reminds us of Christ "Who did no sin...." and sura 19:19 speaks of Christ as being a "righteous son."

The Koran affirms that Jesus was **not** God in sura 3:59, 62, and 4:171. The New Testament clearly teaches that He **was** and **is** God. Jesus said in John 10:30: "I and my Father are one." And in John 14:9: "he that hath seen me hath seen the Father." John 1:1, 18; 20:28; Romans 9:5; Titus 2:13; and Hebrews 1:8, 10:12 all affirm His deity. Jesus may not be the Son of God in sura 4:171 but then He is if you continue to read 19:17-21. It seems Allah just couldn't make up his mind. That's bad for a god!

According to sura 4:157-158, Christ did not die on the cross. "Yet they slew him not, and they crucified him not, but they had only his likeness." We are told that God substituted someone else (many say it was Judas!) in His place. Wonder why a sovereign God has to use subterfuge to accomplish His purpose? And what would be His purpose in deceiving the disciples, the authorities, and the religious leaders? Philippians 2:5-8 clearly states that Christ died for all mankind and verse 9 says He is exalted far above every name. That would include Mohammed. John 19:32-33 tells us that when the soldiers came to break the legs of the three crucified men, they did not break Christ's legs because "he was dead already."

The Hadith also teaches Christ's virgin birth, perfect life, and His miracles. The Koran supports the Bible teaching that Christ was born of the Virgin Mary in sura 3:47. "How shall I have a son when no man has touched me?" Other translations end with, "when I am a virgin...?"

The Koran attacks the Trinity in sura 5:75: "The Mesiah (Jesus), son of (Mary), was no more than a Messenger...." In sura 5:116 Allah really got confused when he said, "And when God shall say, 'O Jesus son of Mary hast thou said unto mankind, 'Take me and my mother as two Gods besides God?'" The highly acclaimed Muslim commentator al-Baidawi said that Christians made the Trinity consist of God, Christ, and **Mary**! And over a billion Muslims are trusting their eternal souls to that "holy" book! I John 5:7 clearly teaches the Trinity.

ISLAM CONFUSES BIBLE TRUTH

Mohammed tried to use people and incidents from the Bible to clothe Islam with some respectability and give Islam a historical past that it does not have. He put words in the mouths of the Old Testament characters that were biblically untrue and often ludicrous. He created a history that never happened. Maybe he was the first to take advantage of "creative" writing.

We are told in sura 5:78 that David and Jesus cursed the children of Israel because they disobeyed Allah. Well, the Jews sure disobeyed God but David did not curse them for it.

The Koran's tale regarding Joseph and Potiphar's wife is unintelligible: Joseph wants to sin with her, but he sees a vision [of his father] at the window. Many women laughed at Potiphar's wife because of her longing for Joseph, and she invited them to see him for themselves. When they came, they were so impressed with him that they cut themselves with knives! Was that a desert declaration of devotion?

The Koran tells us that Haman lived in Egypt during the days of Moses and he worked for Pharaoh in building the Tower of Babel (see suras 28:38; 29:39; 40:24) but most Christians know Haman lived in Persia working as the flunky of King Ahasuerus. Mohammed was only off by a thousand years and a thousand miles! Moreover, Pharaoh did not build the Tower of Babel! Not just mistakes but massive mishmash!

In sura 9:30, Mohammed made another mistake about Jews believing that Ezra was the Son of God. In addition, we discover in Hadith vol. 6, book 60, number 380 that the angel Gabriel has 600 wings according to the Prophet. Well, that's always good information to know. But it gets better! We also learn that demons helped Solomon build the Temple, and Solomon had the ability to talk with birds. If Solomon talked to the birds, he spent too much time at his wine cup!

We discover in sura 7:10-12 that Allah told the angels to bow to Adam at his creation but Satan (Eblis) refused and was cast out of Paradise. We also discover from Hadith, vol. 4, book 55, number 543 that "The Prophet said, 'Allah created Adam, making him 60 cubits tall.'" Then number 544 informs us that wives in Paradise all look alike and will also be 60 cubits tall! Does any Muslim with an IQ equivalent to his hat size really believe such poppycock?

Sura 19:28-29 reveals that after the birth of Christ people came to Mary and said, "O Mary, now you have done an extraordinary thing! O sister of Aaron! Your father was not a bad man, nor was your mother a whore!" Mohammed confused Mary, the mother of Christ, with Miriam, the sister of Moses and Aaron! Sura 3:46 tells of baby Jesus speaking from the cradle, and 3:49 reveals the old fable that Christ gave life to birds of clay! Mohammed couldn't even come up with original fables!

Sura 19:10 (also 3:41) informs us that Zacharias could not speak for three days before John was born, but Luke 1:20 tells us he did not speak for the entire time of the pregnancy.

Muslims teach that Ishmael, not Isaac, was taken to be sacrificed (sura 37:100-112) and the Land of Promise belongs to Ishmael's descendants. They also teach in sura 6:74 that Abraham's father's name was Azar. Abraham lived in Mecca according to sura 14:37, not in Haran (and later in Hebron). Furthermore, in sura 21:68-69 we discover that Abraham was thrown into the fire by Nimrod. Mohammed didn't know that Nimrod lived hundreds of years before Abraham!

Mohammed tells us in sura 20:87, 95 that Aaron made the golden calf in the wilderness at the suggestion of "the Samaritan." There were no Samaritans until hundreds of years later!

Gabriel, who Mohammed taught was the Holy Spirit, opened Mohammed's chest and washed his insides then took wisdom and faith and poured them into his chest (Hadith, vol. 1, book 8, number 345). I'm not sure whether Gabriel or an assistant closed.

Such confusion is not unusual since Mohammed could not read, according to most historians, and picked up bits and pieces of Bible stories as he heard them around the caravan campfires.

ISLAM CONFUSES SCIENTIFIC FACTS

Mohammed didn't know any more about science than he did the Bible! In sura 27:61 he taught that the earth is a fixed object and in 16:15 he "revealed" that the mountains are to provide stability to the earth "lest it should shake with you." But he becomes even more confused in 18:86 where he taught that the sun sets in a "spring of black muddy (or hot) water." In 36:40 we discover that the sun will not "overtake the moon." He thought the sun and moon traveled around the earth.

I'm sorry, but it does get worse! In 67:5, we learn that Allah created the stars to adorn "the nearest [lowest] heaven," and they are missiles "to drive away the devils...." Of course, the stars are not in the lowest heaven

and no sane person believes they are used to pelt "the devils." Mohammed did not know that the moon was not in the midst of the stars, and is
less than 250,000 miles from earth. He would be shocked to discover that
our nearest star is 100 million times farther from earth!

INCONSISTENCIES IN THE KORAN

We are told in sura 54:49-50 that Allah created everything "in the twin-
kling of an eye" then in 41:9 and 12 we discover it took a little longer–"two
days." But it gets worse because in 41:10 it took "four days" then in 7:54;
10:3; and 32:4 it took "six days." It seems Allah didn't remember how long
it took him to create everything. Seems as if the longer you read the more
time it took! Sura 77:20 tells us that Allah created man from semen and
then sura 21:30; 25:54; and 24:45 tell us that all living things were created
out of water. Speaking of water, Mohammed has the Flood taking place
during the time of Moses, not Noah! (See sura 7:137.)

The Koran forbids wine in sura 2:219, yet sura 16:67 permits drinking
wine, and we are assured there will be plenty of wine in Paradise.

In sura 24:2-4, Allah requires 100 lashes for fornication for unmarried
persons (although slaves received only 50): "The woman and man guilty
of fornication, flog each of them with a hundred stripes; let not pity move
you in their case." Muslims have required stoning for centuries for married people, contrary to the Koran. Furthermore, according to sura 4:3,
a Muslim may cohabit with any female slave and sura 4:24 permits any
Muslim to take a married woman if she is a slave. Christ told us not even
to lust after a woman!

SOCIAL LIFE

Mohammed tells us in sura 3:106-107 that only white people will be saved.
Blacks are damned! Yet Black Muslims insist that Christianity is the white
man's religion and Islam is the black man's religion. Wrong again!

Muslims have been buying and selling black slaves for centuries. The
Hadith often refers to Mohammed as being a white man, and Mohammed called Blacks, "raisin" heads in vol. 1, book 11, number 662. There
are various references to Mohammed owning black slaves, and need I remind everyone that Christ came to set men free? And it was white Christians in England and America who set the slaves free!

Mohammed had very definite ideas about what to do about drunks, and it was not to talk them out of drinking or drying them out. He thought it best to beat drunks!

Bukhari vol. 8, book 81, number 772:

Narrated Abu Huraira: A drunk was brought to the Prophet and he ordered him to be beaten (lashed). Some of us beat him with our hands, and some with their shoes, and some with their garments (twisted in the form of a lash). When that drunk had left, a man said, "What is wrong with him? May Allah disgrace him!" Allah's Apostle said, "Do not help Satan against your (Muslim) brother."

The Prophet would chop off the hand of his daughter if she stole something! Of course, **he** was a thief, but that was different.

Bukhari vol. 8, book 81, number 778:

Narrated 'Aisha: Usama approached the Prophet on behalf of a woman (who had committed theft). The prophet said, "The people before you were destroyed because they used to inflict the legal punishments on the poor and forgive the rich. By Him in Whose Hand my soul is! If Fatima (the daughter of the Prophet) did that (i.e., stole), I would cut off her hand."

It is dangerous to look into a Muslim's house. In fact, one could lose an eye.

Bukhari vol. 9, book 83, number 38:

Narrated Sahl bin Sa'd As-Sa'idi: A man peeped through a hole in the door of Allah's Apostle's house, and at that time, Allah's Apostle had a Midri (an iron comb or bar) with which he was rubbing his head. So when Allah's Apostle saw him, he said (to him), "If I had been sure that you were looking at me (through the door), I would have poked your eye with this (sharp iron bar)." Allah's Apostle added, "The asking for permission to enter has been enjoined so that one may not look unlawfully (at what there is in the house without the permission of its people)."

Animal lovers of PETA (People Eating Tasty Animals) will not be thrilled with Mohammed since vol. 4, book 54, number 540 reveals: "Allah's Apostle ordered that the dogs should be killed."

It is one thing to have animal lovers angry with you but to purposely antagonize women is close to suicidal! Sura 4:34 states: "Men are the managers of the affairs of women....Those you fear may be rebellious–admonish; banish them to their couches and beat them." "Beat" means to "scourge them." Muslim television programs give explicit instructions on how to beat a wife, where on her body to beat her, and what to use in the beating.

Women are ideal in the bedroom and kitchen but bad news elsewhere according to Mohammed. One hadith has him saying, "Three things can interrupt prayers if they pass in front of someone praying: a black dog, a woman, and an ass."[20] Mohammed commands that "The woman should never refuse her husband even on the saddle of a horse" or another version says, "on the top of a hot oven." Hey, a wife should seek to satisfy her husband (as he should seek to satisfy her), but on top of a burning stove!

According to vol. 1, book 2, number 28; vol. 1, book 6, number 301; and vol. 2, book 18, number 161 "The Prophet said, 'I was shown the Hell-fire and that the majority of its dwellers were women." Mohammed didn't think women had much chance for Paradise and he didn't help make their earthly existence much of a paradise either. He didn't think a woman had much of a mind. In vol. 3, book 48, number 826, "The Prophet said, 'Isn't the witness of a woman equal to half of that of a man?' The women said, 'Yes,' He said, 'This is because of the deficiency of a woman's mind.'"

Homosexuality is condemned in the Koran, yet it has been practiced in Islam for hundreds of years with only sporadic times of punishment. Sura 7:80, 81 is rather blunt: "And Lot said to his people: Do you commit indecent acts that no nation has ever committed before? You lust after men in preference to women. You really are a degenerate people." Well, I didn't say Mohammed was wrong **every** time he opened his mouth! Again in sura 4:16: "If two men among you commit indecency, punish them both." Sura 26:165-166 and sura 27:55 further condemns perversion; however, sura 52:24 seems to sanction perversion to faithful Muslims: "And there shall wait on them young boys of their own, as fair as virgin pearls." We do know that some of the early Muslim leaders (caliphs) were homosexuals (even the famous Saladin in the twelfth century) while other caliphs executed homosexuals.

SUPERSTITIONS

The Koran is littered with seventh-century Arabian superstition such as the evil eye! Mohammed was asked, "O Prophet, the family of Jafar are affected by the baneful influences of an evil eye; may I use spells for them or not?" Mohammed replies, "Yes, for if there were anything in the world which would overcome fate, it would be an evil eye."[21]

In sura 18:8-26, the old legend of the seven sleepers is retold as a revelation from God! Edward Gibbon says that Mohammed probably heard this tale many times during his trading days with the caravans. It seems that seven youths fled to a cave to escape persecution and their pursuers sealed up the cave. However, the youths survived and walked out about 300 years later unharmed! This is a famous tale that Mohammed treated as his own.

Vol. 5, book 58, number 200 reveals something that I've always wondered about: the spirits or jinn eat dung and bones. Now **you** know!

ABSURDITIES

Muslims learn that Mohammed has given explicit instructions on when and how to urinate. He said:

> One of the major sins is not to protect oneself [one's clothes and body] from one's urine [i.e., from being soiled with it]. Once the Prophet, while passing one of the grave-yards of Medina or Mecca, heard the voices of two persons being tortured in their graves.

> The Prophet then added, "yes! (they are being tortured for a major sin). Indeed, one of them never saved himself from being soiled with his urine" (vol. 1, book 4, number 215).

Mohammed's rules for taking care of the daily personal needs that everyone has: "Don't face Mecca when urinating or defecating. Don't use your right hand to hold or clean yourself. And wash all your private parts after taking care of these personal chores." (See Hadith vol. 1, book 4, numbers 146-157.)

Mohammed was obsessed with urine, yet he told his followers to drink a concoction of camel's urine and milk! (See Hadith vol. 1, book 4, number 234.) My grandkids would say that Mohammed was a weirdo. I concur. Remember that Muslims are bound by what the Koran and Hadith teach. A Muslim leader's ideas don't matter. What matters is the teaching from the Arabian Desert of the seventh century.

Mohammed warned people that if they slept during the mosque service or did not get up for morning prayers Satan would urinate in their ears!

Yes, read vol. 2, book 21, number 245. Mohammed also revealed something that eye, ear, and nose specialists still don't know: that Satan stays all night in the upper part of the nose according to vol. 4, book 54, number 516. Don't look at me like that. I don't explain them, I only report them!

Vol. 1, book 8, number 436 promises us that the angels ask Allah's forgiveness for anyone who passes wind while he is at his praying place. At another place, we are told, "When he enters the mosque he is considered in prayer as long as he is waiting for the prayer and the angels keep on asking for Allah's forgiveness for him and they keep on saying: 'O Allah! Be Merciful to him, O Allah! Forgive him, as long as he keeps on sitting at his praying place and does not pass wind." (See vol. 1, book 8, number 436.)

Faithful Muslims are promised that they will be protected from poison or major powers if they eat seven dates every morning. (See vol. 7, book 65, number 356.) Do intelligent Muslims really believe such poppycock? Do they really know the poppycock that is taught in the Koran and the Hadith?

HATRED IN THE HOLY BOOKS

There is much hatred in the Koran and the Hadith, with love almost absent. Love for fellowmen is absent. Allah doesn't do much loving, but there is much about who he (Allah) does **not** love. He does not love the unjust (3:57; 3:140); nor the extravagant (6:141); nor those who "exceed the limits" (7:55); nor the proud (16:23); nor the ungrateful (22:38); nor mischief-makers (28:77); nor unbelievers (30:45). My Bible tells me in many places that God loves the world.

Allah showed his hatred in sura 5:60 where he changed people into apes and hogs: "They whom God hath cursed and with whom He hath been angry–some of them hath He changed into apes and swine…." In sura 7:163-166, Mohammed regurgitates the old Arabian fable of a village whose citizens were turned into apes because they fished on the Sabbath! Mohammed's fables and heresies weren't even original!

INTOLERANCE OF ISLAM

Muslims leaders have told me that Muslims have the right to decide what they wish to believe of the Hadith; however, that is modern propaganda developed because Islamic belief would turn all thinking people away

161

from Islam. The following quotations prove the intolerance of Islam:

> *Bukhari vol. 9, book 84, number 57: Narrated 'Ikrima: Some Za-nadiqa (atheists) were brought to 'Ali and he burnt them. The news of this event, reached Ibn 'Abbas who said, "If I had been in his place, I would not have burnt them, as Allah's Apostle forbade it, saying, 'Do not punish anybody with Allah's punishment (fire).' I would have killed them according to the statement of Allah's apostle, 'whoever changed his Islamic religion, then kill him.' "*

> *Bukhari vol. 9, book 84, number 58: Narrated Abu Burda: Abu Musa said, "I came to the Prophet along with two men (from the tribe) of Ash'ariyin, one on my right and the other on my left, while Allah's Apostle was brushing his teeth (with a Siwak), and both men asked him for some employment. The Prophet said, 'O Abu Musa (O 'Abdullah bin Qais!).' I said, 'By Him Who sent you with the Truth, these two men did not tell me what was in their hearts and I did not feel (realize) that they were seeking employ-ment.' As if I were looking now at his Siwak being drawn to a corner under his lips, and he said, 'We never (or, we do not) ap-point for our affairs anyone who seeks to be employed. But O Abu Musa! (or 'Abdullah bin Qais!) Go to Yemen.'" The Prophet then sent Mu'adh bin Jabal after him and when Mu'adh reached him, he spread out a cushion for him and requested him to get down (and sit on the cushion). Behold: There was a fettered man be-side Abu Muisa. Mu'adh asked, "Who is this (man)?" Abu Muisa said, "He was a Jew and became a Muslim and then reverted back to Judaism." Then Abu Muisa requested Mu'adh to sit down but Mu'adh said, "I will not sit down till he has been killed. This is the judgment of Allah and his apostle (for such cases) and repeated it thrice. Then Abu Musa ordered that the man be killed, and he was killed. Abu Musa added, "Then we discussed the night prayers and one of us said, 'I pray and sleep, and I hope that Allah will reward me for my sleep as well as for my prayers.'"*

The Koran is full of inconsistencies, superstitions, absurd stories about genies, fables from Arabian folklore, tales from numerous apocryphal works, Jewish Talmud, etc., yet the gullible believe that it came from the throne of a holy God! Their "holy" books are filled with mistakes, mish-mash, and madness. How could anyone in his or her right mind trust their eternal souls to the "holy" books of Islam?

References:

1   *The Concise Encyclopedia of Islam,* ed. Cyril Classe, London: Stacey Inter., 1989, p. 228.

2   Cited by Ibn Warraq, *Why I Am Not a Muslim,* 170.

3   Ibid., p. 154

4   Robert Morey, *The Islamic Invasion,* Harvest House, Eugene, OR, 1992, p. 125.

5   Thomas Carlyle, *On Heroes, Hero-worship, and the Heroes in History,* First Published 1881, Re. Dossier Press, New York, 2015, pp. 64-67, 1841.

6   Cited in *Why I am Not a Muslim,* p. 113.

7   Julian Obermann, "Islamic Origins: A Study in Background and Foundation." In *The Arab Heritage.* Nabih Faris, ed. Princeton, 1944, p. 94.

8   Ali Dashti, *Twenty-three Years: A Study of the Prophetic Career of Mohammed,* London, 1985, p. 50.

9   Salmon Reinach, *Orpheus: A History of Religion,* New York: Livercraft, Inc. 1932, p. 176.

10   *The Concise Encyclopedia of Islam,* p. 231.

11   Dashti, p. 50.

12   Arthur Jeffery, *The Foreign Vocabulary of the Quran,* Baroda: Oriental Institute, 1938, number 79.

13   Edward Sell, *Studies in Islam,* Diocesan Press, London, 1928. p. 226.

14   John McClintock and James Strong, *Cyclopedia of Biblical, Theological, and Ecclesiastical Literature* Baker, Grand Rapids, 1981, V:152.

15   *The Concise Encyclopedia of Islam,* p. 230.

16   Dashti, p. 155.

17   Morey, p. 115.

18   Dashti, p. 98.

19   Ibid. p. 155.

20   Warraq, p. 301.

21   Ibid., p. 49.

Chapter Twelve

Holy Hatred of Christians!

Television pundits have been talking incessantly about terrorism, but few are talking about motives. So I will. What could make people hate America so much that they would fly a plane into a building and kill themselves and innocent people? It appears that Muslims pursue death because they hate their lives. First of all, many of them don't hate Americans but they hate our Government. There is a difference. But why don't they hate other governments as much as they hate ours? Most countries usually don't meddle in the affairs of other nations. Muslims do have some hatred toward Americans because of our corrupting influence of their culture.

Following the September 11 disasters, a militant Islamic group in Pakistan held up a sign that was flashed all over the earth: AMERICANS, THINK! WHY YOU ARE HATED ALL OVER THE WORLD. Inquiring minds want to know the answer.

Sheikh Omar said of terrorist attacks: "The question is not who did it, but why America creates more enemies than friends." No, we must chase down all terrorists and punish them for their crimes but the sheikh asked a good question. Are some pundits correct when they tell us that the Muslims envy our success and covet our "good life?" If they covet our "good life," they don't get it by flying planes into buildings or other acts of terror. The fact is they hate us for what we believe and what we don't believe.

AMERICA HAD IT COMING

One conservative wrote that the U.S. is a target for terrorists "because we are powerful, rich and good." Sheikh Omar Bakri Mohammed, founder and leader of the radical Al Muhajiroun group, told *The Times of India*, "Yes, it is Muslims who have done this. There is no one else who would feel that much anger against America." A London Muslim cleric added, "America had it coming."

No, we didn't have it coming, but we should have seen it coming! What else could we expect after many years of bombing Arab cities and aspirin factories, boycotting them resulting in over a million civilian deaths in Iraq, and the U.S. knee-jerk support of their enemies? Example: Former U.S. Ambassador to the U.N., Madeleine Albright told Lesley Stahl of *CBS* that 500,000 dead Iraqi children, killed by U.S. sanctions, was morally justified to get Saddam! She said, "We think the price is worth it."[1]

Muslim mothers may think that their children might as well die as martyrs as to die by mortars. Sure, it is warped thinking, but hearing the Koran every day for a lifetime and other contributing factors could lead to that kind of thinking. I have yet to hear any politician successfully justify killing innocent children on a massive scale. Can you justify the deaths of more than 500,000 children whom God loves as much as yours? Dare I write that God loves Arab babies as much as He does Israeli babies! Now, surely **that** makes me an anti-Semite! On the other hand, maybe it simply makes me a consistent Christian.

U. S. POLICIES

The American Government is hated because of such policies and because our policies over the past 50 years have not been even-handed. George Washington warned us about getting involved with other nations, but we have totally disregarded his warning. Thomas Jefferson said, "Peace, commerce and honest friendship with all nations; entangling alliances with none." Jefferson did not believe in expanding the U.S. Empire to Europe.

America has not followed Jefferson's advice. An obvious example is our involvement with Israel. We have not been even-handed in the treatment of Israel and the Arab states. We have almost given Israel a blank check since her founding over 50 years ago. We are now giving them over 3 billion dollars per year! I think it is time for Israel to pay its own bills. Does **that** make me anti-Semitic?

I have been to Israel and the Arab states about 13 times since 1967. Sharon, Begin, Peres, and other Jewish leaders have briefed me, along with about 50 other U.S. religious leaders. I have often walked the streets of Jerusalem, Jericho, Tiberias, and even Beersheba and Hebron, without apprehension, except in Hebron. I have walked upon the Golan Heights amid the bunkers and other defenses even before the landmines had been removed following one of their wars. I have seen young Arabs throw stones at Americans (including my vehicle) and wondered how they developed such hatred so young. Now I know. The U.S. helped promote animosity by our policies, but promoting animosity is not the same as producing terrorism. Some Islamic leaders are doing that right here in America! Muslims think they have a duty to conquer America and will use any excuse as justification.

Israel has a right to exist. I am thrilled that they are a nation, but I don't want to continue funding them. I also refuse to assume that what they do is justified by the circumstances. It is a fact that Israel has a policy of torture, holding people for months without trial, carrying out political assassinations anywhere in the world, and over-reacting to rock-throwing youths by responding with bullets and tanks! However, we must remember that Israel is opposed by 44 Muslims nations consisting of one billion people! Moreover, Israelis are much friendlier to America than any Muslim nation.

ISRAELI POLICIES

I have been in the homes of Israeli and Arab friends. One long-time friend, a Christian businessman in Jerusalem, is a Christian Arab from a wealthy family. The Israelis took his father's prime property in Jerusalem without compensation. I always thought that was thievery. If it happened to your family, you would consider it thievery, but the Israelis got a pass. Why? Well, because they are God's chosen people, but what does that have to do with anything? Do "God's chosen people" not have to abide by the Ten Commandments? How about the rule of law?

My Arab friend loves Americans but hates our government because we have permitted Israel to operate outside normal parameters. I will not surrender my right and responsibility to hold Israel to the same standard I demand of other nations, even if bigots and non-thinkers call me an "anti-Semite."

I am not a pacifist. I believe in self-defence personally and nationally, but I don't believe it is wise to get involved in every beer-hall brawl in town.

We must permit Israel to form its own policies, fund its own military, and fight its own battles. The U.S. has no legal or moral right to assume the position as policeman of the world. In fact, if we are consistent, we have no more rights than the smallest nation in the world. We must respect the sovereignty of every other nation and defend our sovereignty against every incursion, including that coming from the United Nations. Of course, we have every right, even an obligation to hunt down, try, convict, and execute all perpetrators of the terrorist attacks against us from the 1993 and 2001 Trade Center attacks to Boston to San Bernardino, but we must keep in mind that some of our policies for the last fifty years are part of the equation as we try to find an answer for such dedicated terror against innocent people.

ISLAM WAS THE FUTURE

Many Muslims all over the world have been anti-American for fifty years because they perceive us as the supporter, sustainer, and supplier of Israel. They consider Saudi Arabia holy ground since it is the land of Mohammed and is the location of their main mosque in Mecca. That U.S. troops (infidels) were stationed in Saudi Arabia inflamed them further; but in 2003 the 10,000 U.S. troops were removed. Muslims, in general, have hated the West for hundreds of years because of the Crusades and for sundry other reasons.

One reason for Muslim hatred and resentment of the U.S. is our success, but it is more than that. Muslims remember that they were on the march during the Middle Ages. Europeans lived in squalor except for the lords of the manors. Europeans were bathing every few months when Muslims bathed daily. Muslim ships, loaded with trade goods from afar, plied the open seas and provided the best the world had to offer. They built libraries, universities, and mosques all over the Middle East and Europe. Their armies seemed invincible. They were the future.

Then something happened: the Crusades occupied much of their time for more than two hundred years. One Crusade after another was fought seeking to dislodge Islamic rule from the Middle East. Huge numbers of "Christians" traveled to the Middle East to "fight the Turks" and consequently were exposed to other cultures, inventions, opportunities, and goods. While the Muslims had many great military victories, they also were humiliated many times. Then something else happened.

MUSLIMS AS LOSERS

Columbus discovered America. Other mariners discovered ocean routes to exotic places. Gold, silver, ivory, and other trade goods were brought to European cities. Universities, hospitals, and other institutions were established in all the major European cities. Armies and navies were built and the Muslim tide began to recede. "Christian" Europe was on the march, and momentum was no longer with Islam but with Christianity. Muslims slowly lost their grip and everything slipped from their hands. They have been trying to hang on to it but that is like trying to hold on to a greased pig.

Muslims watched in horror as their place in the world slipped from first to last, or almost last. Their great achievements were no longer remembered, and they have watched as America became the world leader in 200 years. Muslims are looking at their "glorious" past as they and the whole world are aware of their galling inferiority. They dwell on their "glorious" past until they are jerked back into their gloomy present. They recognize themselves as losers while non-Muslims are winners. They realize that America saved the world from Germany in 1914 (when Muslims supported Germany) and we went on to pull England and France from the grip of Nazi Germany in 1945. In recent years, they watched as Communism was discredited, though not decapitated, and the Berlin Wall came down because of America.

FALSE PRAISE

Barack Obama's dedication to Islam may have driven him into demonstrative error when he praised Islam profusely. Or, he may be a fool and is simply repeating what some other fool has uttered. Or, he might be a fraud in that he knows the claims are false but wanting to give credibility to Islam, he promulgates a falsehood. He is weaving a cloak to hide the naked lies of Islam. My purpose is to lift the cloak and reveal the ugly, uncomfortable, and ungodly side of Islam. It is a Trojan Horse and their overwhelming hordes could destroy our nation.

A leading Muslim said, "The Islamic civilization was one of the most amazing that history has ever known." That was tunnel vision and wishful thinking if not skewed, dishonest history. Such boastful claims are even more solemn, shameless, and scandalous when spoken by the President of the U.S.A.

The following grandiose claims are a pathetic example of desperate Muslim leaders who make false claims hoping to impress the gullible and feeble-minded. I could provide many more such false claims.

Muslims declare that Columbus had a Muslim navigator but he did not. He did have a Spaniard who spoke Arabic. Big difference. However, Vasco da Gama did have an Arab pilot when he sailed down the east coast of Africa.

The Muslim claim for the invention of glassmaking is totally bogus since glass can be traced back to 3500 B.C. in Mesopotamia.

Islamic fanatics tell us a Muslim was the first to test the principle of flying when Abbas ibn Firnas jumped from the top of the Grand Mosque in Cordoba, Spain in A.D. 852. He hoped to glide like a bird but he fell like a rock. Moreover, the Chinese developed kites 3,000 years ago and built a flying machine about A.D. 320. In the book *Pao Phu Tzu*, dated A.D. 320, Ko Hung states: "Some have made flying cars with wood, using ox-leather straps fastened to returning blades to set the machines in motion." The Wright Brothers expanded on the Chinese efforts in 1903 when they flew their plane 59 seconds over a North Carolina beach.

Desperate Muslims even take credit for bathing and soap invention! If Muslims would read the Old Testament they would discover the emphasis on cleanliness. Moreover, I have seen baths in Greece, Rome, and all over the Middle East that go back more than 2,000 years. The "Muslim" who allegedly developed soap in the late 1,700s was not even a Muslim! He was reared in a Muslim home but became a Christian and one of his grandsons became a preacher! Furthermore, soap making goes back to Babylon in 2,800 B.C. Such spurious Muslim claims show desperation.

Muslims have long taken credit for architecture especially the pointed arch that is so common all over Europe; however, it is a fact that the pointed arch goes back to the Assyrians as early as 722 B.C.

Dishonest Muslim hacks, without even a suppressed giggle, tell us that Muslims developed surgical instruments in the 10th century that are almost the same as those in use today. They even take credit for the use of catgut and for revealing information about circulation of the blood. The truth is that a Greek surgeon's home in ancient Pompeii (A.D. 79) revealed many surgical instruments that are the same design as today. That means Muslims are lying.

Furthermore, catgut was used by Greek physician Galenus (A.D. 129-

217) and Muslim claims of discovering the circulation of the blood is also bogus since it was described in the *Chinese Book of Medicine* about 300 B.C.! William Harvey, "Physician Extraordinary" to King James I, was the first to explain in the early 1600s how the heart pumped blood through the body in a continuous manner and in one direction. Harvey was a Christian, not a Muslim.

Deceptive Muslims even claim they were the first to proclaim the earth is round in the 8th century even though the Bible clearly declares the earth is a sphere in Isaiah 40:22. Muslims proved their deception when Saudi Arabia Sheik Abdul-Aziz Ibn Baaz recently declared "The earth is flat. Whoever claims it is round is an atheist deserving of punishment." Which is it—round or flat? But it gets worse because in October 2007 on Iraqi TV, a Muslim **scientist** authoritatively affirmed that the Earth is flat! Moreover, he informed his audience that the Sun is much smaller than the Earth and revolves around it!

Why all this disingenuousness, distortion, and dishonesty? It is because Islam has no credibility with informed people. So, Islamic followers try to prop it up and make it more respectable. Like angry atheists, they believe if they repeat their lies often enough, uninformed people will believe it is truth. It won't work.

No, Obama was wrong. Muslims made absolutely no contribution to America's founding or development. They are doing their best to destroy America as we have known it.

As proved above, Muslims blow smoke when they boast about their lasting accomplishments. What they did give to the world was a backward, barbaric, and bloody religion. Winston Churchill declared, "Individual Muslims may show splendid qualities, but the influence of the religion paralyses the social development of those who follow it. **No stronger retrograde force exists in the world.**"[2] Churchill called it right long before others.

But then, I'm not supposed to mention that fact or at least I should say that "a good religion was hijacked." That is also untrue.

Muslims see in the U.S. all that they should have, could have, and would have been—only if! While they hate Israel, they also hate our way of life, freedom, success, money, power, arrogance, and materialism. As they wish to drive Israel into the sea, they would also like to bring America to her knees. September 11, the Boston bombing, San Bernardino, etc., were part of their international conspiracy to accomplish that objective.

171

U.S. OUT OF THE MIDDLE EAST

Muslims also want us out of all Middle East countries, and with that I concur. They consider Saudi Arabia holy land, and they believe "infidels" have been camping there. Bin Laden made it very clear that we were trespassing on holy land with our troops in Saudi Arabia, and he (along with other Muslim leaders) wanted us out of "their" land. Even so, I'm convinced that some Muslim terrorist leaders want to dislodge the royal family and make Saudi Arabia their own cash cow. They are not unmindful of the petro-dollars that will flow into the treasury from the oil fields. I am fearful that if the U.S. goes after a terrorist state such as Iran or Syria, killing thousands of innocent people, it will inflame and unite the whole Arab/Islamic world against us. I'm convinced that there will be a last ditch effort to use weapons of mass destruction against the U.S. or Israel.

MUSLIMS' CRUSADE

Osama bin Laden used inflammatory rhetoric to energize Muslims around the world to his political and religious philosophy:

> Despite the great devastation inflicted on the Iraqi people by the crusader-Zionist alliance, and despite the huge number of those killed, which has exceeded 1 million...despite all this, the Americans are once again trying to repeat the horrific massacres, as though they are not content with the protracted blockade imposed after the ferocious war or the fragmentation and devastation.
>
> We–with God's help–call on every Muslim who believes in God and wishes to be rewarded to comply with God's order to kill the Americans and plunder their money wherever and whenever they find it. We also call on Muslim ulema, leaders, youths, and soldiers to launch the raid on Satan's U.S. troops and the devil's supporters allying with them, and to displace those who are behind them so that they may learn a lesson.
>
> The ruling to kill the Americans and their allies–civilians and military–is an individual duty for **every** Muslim who can do it in any country in which it is possible to do it, in order to liberate the al-Aqsa Mosque and the holy mosque [Mecca] from their grip, and in order for their armies to move out of all the lands of Islam, defeated and unable to threaten any Muslim.[3]

The late bin Laden issued a holy war against Israel, America, and her allies until Islam is supreme. Note his use of "crusader." It is not only a clash of cultures, but also a clash of religions. In a video delivered to Pakistani TV in early November of 2001, bin Laden said the conflict in Afghanistan was "primarily a religious war" between Christianity and Islam. Of Bush's "crusade," he said, "it is a certain fact that Bush carried the cross high.... Whoever stands behind Bush has committed an act that stands as annulment of their Islam." Here again the master terrorist referred to "crusade" and the "cross" and "a clash of religions." The Muslim terrorists are still fighting the Catholics of the Crusades!

You may remember that former President Bush originally used "Crusade" in giving a name to his war on terrorism! Bad choice of words as the following chapter will support.

FOUNDATION FOR CATHOLIC CHURCH

Most people think that the Roman Catholic Church started with the Apostle Peter with each succeeding pastor taking the title of Pope. Others think the Roman Catholic Church began on a Monday morning at 9:00 on a given day. Not so. It all happened very slowly. In fact, there were some good preachers (priests) in the Church for a long time.

During A.D. 68, Rome was in turmoil. The city had burned, resulting in Nero's suicide. Vespasian was now on the mighty Roman throne and sent Titus to Jerusalem to put out some political fires in that irascible city where 600,000 rebels had gathered. Titus arrived in February of 70, at the head of 80,000 troops. He also had thousands of war machines (I would call them "wallbusters") to wage war against a city. General Titus sought their surrender but was met with ridicule and had massive stones and hot oil hurled at his army.

Each day the Romans crucified hundreds of Jewish prisoners in full view of those Jews on the walls. Soon the black horse of famine galloped through the streets of the holy city and mothers ate their own dead children. Josephus said that the streets were clogged with the dead. The Temple was torched and as it burned, the defeated, desperate, and defiant Jews fell on their swords and others jumped into the flames. Josephus reported that 1,197,000 Jews were killed in the siege and its aftermath. Durant wrote that no people in history fought so tenaciously for liberty as the Jews nor had any people fought against such odds.[4]

Following the destruction of the Temple and the fall of Jerusalem, Judaism hid in fear while its offspring, Christianity, went out to witness about Christ to the world.[5] The Christians had dark periods of bloody persecution; however, their numbers continued to increase. Churches were established all over the land and extended their influence throughout Asia Minor and into Europe.

The greatest drama in human history was to see a relatively small group of Christians (hated, scorned, libeled, jailed, and tortured by numerous Roman dictators) bearing all their troubles, tests, and trials with tenacity, yet multiplying amid all the oppression, and finally overcoming and outlasting the mightiest state that had ever existed. Durant aptly wrote, "Caesar and Christ had met in the arena, and Christ had won."[6]

THE DIVIDED EMPIRE

Muslims have been told about the success of Islam during its early years as it raced across the Middle East, Asia, and Europe creating an impressive empire as they subdued and humiliated "infidels" along their path. The Western Roman Empire, centered in Rome, was to become the Holy Roman Empire but by 285 it had become so large that it was impossible to govern. Emperor Diocletian split the empire in two with the new entity known as the Eastern Empire with the seat in what was later Constantinople. Both empires were known as "The Roman Empire" although the Eastern part became Greek rather than Latin. Voltaire opined that the Holy Roman Empire was neither holy, Roman, nor an empire. Many historians agree.

Few Romans thought there were two empires but one massive empire ruled by two men, one in Rome and the other in Byzantium which was a Greek colony well-positioned astride the trade routes between East and West. The new city divided Europe from Asia. The Eastern Empire was ruled by Licinius in Byzantium, later known as Constantinople, now known as Istanbul. Constantine, after his alleged conversion to Christ in the early 300s, built a city he called Constantinople–the "new Rome" and moved the seat of the empire there in 330. Byzantine (known as the Eastern Byzantine Empire) was ruled by Licinius. The Eastern Empire lasted until 1453 when it was overrun by Muslim hordes. Constantine and Licinius signed the Edit of Milan (A.D. 313) that permitted Christians to meet without persecution from the state. While Rome continued to disintegrate, it was held together by Christian Churches as represented by the Church at Rome that slowly morphed into the Roman Catholic Church.

The Byzantine and Sasanian (Persia, now Iran) Empires from 224 to 651 fought for hundreds of years with each having occasional success. In 626 the Persians (Sasanians) laid siege to Constantinople but the siege ended with the Persians aborting their efforts. The almost constant fighting for hundreds of years between the Byzantine Empire and the Persian Empire devastated, discouraged, and debilitated the Persians setting them up to be subdued by the Muslim forces in 637.

With a dwindling Roman Empire, a depleted Persian Empire, and an extended Byzantine Empire, the stage was set for Muslims to "do their thing," and they did. Muslim troops, by the mid-700s, conquered Iran, Iraq, Syria, Palestine, Egypt, North Africa, and Spain. They even penetrated into India and for a time into France. Muslims were on the march and influenced the world for hundreds of years. Muslim scholars translated hundreds of Greek classics into Arabic then into Latin making them available to European scholars during the Middle Ages. Muslims were not known for original thinking but they were responsible for transferring major masterpieces to other cultures.

ROMAN CATHOLICISM ARRIVES

By A.D. 590, the situation changed relating to Christian churches. Whereas each pastor (bishop) had been equal to all others (whatever the size of the church and city in which it was located), now there was an organizational hierarchy and papacy of the Roman Catholic Church. In A.D. 445, the Roman Emperor recognized the primacy of the Roman bishop and Leo I, who ruled from 440 to 461, was the first Roman bishop to take the title of pope. (No, it was not Peter!) Leo claimed that as the Bishop of Rome, he had authority over all other churches.

When Rome fell in A.D. 475, the Dark Ages began. Alaric attacked and seized Rome in 410, and the Roman legions withdrew from Britain to protect the city. By 425, barbarians settled into the Roman provinces in southern Spain (Vandals), in Dalmatia (Ostrogoths), etc. Rome was crumbling. By 436, the last Roman troops had left Britain to return home, but without providing necessary protection to the Imperial City. In 455, the Vandals sacked Rome and the citizens were in panic. Mighty Rome was only a ghost of itself.

CHRISTENDOM SPLITS

The Roman Church experienced many heresies and grew wealthy but weak. Cyprian complained that the Christians were "mad about money, that Christian women painted their faces; that bishops held lucrative offices of state, made fortunes, lent money at usurious interest, and denied their faith at the first sign of danger." While Christianity "converted" the world, it seems the world converted Christianity![7] The corruption got progressively worse until the Reformation in the 1500s.

Power shifted from Rome to Constantinople, the capital of the Eastern Roman Empire (Byzantine), and while Europe was in the throes of the Dark Ages with trade, invention, etc., almost at a standstill, the Byzantine Empire was booming. Constantinople was becoming the center of world trade.[8] When London and Paris were small towns, Constantinople was the largest, richest city in medieval Europe.[9]

The remnant of the old Roman Empire was ruled from what is now Istanbul in Turkey, first known as Byzantium, then Constantinople. The Byzantine Emperors abandoned Roman Catholicism for what is now known as the Eastern Orthodox Church. The great Byzantine cathedral of Sophia was the spiritual center of the Byzantine Empire until the advance of Islam.

Christendom formally split like a ripe watermelon into east and west in A.D. 1054. They became the Greek or Eastern Orthodox Church in Constantinople and the Roman Catholic Church in Rome. Their split was over very **serious** issues such as: What type of bread should be used in communion? Must the priests wear beards? Is a weekly fast required? Much like today! It also involved the normal power play: should the top honcho in Constantinople (the Patriarch) be forced to recognize the Pope as supreme ruler of the churches? Like most splits, the two preachers (Pope and Patriarch) kicked each other out of their portion of "Christianity"! In 1453, Constantinople and the Eastern Roman Empire (Byzantine) fell to the Muslims.

MILITANT MUSLIMS ON THE MARCH

By this time, the Muslims had been on the march for hundreds of years. Within 20 years of Mohammed's death (632), the Muslims erupted out of the Arabian Peninsula and conquered Iraq, Syria, Palestine, Egypt, and western Iran. Then Muslim ships sailed the "Roman lake" (Mediterranean Sea) and took Cyprus in 649, Carthage in 698, Tunis in 700, and Gibraltar in 711. From there they ripped into Spain in 711-716 and on to France in 720.[10]

Islam advanced into Europe via the Iberian Peninsula (Spain and Portugal) in 711, and fighting continued between Muslims and Catholics for hundreds of years. By the middle of the eleventh century, "Christian" forces managed to retake about half the peninsula and the Pope got into the act. He told citizens of other nations to come to the aid of their fellow "Christians" and drive the Muslims out of Europe. To make it palatable to them, he offered them limited indulgences (forgiveness of sins) to fight for the cause. This reconquest is known as Reconquista and is considered by some to be the unofficial "first" Crusade.

In 1009, the Muslims ordered the destruction of the Church of the Holy Sepulchre in Jerusalem. Some 30,000 Christian buildings are said to have been destroyed at that time. In 1076, Seljuk Turks occupied Jerusalem. They came from the borders of China and had been converted to Islam, and they followed Mohammed by persecuting Christians and Jews.

During those years, the Roman Catholic Church was festering with corruption from the lowest, uneducated, unsophisticated, unconcerned priest to the pompous pugilistic popes squatting on the plush throne in Rome (or wherever).

CATHOLIC CHURCH CORRUPTION

In our day, the Roman Church is in a similar crises since it has been revealed that homosexual clergy have preyed on helpless boys from age 11 to 14 and some as young as 3. That has gone on for more than 30 years with subsequent cover-ups by the higher ups. From 2001 to 2010, the Vatican looked into sex abuse allegations by 3,000 priests that dated back fifty years.

Even Boston's Cardinal Law was forced to resign in December of 2002 because of his unethical, unlawful, and unscriptural handling of homosexual priests who preyed on young boys and his subsequent cover-up. The cover-up was accomplished by transferring priests across the country, ignoring the problem, and stonewalling. The problem is worldwide.

Some major Catholic leaders will go to jail if there is any justice left in the U.S. Of course, any clergyman (Catholic, Baptist, or whatever) who abuses males or females should go to the clinker for 25 years or more!

CORRUPTION IN THE MIDDLE AGES

But the Church corruption has a long and dreary history. Manchester quotes Abbot Johannes Trithemius' evaluation of his own monks thusly: "The whole day is spent in filthy talk; their whole time is given to play

177

and gluttony....They neither fear nor love God; they have no thought of the life to come, preferring their fleshly lusts to the needs of the soul.... They scorn the vow of poverty, know not that of chastity, revile that of obedience....The smoke of their filth ascends all around."[11] It was not unusual for women who came to the confessional to be offered absolution in exchange for sex in the very cramped booth! There is documentary evidence of priestly immorality in almost **every** town in the Italian peninsula, according to Manchester.

With the incredible priestly immorality, including the selling of priestly positions, appointing **children** to official religious office, and other corruption, the Roman Church in Europe was in convulsions. The stage was now set for the Crusades, probably the greatest tragedy in church history.

CATHOLIC CRUSADES

The Crusades were also one of the most unnecessary events in history. The Muslims were harassing Christian pilgrims in the Holy City and on their travel route; that distressing news disturbed the Roman pontiff. When the timid emperor, Alexius Comnenus, thought Constantinople might fall, he appealed for help to none other than the Pope himself. Pope Urban was ready and willing to commit to a crusade. Urban, the Roman Catholic pope thought his help in defending the Eastern Empire in Constantinople might ingratiate himself to the Greek Orthodox Patriarch and at the same time take the city of Jerusalem from the infidels. A crusade would become a unifying cause for all "Christians." How could he lose? It was a win-win situation. His attempt to help the top honcho in Constantinople would also strengthen the Pope's weak position.

The Roman Pope was heartbroken over the church split in 1054, and thought his calling for a crusade against the Turks would establish his long-time claim as Pope of all "Christians" in the East and West. He would show his power and influence to the Greek Patriarch with a trek into the heart of the Muslim world with his army of "Christians." (And no doubt there were some Christians in the crowd.)

It was in 1095 that Urban called a council in central France and urged all his bishops and abbots to bring their respective secular lords and knights to the meeting. Urban touched all their "buttons" during his sermon. He described the Holy City and Holy Sepulchre in infidel hands. He talked of the land of "milk and honey" and of carving out their own kingdoms in the Holy Land. He promised that the families of those who "took up the cross" would be protected and debts would be suspended during the crusade. Finally, he took a page out of Mohammed's own book when he promised plenary indulgence for their sins! Heaven for martyrdom! If they lived, they would be little kings in the Holy Land. If they died, they would go straight to Heaven. The only thing missing was 72 dark-eyed virgins waiting for each crusader!

Witnesses reported that the crowd yelled, "God wishes it. God wishes it." And a cardinal fell to his knees in convulsive trembling. (It must have been a very effective sermon!) Prominent lords and common people rushed forward "at the invitation" to take up the cross. They grabbed red cloth and cut crosses and sewed them on the fronts of their tunics. All over Europe "Christians" made plans to "take up the cross" to do battle with the hated Muslims.

The First (of eight Crusades) was the only one that could be called a success. Moreover, it was successful not because of the fighting ability of the Crusaders but because the Muslims had been getting weaker for many years. As the Crusaders advanced toward Jerusalem, they killed thousands of Jews in their trek through the Rhineland; after all, the Jews were unbelievers too! After battles along the way, they finally took Jerusalem and quickly slaughtered 70,000 civilians in cold blood!

There were eight major crusades to free Jerusalem from the pagan Muslims, and all were disgraceful. The crusades solidified the foundation for Muslim hatred of all things "Christian."

References:

1   "60 Minutes."

2   Winston Churchill, *The River War,* Vol. II, First Ed., London: Longsman Green & Co., 1899, pp 248-250.

3   Bin Laden's statement issued Feb. 23, 1998, by the World Islamic Front, "Jihad Against Jews and Crusaders."

4   Will Durant, The *Story of Civilization,* Book 3, 1944, p. 542.

5   Ibid., 549.

6   Ibid., 652.

7   Ibid., 657.

8   *The Record of Mankind,* fourth ed., Roehm, Buske, Webster, and Wesley, D.C. Heath and Co., Lexington, Mass., 1970, p. 125.

9   Ibid., 125, 126.

10 *The Oxford History of Islam,* ed., John L. Esposita, Oxford University Press, 1999, p. 71.

11 William Manchester, *A World Lit Only by Fire,* Little, Brown and Co., Boston, 1992, pp. 128, 129.

Chapter Thirteen

Crusades: Preached by Popes and Punished by God!

C hristopher Columbus was convinced that God had chosen him to lead a Crusade against the Muslims who controlled the Holy Land in the early 1400s. He did not see that dream fulfilled; however, those who had already fought in the Crusades discovered the dream was, in reality, a nightmare. The Crusades forever changed the face of the world and set the stage for the Reformation in the sixteenth century and the nightmare of terrorism the free world faces today.

The Crusades were one of the darkest periods in the history of man. They were preached by popes, promoted by priests, planned by potentates, and will someday be punished by God. Most of the Crusaders were no better than the Muslims who were the objects of their hatred. They called the Muslims "unbelievers," but most of the Crusaders were also unbelievers, as well as being thieves and killers. While Catholics and many Baptists profess faith in Christ, most reject His clear teachings.

How could a church even consider the slaughter of innocent people? While I am not a pacifist, I also don't believe in butchery and cruelty. I do believe Christians have a right to defend themselves and an obligation to defend the family even at the cost of another's life. A rapist or thief needs to realize that getting shot is an occupational hazard of being a rapist or thief. That principle of defense of family carries over to the defense of one's country. I have no respect for those who refuse to fight for their freedom, while others do fight and die so all of us, including cowards and pacifists, can be free and safe.

A JUST WAR

Isidore of Seville, five hundred years before the Crusades, stated, "That war is lawful and just which is waged upon command in order to recover property or to repel attack." You would think that anyone would agree with that statement; however, many limp-wristed sissies tell us it is better to be Red than dead, and then they try to appeal to the Bible for support of their warped doctrine of peace at any price.

Isidore continued: "There are four types of war: that is just, unjust, civil and more than civil. Just war is that which is fought after the enemy was warned concerning the unjust loss of holdings or for the sake of fending off enemies. Unjust war is that which is begun from wrath rather than lawful reason. Cicero speaks of this in his *Republic* (3,35): 'Unjust wars are those begun without a reason. For there is no just reason for war outside of just vengeance or self defense.' And Cicero added this shortly afterward: 'No war is to be considered just unless it was openly announced and declared, unless reparation has first been demanded.'"[1]

In 1209, Pope Innocent III encouraged the King of Denmark to go a step or two further. The Pope was not only interested in recovering property and repelling attack, he wanted the king "to extirpate the error of paganism and spread the frontiers of the Christian faith." The king would also share in the Indulgences if he managed to spread the Pope's religion. Indulgences provided forgiveness of past and future sins and were granted for favors done to and for the Roman Catholic Church, or for money given to the Church.

INDULGENCES

In return for a sum of money or for service to the Church, the Pope would grant a dispensation or license either to excuse or to permit an action which was sinful. Furthermore, if anyone had been to the confessional and had been given a very heavy penance to absolve his sins, he could pay the Church money instead of carrying out the required duty to pay for his offences. These practices made the Church very prosperous and the commoners very poor.

These indulgences were one of the major reasons for Luther's break with Rome. The church had become a money-machine as indulgences were sold all over Europe. Tetzel, a Dominican friar, promised poverty-stricken villagers, "I have here the passports...to lead the human soul to the celestial joys of Paradise."[2] So, a person could purchase his way to heaven and even guarantee that the dead in hell could escape eternal torment. Tetzel promised relatives of dead loved ones, "As soon as the coin rings in the bowl, the soul for whom it is paid will fly out of purgatory and straight to heaven." What concerned person would refuse to give his last coin to release his beloved relative from the flames of "purgatory"? It was a powerful tool but it backfired on the church in later years.

If a king, knight, or common citizen went on a Crusade, he received total forgiveness of all sins, past and future. Those guilty of robbery, rape, or murder would receive total forgiveness of sins and at death pass by Purgatory right into heaven! They thought it was a good deal.

NOT FIGHTING BUT FOOLERY

"Saint" Bernard forbade any truce with the pagans "until such time as, with God's help, they shall be either converted or wiped out." Convert 'um or kill 'um–a choice of being baptized or buried. Therefore, we see a progression from the legitimate use of force to its illegitimate use to "spread the frontiers of the Christian faith" which, in effect, is not possible.

Pope Innocent IV, in the middle of the thirteenth century, tried to justify the Crusades by affirming that the Holy Land was Christian property and the Crusades were actions to recover land that rightfully belonged to Christians. But thinkers weren't buying.

There was another reason war with the Turks was acceptable to the general population. The Muslims were dangerous people and they harassed Christians and refused to permit preachers of the gospel to preach in their lands, so war with them was acceptable and even desirable.

Later, schismatics were considered a **greater** threat to the Church than the threat of the Muslims in the Holy Land, so it was all right to behead, to burn at the stake, and to persecute Christians who dared disagree with Rome! (This was before the first ecumenical council!)

A pope or one of his designates would preach a Crusade asking all strong, able-bodied people to join in the "noble" cause to "take the cross." To persuade knights to "take up the cross," Pope Urban ridiculed the old knight (who stayed home) and compared him with the knight who left all to "fight for Christ." He said, "Let those who, for a long time, have been robbers, now become knights. Let those who have been fighting against their brothers and relatives now fight in a proper way against the barbarians. Let those who have been serving as mercenaries for small pay now obtain the eternal reward."[3]

St. Bernard continued the thought when he said: "For how long will your men continue to shed Christian blood, for how long will they continue to fight amongst themselves? You attack one another, you slay one another and by one another you are slain. What is this savage craving of yours? Put a stop to it now, for it is not fighting but foolery. So to risk both soul and body is not brave but shocking, is not strength but folly. But now O mighty soldiers, O men of war, you have a cause for which you can fight without danger to your souls; a cause in which to conquer is glorious and for which to die is gain."[4] Sounds as if they took their cue from the Muslims.

RELIGIOUS RABBLE ROUSER

Bernie's teaching is not much different from the Muslims who taught that if a man were to die in battle against infidels (those who were not Muslims), he would upon entering heaven experience a thousand sexual climaxes in one! Nonetheless, Bernie and his Catholic friends were preaching a "Holy War" against the hated Muslims.

Catholics were offered full salvation and forgiveness of all sins if they took a vow to go on the Crusade. This is the oldest religion in the world, the false religion of works. Listen to Bernard whip up the crowd: "Go forward then in security, knights, and drive off without fear the enemies of the Cross of Christ, certain that neither death nor life can separate you from the love of God which is in Jesus Christ.... How glorious are those who return victorious from the battle! How happy are those who die as martyrs in the battle! Rejoice, courageous athlete, if you survive and are victor in the Lord; but rejoice and glory the more if you die and are joined to the Lord. For your life is fruitful and your victory glorious. For if those who die in the Lord are blessed, how much more so are those who die for the Lord."[5]

How could Bernard, whom Martin Luther called a "God-fearing and holy monk," use his talent as a "stem-winding" speaker to rouse the rabble (and the nobles) to such an ignoble cause as the Crusades? Bernard also wrote the hymn, "Jesus, the Very Thought Thee," but Bernard was not thinking of Jesus when he called the "faithful" (and some were no doubt faithful) to "take up the Cross" and take the Holy Land for Christ. In fact, Bernie wasn't even thinking when he got involved with a corrupt pope to baptize Europe and the Middle East with blood.

SOME WERE SINCERE

When a man took the public vow to go on a Crusade, he was to sew a cross on his clothing and he was legally bound to fulfill that oath. If he could not keep his oath because of sickness or death, his son was expected to keep it. If a man simply refused to keep it, he was threatened with excommunication. His vow was legally binding upon him and his family. Those who stitched a red cross on their clothing were promised that their family would be protected (if left behind) and any debts or legal problems would be delayed for the years they would be on their "Holy Land" trip. Some were glad to be away from the little woman and others were pleased to escape debts and other problems. Others were excited about the possibility of a good fight and the promise of free estates after the victory. Still others were sincere people who were only following the leader of the Roman Catholic Church.

Of course it needs to be said that sincere people died in the blood and mud of a hot battle fought at the gates of some unknown city, while the pope and his prelates lived well, warm, and worldly in a secure palace hundreds of miles away from the tip of the longest shot arrow.

FIGHTING BISHOPS KISS AND MAKE UP

The "Christian" world had split like a ripe watermelon in the eleventh century. Emperor Alexius, who was also the Bishop of Constantinople, excommunicated the Bishop of Rome (the Pope), who in turn excommunicated him! Christendom was now divided between the Roman Catholic Church (with headquarters in Rome) and the Eastern Orthodox Church (with headquarters in Constantinople). In 1071, the Turks defeated the Byzantine warriors at the Battle of Manzikert, leaving Constantinople exposed to Muslim attack. Meanwhile, Christians were being ambushed during their "Holy Land trip" to Jerusalem.

There was no longer one Holy Roman Empire, and with the Byzantine Empire in Constantinople under threat from the Turks, the Emperor Alexius swallowed his pride and requested help from Pope Urban II in Rome. This plea for help was a good opportunity for Pope Urban to regain some influence over Constantinople and to also fulfill his obligation to protect the rights of Christendom. He couldn't lose. But the fact is, he couldn't win.

Pope Urban started the Crusade ball rolling when he personally preached the First Crusade throughout France. He did so after the appeal from the Byzantine emperor for help in defending the Church against the Turks who were almost at the gates of Constantinople. He believed that cooperation might also help draw the Latin and Greek churches closer together, but it might also liberate Jerusalem from the pagans. I can hear Pope Urban say to the Crusaders at their going away party, "Now fellows, after you protect Constantinople, run over to Jerusalem and take it away from a handful of Turks."

WHAT A SERMON!

Pope Urban spoke to the Council of Clermont (France) on November 27, 1095, and later from a platform to 10,000 church leaders and peasants. As he preached on the final day of the council, the people sat on the grass outside of town. Urban was surrounded by his Italian Guard and about 200 bishops and hundreds of priests. It was **some** denominational conclave, that's for sure.

There are various reports of his sermon, and one of the most famous is by Fulcher of Chartres: "On this account I, or rather the Lord, beseech you as Christ's heralds to publish this everywhere and to persuade all people of whatever rank, foot-soldiers and knights, poor and rich, to carry aid promptly to those Christians and to destroy that vile race from the lands of our friends. I say this to those who are present, it is meant also for those who are absent. Moreover, Christ commands it." I would like to know how the Pope knew that "Christ commands it." Oh, the crimes that have been committed in His name!

The "infallible" Pope went on and on and on: "Let those who for a long time, have been robbers, now become knights. Let those who have been fighting against their brothers and relatives now fight in a proper way against the barbarians. Let those who have been serving as mercenaries for small pay now obtain the eternal reward. Let those who have been wearing themselves out in both body and soul now work for a double honor. Behold! On this side will be the sorrowful and poor, on that, the rich; on this side, the enemies of the Lord, on that, his friends. Let those who go, not put off the journey, but rent their lands and collect money for their expenses; and as soon as winter is over and spring comes, let them eagerly set out on the way with God as their guide"[6]

ARROGANCE AND AUDACITY

To his credit, the Pope threatened strong sanctions against anyone who did any evil to the women, children, goods, or properties of anyone engaged in the Crusade; however, he was not very concerned about those who were **not** involved in the Crusade. Various church leaders did try to protect Jews in different cities along the crusade route, usually without success.

Urban was considered as a heavenly (wrong direction) trumpet, summoning the sons of the Holy Roman Catholic Church from several parts of the world to free the Eastern Church. Those who refused to take up the sword for Rome were ungrateful wretches who would face the pope on Judgment Day. Each pope issuing a general call for holy warriors wrote, "We firmly state on behalf of the Apostle that they should know that they will have to reply to us on this matter in the presence of the Dreadful Judge on the Last Day of Severe Judgment."[7] What arrogance and audacity without accuracy! I don't believe the "Apostle" would appreciate the pope's speaking for him, and I am sure the popes will be too occupied in giving an account for themselves at the Judgment to hear the excuse of some peasant for not picking up a rusty sword and going after the Turks.

Remember that the Roman Church recognized no boundaries. The power of the pope transcended nations, languages, and customs. The popes often ordered kings around. In the middle of the eighth century, Pope Zacharias removed King Childeric of the Franks from the throne, and Pope Gregory humiliated King Henry IV by making him stand (barefoot) in his (the Pope's) courtyard for three days in January before he would see him! How could a pope effectively command a king and make it stick? He could launch a Crusade against him or threaten interdiction which is to excommunicate **all** the people in the nation!

HATE THE TURKS

The popes were often not very successful in raising men to spill their blood in a "holy war" or to spend their funds (and years) in the liberation of Jerusalem. Sometime the hatred of one king for another king was more intense than his fear (or respect) for the pope. The kings were too busy fussing and fighting each other to care about fighting the Muslims. Pope Innocent III thought that was a dirty shame and seethed with what he would call righteous indignation. In his preamble to the encyclical of 1198 (proclaiming the bloody Fourth Crusade), he self-righteously said: "Now indeed…while our princes pursue one another with inexorable hatred, while each strives to vindicate his injuries, suffered at the hands of another, there is not one who is moved at the injury suffered by the Crucified One….Already our enemies insult us, saying, 'Where is your God, who cannot free himself or you from our hands?'"[8]

Ironically, he was saying that the kings and princes should be ashamed for the hatred they had for each other–they should hate the Turks instead. This bloody pope was a self-righteous tyrant who used God to consolidate his own power, and for him to criticize the kings for their hatred of others was like Donald Trump accusing Ben Carson of being brash, bold, and brazen.

PREACHING THE CRUSADE

The popes **finally** (they were slow learners) realized that the mere publishing of a papal bull would not raise an army or fill their coffers with gold. Therefore, they sent out priests to raise money for an attack on innocent women and children, calling it the "preaching of the cross." The popes even granted Indulgences for those who **listened** to the sermon of the vicars of violence. Things were so bad, the popes resorted to taxing the churches and priests, and that idea was no more popular then than it is today. Two things were sure: death and taxes, but death was far more prevalent and more permanent than taxes.

A Roman Catholic clergyman usually preached a Crusade, following orders from Rome, trying to convince the locals to leave home for an exciting journey to Jerusalem. Those accepting the responsibility were supposed to be fighting men or men who could make a contribution to the "cause." Each man must also have his wife's permission since he would be gone for a long time (usually forever) and she would be deprived of her "marital rights." Pope Innocent III got so desperate for troops in the thirteenth century that he no longer insisted on a wife's permission.

There is no doubt that many courageous, sincere men went on a Crusade, especially the First Crusade; Constantinople **was** being threatened, and the Turks were among the most cruel and vicious people alive. Escaping a life of backbreaking toil (without possibilities of improvement) motivated others to join the Crusade. There were many examples of great courage and little honor–great devotion to a cause and little understanding of concepts. Idealism was besmirched by voracious greed and unbridled cruelty. The gentle voice of the Savior was unheard as the bloody sword was unsheathed. T. S. Eliot said of them, "Among [them] were a few good men, many who were evil, And most who were neither, Like all men in all places."[9]

FIRST CRUSADE

Peter the Hermit accepted Pope Urban's challenge and went throughout France "preaching the cross" and raised an army that was scheduled to leave on August 15, 1096 in the First Crusade. The wealthy made elaborate plans for departure and the poor sold their few belongings and waited for that fateful day in August. The leadership of the First Crusade was made up of several high nobles and a papal legate (the pope's envoy). The best known of these leaders included Bohemond of Taranto, Raymond of Toulouse, Hugh of Vermandois, Godfrey of Bouillon, Baldwin of Boulogne, Robert of Flanders, and Robert of Normandy. The papal legate was the Bishop of Le Puy, Adhmar.

How pathetic to see thousands of poor people with ox-drawn, two-wheeled carts bearing all their worldly goods while their small children asked at every walled city if this were Jerusalem. The rich often took their families, servants, and food, while the poor ate what they found. Soon they were all starving together. Through rain, mud, pain, and sickness they pushed with "hell licking at their heels" at every step. They had to keep going if they wanted to earn forgiveness of sins and a good seat in Heaven; and they were sure of Heaven (Didn't the Pope, priests, and prelates tell them so?), as long as they kept decapitating the infidels with a dull blade. The duller, the better. However, they started their slaughter long before reaching the Middle East. Since Jews were infidels, did they not qualify to be put to the sword? That's what Pope Urban had preached, so whop, whop, and off went numerous Jewish heads in villages throughout Germany.

HOLY MISSION

By now they had attracted 40,000 "Crusaders" each with a red cross stitched onto his clothing. In Cologne, the Archbishop opened his palace to protect the Jews, but the determined mob broke down the doors and slaughtered everyone inside, killing over 10,000 in that one incident. The Jews were given an opportunity to be "converted" just before they were beheaded and the prettiest Jewish girls were raped by those who had "taken the vow."

When this slow-moving pack of vermin reached Hungary, it was altogether different in every way. The large, beautiful cities were behind them and now they only saw small villages of thatched huts that housed, for the most part, cattle-raisers. However, the peasants were glad to share what they had with the "pilgrims." The cattle-raisers did have fields and barns rich in foodstuffs, food that the pilgrims assumed belonged to them since they were going to fight a "holy" war. The looters took what they wanted, then set fire to the wheat stores while their kind hosts watched in dismay and unbelief. Then they took what women they wanted, and if a sensitive conscience whimpered a cry of protest, it was stifled for, after all, they were on a "holy" mission and a "holy" mission seems to justify everything. Or so they thought. Besides, the pope, Constantinople, and Jerusalem were far away.

Peter the Hermit cautioned them to act like Christians, but they ridiculed him and moved on to Moysson which they planned to sack as they had the other villages. But the timid citizens had learned their lesson, and they ambushed the butchers and pushed them back into a flooded river to perish. The hungry survivors trekked back to France to be mocked by their own people (who had wisely stayed home).

NEXT STOP: CONSTANTINOPLE

Of course, there were many groups of pilgrims who were headed for Constantinople at the same time. Some were more disciplined than others, but few made it. Henry Treece wrote: "Of a total of 300,000 Crusaders who had started off in such haste, only a third survived the first stage of the journey. Those who struggled on into Constantinople were like walking corpses, brutalized beyond all measure and no longer Christians of even the most primitive sort. Behind them a train of bones reached back to the Rhineland and to France"[10]

During July of 1096, this tattered "army" started straggling into Constantinople and was treated graciously by the Emperor who had invited them to make the journey. They were given lodging outside the city and after satisfying their hunger, they went on another rampage setting fire to the palatial homes, looting the churches, and slaughtering all who tried to stop them. Even the most crude and brutal among them knew this was wrong because the safety of Constantinople was one of the reasons they were there, but no cause to fret; didn't Pope Urban promise forgiveness of all sins? So, on with the murder and mayhem.

The Emperor could have set his troops upon his "friends," but instead he ordered the Crusaders to attack the Turks of Kiliz Arslan. Finally, they would get a chance to put the Muslims to the sword and dispatch them to meet their already departed leader, Mohammed. Therefore, 100,000 peasants crossed the straits into Roum. They found a deserted castle (a trap laid by the wily Turks) and took it without any bloodshed. The Turks then surrounded the castle that was gorged with European peasants who thought they had won an easy victory. It was a dry "victory" because there was no water and after eight days of torment, the "Christian" mob surrendered to the Turks with the understanding that all prisoners would be spared.

After the surrender, all the Crusaders were butchered or sold into slavery. Muslim archers used those who were not acceptable as slaves for target practice. The Turks celebrated their victory by erecting a monument of bones that was "most conspicuous in height and breadth and depth." So ended the first wave of the First Crusade to defend Constantinople, to bring the two church groups together, and to liberate Jerusalem from the Muslims. Yes, the dream had become a nightmare.

CONSTANTINOPLE THEN ANTIOCH

The next wave of Crusaders was not composed of peasants but of great noblemen and princes who got started late and did not arrive in Constantinople until May of 1097. There were about 600,000 experienced soldiers who expected victory over the Muslims and a lot of loot for their trouble. However, since they were of such mixed nationalities they could not decide on a leader; so they broke up into four divisions, each with its own general. When those four armies reached Constantinople, the Emperor convinced three of the generals to swear allegiance to him for he knew he could not withstand a battle with the Turks **and** the four armies of "liberation."

Next stop, the gates of Jerusalem. Well, not exactly the **next** stop, for there were a few problems such as a desert and a mountain range to cross, then Antioch to take, **then** Jerusalem. Antioch was a city of silk, gold, silver, and beautiful works of art, and the noblemen wanted their share before taking Jerusalem. They surrounded the well-defended city and lived off the fruit and grain they discovered while waiting for the siege to begin. However, the food ran out and a couple of the leaders took a force of 20,000 men to search the countryside for food. While they were gone, the Turks attacked the weakened force, inflicting them with great loss.

The Crusaders stopped all food supplies from entering Antioch and after numerous battles with thousands killed on both sides, they made a bargain with one of the Turkish leaders to betray the city. The traitor opened the gate one night and permitted the Crusaders to commandeer the outer wall. Although the Crusaders had promised safety to the Turks, they massacred everyone they could find–soldiers and civilians. Other Turks escaped to a citadel on a hill. Three days later, Kerboga of Monsul arrived with 200,000 Muslims to continue the struggle with the Crusaders. The Crusaders had kept food from the city and now they occupied it and they were hungry again. They ate their horses to stay alive. Then 200,000 angry, well-fed Muslims who were anxious to avenge the slaughter of the soldiers and citizens of Antioch surrounded them. "Pope Urban, where are you when we need you?"

TELLER-OF-TALL-TALES

A meek priest Peter Bartholomew, accompanying the Crusaders, told them that he had seen a vision where Christ warned them about having intercourse with Muslim women. Tancred, the Crusade leader, then swore that he would assault the gates of Jerusalem if he only had forty knights. The priest had another vision from St. Andrew informing him that the actual lance used by the Roman soldier that had pierced Christ was in the Church of St. Peter in Antioch. That lance would guarantee victory to the side that raised it in battle, so he said.

The Roman lance transformed the Crusaders as they marched through the gates into battle with the Turks. They were so hypnotized that they marched and rode through a shower of arrows not even aware of being pierced. The Turks were panic-stricken. The Crusaders pointed toward the mountain and "saw" thousands of soldiers led by St. George coming to rescue them. Of course, no soldiers were there, but it worked. The Turks turned their horses and fled pursued by the European "nobles." The

Syrians and Armenians (of that area) rode to the mountains and cut off the retreating Turks and killed all they could.

The Crusaders re-entered the city to discover that the Muslims who had fled to the citadel on the hill had surrendered and some even became "Christians." The others were permitted to leave the city unharmed. The Norman faction of the Crusade had a hunch that the priest was not so much a see-er-of-visions but a teller-of-tall-tales. They accused him of planting the lance and telling a false story to whip up emotions. They made the priest run through two large fires twice to prove that he was Someone Special. To the surprise of the priest and the crowd, he survived the test of fire and that made him a very special person, one to be admired and sought after. Moreover, they sought after him, all at once. The crowd rushed him to get a "holy relic" from him that might protect them in the following battles. They pulled out his hair, tore off his burned clothes, and almost tore him apart heedless of his cries. As the soldiers walked away with their relics, the priest lay dying on the ground as a sacrifice to the mad mob.

ON TO JERUSALEM

Finally, nothing stood between the mob and Jerusalem! Most people assume that Jerusalem was populated by Jews but not so. Palestine and Syria were within the boundaries of the Roman Empire and became mainly "Christian." The Jewish population of Jerusalem had been largely dispersed by pagan Roman authorities following the Jewish anti-Roman revolts of A.D. 66-70 and 132-135, and few Jews remained in the area.

When Titus took Jerusalem on September 8, 70 A.D., over a million Jews were slaughtered and 97,000 were taken captive. Josephus reports that the streets were clogged with bodies and during the famine, mothers ate their own children. He reports that one Mary took her infant son, knowing he would become a slave, and killed him. Then she roasted him and ate half his body, "hiding away the rest." When thieves arrived at her door, having smelled the meat cooking, they demanded the food. When shown what she had to offer, they recoiled in horror. She taunted them "for being weaklings who couldn't bring themselves to do what a woman had done."[11] The Temple and other buildings were burned with thousands dying within them. The escaping Jews dispersed all over the Empire, while others were put to work in the Roman mines.[12]

Therefore, the Jews were not in great abundance even in the eleventh century. Arab Muslims had governed the Holy City for many generations and the Christian and Jewish inhabitants lived as second-class citizens with their Muslim masters. ("Christian" Crusaders wanted to take the city from the Muslims and the few Jews that were there.) As the Crusaders approached the city, all the Christians were expelled from the city in preparation for the inevitable siege.

SIEGE OF JERUSALEM

The battle for Antioch had lasted almost nine months, and after a five-month rest, the army (now only 25,000 of the original 600,000) moved upon the Holy City. The siege of Jerusalem began on June 7, 1099, and after a lengthy battle, the "Christians" broke into the city and the maddened maniacs ran through the streets of Jerusalem driving all before them into a temple where they were butchered. Of course, the Crusaders' "noble" motive was to kill a Turk for Christ, as if Christ had anything to do with the whole Crusade movement. They slaughtered men, women, and children throughout the day and well into the night. As the sun rose, they discovered about 6,000 Jews who had fled to a synagogue for refuge. They torched the synagogue and burned the people alive. The surviving Muslims had fled to the Mosque of al Aqsa in the southeastern quarter of the city. The Crusaders broke down the doors and slaughtered an estimated 30,000 Muslims.

Such acts of "Christian" brutality cannot be defended in any way; however, an explanation for it could be the brutality perpetrated by the Muslims in their conquests from the Arabian Desert into Spain. While the "Christian" brutality was deplorable, it is also a reminder of the Biblical truth that men, families, and nations reap what they sow.

So ended the battle for Jerusalem and immediately a king was chosen establishing the Kingdom of Jerusalem. The Holy City was now in the hands of the Roman Catholic Church. The final result of the First Crusade was the establishment of four Latin "states" or "kingdoms" in the Middle East: the County of Edessa, the Principality of Antioch, the County of Tripoli and the Kingdom of Jerusalem. Jerusalem exercised an ambiguous political control over the other three.

CONTINUING CRUSADES

In 1144, the Turks had regrouped and took the northern outposts of the Kingdom of Edessa. So, guess what. Another Crusade was preached by Bernard in 1146 and led by King Louis VII of France and Emperor Conrad III. Again, this Crusade was not successful and Bernard's reputation lost its luster. Though disgraced, he was honored by the Church for his "faithfulness" to the cause: killing Muslims.

A few years later Saladin united the Muslim world from Cairo to Baghdad, and he preached a "Holy War" against the Christians. Fair enough. If a Roman Catholic Pope can preach hatred, who says a Turk can't do the same? In 1187 the Turks took Jerusalem again. It was now time for Crusade number three, led by Emperor Frederick I, King Philip Augustus, and King Richard. They were determined to retake Jerusalem but failed, so why not try crusade number four? Pope Innocent III was now the Man in Charge at Rome, and he was the first pope to claim a divine supremacy over all civil rulers! That proclamation resulted in a massive dark storm that lasted hundreds of years in Europe.

The Fourth Crusade never reached Jerusalem, but in 1204, the Crusaders did make it to Constantinople (the greatest city in Christendom) which they attacked and burned, resulting in Emperor Alexius III fleeing the city and his imprisoned brother replacing him. Pope Innocent III had forbidden the Crusaders to sack the city (after all they were "Christians"), but the Crusade leaders refused to obey the most powerful man on earth!

To his credit, Pope Innocent III had already excommunicated all the Crusaders, but that didn't help the citizens of Constantinople. Remember that the protection of Constantinople was one of the reasons for the First Crusade. The result of this Crusade affects the Roman Catholic and Greek Orthodox Church to this very day. It erected a massive iron door that some say will never be opened between those major divisions of "Christianity."

CHILDREN'S CRUSADE

There were many Crusades for many more years but the most shameful one was the Children's Crusade in 1212. There were two groups: one from France, another from Germany. Thirty thousand children gathered in a French market and started their journey of tears without food, maps, or supplies. Under the leadership of a French peasant boy, Stephen of Vendôme, thousands of boys and girls, many less than twelve years old, traveled to Marseilles. Those who were not drowned in shipwreck were betrayed, starved, and butchered or sold into Egyptian slavery. Others were taken to Baghdad, where eighteen of them were beheaded for refusing to become Muslims. Only **one** of the 30,000 French children ever returned home. A few of the 20,000 German children straggled back over the Alps to their villages to be ridiculed for their altruistic motives. Surely, if any Crusade had sincere motives, this one did; however, sincerity didn't keep it from being foolish, and in the end, tragic.

CRUSADE AGAINST HERETICS

The Crusades continued to evolve from being arguably highly motivated (First Crusade) to the Children's Crusade to a Crusade to "cleanse" the Church of "heretics" in the thirteenth century. The Albigenses (arising in southern France) were people who followed the principles of modern-day Baptists emphasizing:

- a membership of born-again people.
- baptism by immersion only.
- total separation of church and state.
- the Priesthood of all believers.
- the Bible as the sole authority.
- independent, self-governing churches; not dependent on any other church.

Pope Innocent III has been called (well, a lot of things) but he is known as the most powerful man who ever lived. He had that reputation because he had the power to boot **everyone** in a nation out of the Church (thereby damning every soul), if any king of Europe disobeyed him. Innocent was alarmed with the exploding growth of independent churches and tried to control them, but they only wanted to discuss what the Bible had to say about the above distinctives. The Pope became alarmed at the growth of the movement and tried persecution since persuasion didn't work. Eventually, Innocent III declared a Crusade against these "heretics," making the Albigensian Crusade the first against internal enemies of the Church instead of external ones.

Of course, persecution only made these independent churches grow even more until a Roman Catholic historian suggested that about one-third of Europe's population "identified with independent churches!"[13] Innocent also ordered vicious campaigns against the Jews and even threatened European kings with interdiction (excommunicating all citizens) if the kings did not destroy the independent churches within their jurisdiction.[14]

LEGACY OF CRUSADES

However, the independent churches continued to grow as did the Roman Churches' hatred for all "unbelievers." This culminated with the Inquisition of the Middle Ages where Roman Catholic Church tribunals "tried" thousands of Christians and Jews for heresy. Thousands of people were burned at the stake, stoned, drowned, flayed alive, etc. But the independent churches continued to grow until the explosion in the sixteenth century known as the Reformation.

After a hundred or so years of Crusades, some people in Europe began to ask; "If the Pope is infallible why are the Crusades such abysmal failures?" Why, indeed!

The Catholics preached peace and came with a sword while the Muslims preached peace **by** the sword. One was a hypocrite, the other a heretic, and both were unbelievers and deserve our pity and scorn. Catholics would say that the Crusades were the long-term result of the Muslim terror, while modern Muslims would admit that much of their hatred goes back to the Crusades. I say, "A pox on both their houses."

After two hundred years, the Crusades finally sputtered out, and surviving Crusaders returned to their homeports after many months' absence. They staggered off hired ships with their swords, souvenirs, spices, and exaggerated stories of violence, virtue, and valor. As they disembarked from the ships into the arms of their loved ones, no one noticed black rats, infested with disease-laden fleas, running down the tie ropes to the dock. Europe was going to face the Bubonic Plague for hundreds of years, a menace far more vicious than the Muslim hoard.

I am fearful that invading hordes of Muslims and Mexicans are not only distorting religious freedom, destroying our culture but are introducing exotic new diseases, even plagues into a society unable to deal with such attacks. Moreover, we are not prepared to deal with major medical problems. We saw the possibility of this in the scare from the Ebola and Zita viruses. But the biggest threat comes from Islamic terrorists bringing in chemical "bombs" as they cross the border—tonight.

References:

1. Isidore of Seville, *Encyclopedia of Greco-Roman Culture in the 7th century.*
2. William Manchester, *A World Lit Only by Fire, Little, Brown & Company,* Boston, 1992, pp. 134-135.

3. Pope Urban's speech at the Council of Clermont, 1095, according to Fulcher of Chartres.

4. Quoted by Don Boys in *Pilgrims, Puritans and Patriots,* Good Hope Press, Indianapolis, 1983, p. 43.

5. Ibid. pp. 43-44.

6. Edgar Holmes McNeal, eds., *A Source Book for Medieval History,* New York, Scribners, 1905, pp. 513-517.

7. Pope Urban's speech at Council of Clermont.

8. Boys, p. 45.

9. T. S. Eliot, *Collected Poems 1909-1962,* San Diego, 1984, p. 165.

10. Boys, p. 49.

11. F. Josephus, *Josephus Thrones of Blood, A History of the Times of Jesus,* Barbour publishing, undated, p. 223.

12. F. Josephus, *The Works of Flavius Josephus,* vol. 1, trans. William Whiston, Baker Book House, 1974, p. 469.

13. Quoted by Phil Stringer, *Faithful Baptist Witness,* Landmark Baptist Press, Haines City, FL, 1998, p. 86.

14. Ibid., p. 87.

Chapter Fourteen

Reaction to Disasters!

Major terrorist attacks, epidemics, famines, and natural disasters not only have a profound effect upon the political, business, and agricultural life of a nation, they also change people. Our nation is being changed even before catastrophic events take place. There have been charges that Muslim terrorists have carried suitcase nuclear bombs across our southern border and have placed them in major U.S. cities. Others have suggested that smallpox (or worse) germs might be sprayed in crowded areas in many cities thereby producing a massive epidemic of deadly diseases.

We should consider the possibility of horrific, adverse reactions to disaster, and the resultant havoc upon commerce, cultures, churches, and communities as similar diseases and disasters have done in the past. If the next Muslim attack is biological or chemical, we could face the same experiences of people in the past when the pestilence was natural, not manmade.

TROUBLE AHEAD

We are facing turbulent times while government officials are doing things to make us "feel good," such as providing military and "security" people at the airports. Airport security people are goosing little old ladies from Iowa, making grown men drop their pants, etc., while people frequently pass through security into planes with guns, knives, etc. That does **not** make me feel good, warm, or cozy.

Plagues have always influenced human lives in more ways than putting incompetent leaders in power, making certain jobs available, impacting the economy, and changing living conditions. The constant threat of death, misery, fear, and pain changed people.

We can expect the divorce rate to soar even higher, as uninfected mates leave their infected spouses. To whom will judges give the children of those couples–the infected or uninfected mate? Euthanasia and suicide will become acceptable, even legal as the death rate climbs. Some political conservatives will notice the economic foundations cracking under the financial strain of millions of patients and will decide that it is a person's right to do what he wants with his or her body, without state interference. Euthanasia, suicide, and abortion (the unholy trinity) will become respectable and legal. Euthanasia and suicide will become more desirable for some people as the hope for a vaccine and cure becomes more and more distant. People will lose hope, and in despair will end their lives as the HIV-infected "couple" who tied themselves together with a silk rope and jumped to their deaths from the 35th floor of an office building. Similar events happened in every plague.

Since events of history have given us an indication how U.S. civilians, military, and politicians will react in a time of mass destruction, it is certain that Muslims will also pay a price as thoughtless and wicked people see them as "the enemy." Innocent and patriotic Muslims will be identified with the terrorists, and since they are available, when terrorists are not, a pound of flesh will be exacted from them. I expect a massive overreaction to the next terrorist attack upon the U.S. Every Muslim will have a target on his back; unprincipled politicians will declare them fair game to strike back at the enemy. That's another reason why Muslims should go to extremes to explain their disagreement, disapproval, disgust, and disassociation with all terrorist activity. It may help protect them later.

IMPACT OF PLAGUE

There is no doubt that the Plague of Justinian nudged Europe into the Dark Ages, so informed people are aware of the danger posed by repeated terrorist attacks against our nation. Those attacks will affect our constitution, community, commerce, churches, and culture.

The plague of Athens is a good example of how people reacted to plague. Athens was crowded because the rural population swarmed into the city. Attica was the headquarters for large armies in 430 B.C., and conditions were perfect for pestilence. The disease started in Ethiopia and went to Egypt, Libya, and finally reached Athens, packed with people from Attica and the countryside.

Plague victims got severe headaches followed by inflammation of the tongue and pharynx. At the same time, there was sneezing, hoarseness, and coughing. Then there was vomiting, diarrhea, and insatiable thirst. The patient usually died between the seventh and ninth day. Some patients lost their sight, others their memory, before dying. The Athenians were demoralized followed by extreme lawlessness. No one seemed to fear God or man. Honor was a forgotten concept.[1]

In 540 B.C., the Plague of Justinian smacked the Greek Empire with 10,000 deaths per day! When the pestilence had passed, there was so much depravity and general licentiousness that Procopius said it seemed that "only the most wicked were left alive."

PESTILENCE PRODUCES PANIC

Panic was usually the immediate reaction to the appearance of pestilence. Daniel Defoe records how London reacted when the Black Death reached that city in the seventeenth century: "the richer sort of people, especially the nobility and gentry from the west part of the city, thronged out of town with their families and servants in an unusual manner...nothing was to be seen but wagons and carts with goods, women, servants, children, etc.; coaches filled with people of the better sort, and horsemen attending them, and all hurrying away...."[2]

As always, when fear rules, reason flees and intelligent people do dumb things. The "con-ers" came out of the closets and set up shop in proximity to the "con-ees." The sheep were ready to be sheared! Those people still in the city were "running about to fortune-tellers, cunningmen, and astrologers to know their fortune...and this folly presently made the town swarm with a wicked generation of pretenders to magic...."[3] The quacks had long lines of gullible people at their doors every day. Seems to be no end to people wanting to be taken.

The ministers of most denominations warned the people of the charlatans, but their warnings made little impression on the laboring poor whose fears dominated all their passions causing them to throw away their money "in a most distracted manner upon those whimsies."[4] As always, the people who lost their money were those who could least afford to do so.

Other con artists were more subtle than the astrologers, but not much. Notices were posted throughout the city inviting people to get the sure cure for a sure price. The notices read: "Infallible preventive pills against the plague"; "Never-failing preservatives against the infection"; "Sovereign cordials against the corruptions of the air"; "Exact regulations for the conduct of the body in case of an infection"; "Anti-pestilential pills"; and "Incomparable drink against the plague, never found out before." The people spent their hard-earned money for pills, potions, and preservatives, preparing themselves **for** the plague, not against it. In a later plague, infected folk sought to be cured by bathing in urine collected from people who had eaten cabbage!

TIME TO PRAY

Death was on everyone's mind. The talk among the uninfected was about the grave, dying, sickness, fevers, spots, dead carts, etc. They were not much interested in fun and games. Defoe wrote, "the gaming tables, public dancing rooms, and music-houses...were shut-up and suppressed...." He added that "a kind of sadness and horror at those things sat upon the countenances even of the common people."[5] People were not thinking of games but of the grave.

The government encouraged the peoples' devotion by days of prayer and days of fasting and humiliation. Officials asked the people to make public confession of sin and to implore the mercy of God to avert the dreadful judgment which hung over their heads. (Can you imagine the mayor of a major city taking such a position today? No? Well, you can imagine him leading an LGBT parade, can't you?)

People of all persuasions embraced the occasion by flocking to the churches until one could not get near the church doors. The people were saying, "There's a time to play and a time to pray, and this is the time to pray." While many Christians got serious about living for Christ and became cautious in daily activities, Muslims were little affected spiritually by the plague. Their rigid predestination (some would call fatalism) led them to not take any unusual precautions, so they put themselves in danger by exposing themselves to plague carriers.

When people arrived at church, the parish minister was often absent. He had, well, felt "called" to the safe countryside where the prosperous and powerful had fled. The preacher in the pulpit was often a Dissenter (Independent Bible preacher) who had been outlawed a few years earlier!

To be sure, some of the establishment preachers (Church of England) stayed on the job and died of plague, but many fled to safety. The people flocked to packed churches to hear the preachers preach the Word of God to a needy and confused congregation. Many people professed faith in Christ, and great crowds attended; but, when the plague took control, the churches emptied because it was not safe to be near any person who might be infected.

AWAKENED CONSCIENCES

Defoe wrote that many consciences were awakened: "Many hard hearts melted into tears; many a penitent confession was made of crimes long concealed....Many a robbery, many a murder, was then confessed aloud, and nobody surviving [in the home] to record the accounts of it. People might be heard, even into the streets as we passed along, calling upon God for mercy, through Jesus Christ, and saying, 'I have been a thief,' 'I have been an adulterer,' 'I have been a murderer,' and the like, and none durst stop to make the least inquiry into such things or to administer comfort to the poor creatures....Some of the ministers did visit the sick at first and for a little while, but it was not to be done. It would have been present death to have gone into some houses."[6]

The constant atmosphere of death and constant terror drove men to look honestly at their lives and at their religious experience. This resulted in thousands becoming more sincere and placing more emphasis on their personal relationship with Christ. It also led them away from the established churches in various countries. Of course, printing had been invented in 1450, and people were now reading the Bible and doing their own thinking for the first time in over a thousand years. They realized that church membership and church attendance did not produce personal satisfaction or personal salvation, contrary to what they had been taught. Following personal conversion, those new converts (but old church members) lived and died as Christians.

DESPAIR AND DEATH

Christians believed they had a responsibility to help others as a Christian duty, so during times of famine they shared their food; in times of sorrow they wept with the bereaved; and, in times of pestilence, they nursed the sick and dying. The non-Christians and the pagans took notice at such kindness, and at a time when other institutions were discredited and often dissolved, the Christian churches were enhanced. William McNeill wrote, "Pagans fled from the sick and heartlessly abandoned them."[7] Christians stayed and served–and died.

After so much despair and death, a dullness set in. It seemed that people lost their fear of death and had really resigned themselves to death. Defoe wrote: "Towards the latter end men's hearts were hardened, and death was so always before their eyes, that they did not so much concern themselves for the loss of their friends, expecting that themselves should be summoned the next hour."[8] They no longer asked people on the street (with whom they had to do business) how they were nor did they feel a need to inform others that they were not infected. The general attitude was: all were going to die. So now, they went back to church and sat in hot, crowded pews without fear of the next person. It didn't matter. They were all among the walking dead.

Defoe, an outspoken Christian, made a cogent comment in this regard: "Indeed, the zeal which they showed in coming [to church], and the earnestness and affection they showed in their attention to what they heard, made it manifest what a value people would all put upon the worship of God if they thought every day they attended at the church that it would be their last."[9]

GLOOMY FANATICISM

When rumors reached a city that a pestilence was working its way to their area, the social fabric often ripped apart at the seams. To make matters worse, the authorities were often the first to flee to the countryside. Riots, thievery, killings, and plundering of homes were common. The approaching plague was cover for old hatreds and fears to spring to the surface.

One of the most flamboyant results of pestilence was also one of the most despicable, and it came out of religious excess. As I have mentioned, a time of dying was a time to look at one's self, and as is often true, some people became mentally or emotionally unbalanced. Such were the Flagellants or the Brotherhood of the Cross. Those confused, but sincere, people tore off their clothes and beat each other on their naked bodies with scourges, consisting of three lengths of leather with knots. In each knot were iron spikes, sharp as needles.

The movement spread throughout Poland, Hungary, Bohemia, Germany, etc. The fanatics went from town to town spreading their fanaticism, and no doubt, the plague. One historian wrote of the Flagellants: "the gloomy fanaticism which gave rise to them infused a near poison into the despairing minds of the people. Thus, during the fourteenth century, the idea was spread that Jews had been responsible for spreading the pestilence by poisoning wells and infecting the air."[10] He was saying that a poisoned mind produced poisoned thinking and twisted actions, resulting in hatred of Jews and others.

CHRISTIANS DON'T KILL THE INNOCENT

In Mayence, 12,000 Jews were killed when the Flagellants entered the town. In Spain, the Muslims were the "culprits," so they were persecuted. In 1346, all the lepers in Languedoc were burned as suspected well poisoners, while gravediggers were persecuted in other cities. If the haters had opened their eyes, they would have seen that the Jews, Muslims, gravediggers, and others were dying of pestilence like everyone else. Some Jews saved their lives by accepting baptism (sprinkling by the Roman Catholic Church) but were later killed. When non-Catholic Christians tried to assist the helpless Jews, they too were executed.[11]

Church officials did not endorse most of this persecution. Pope Clement VI condemned the massacres and threatened to excommunicate those who harmed the Jews. It must be understood that Bible-believing (and practicing) Christians don't persecute anyone, but **church members** do. However, a "flake" may become a genuine Christian, but he may remain a "flake." Christian converts are always changed but not totally remade (until eternity).

"Christian" is also used generally to identify a specific part of the country, or a city, as in the case of Beirut, Lebanon where the city was divided between "Christians" and Muslims who tried to kill each other. Real Christians don't kill innocent people, take hostages, and blow airplanes out of the sky. Nor do they finance such activities! Church members do, and all real Christians get the flak.

UNSOUND ASSUMPTIONS

The Flagellants were accepted in some cities and mocked in others, but the clergy rejected them almost everywhere because they saw their authority (often an iron grip) being superseded by the fanatics. The fanatics beat themselves and each other while others of their group prayed, but the plague was not assuaged. This, among other things, caused the people to lose confidence in the Roman Catholic Church. The whole episode of the foolish Flagellants represented a reaction against the corruption and growing impotence of the Roman Church.

Some have made unsound assumptions, giving the plague credit for the Reformation. It has been argued that the Black Death led to religious fervor that eventually culminated in the Reformation, and the immediate reaction of the Roman Church was the Inquisition to squelch its success. There was no doubt some connection, but there were many more factors that prompted the Reformation: the corruption of the Roman Catholic Church, the invention of printing, the general population's ability to read, etc.

The persecution of a minority, while never justified, is understandable. Death was stalking the streets. People were buried in mass graves. No one could be trusted, not politicians, priests, nor physicians. Terrified people looked for someone to blame and to hate, and they found them: Jews, Muslims, gravediggers, lepers, and others. Such action is a "scapegoat" response that is as old as man. They felt they had done **something** by placing blame and throwing stones.

SCAPEGOATS

During the sixth century, B.C., when a plague or famine lashed a Greek city, an ugly person would be chosen to take all the evils of the city upon himself. He was fed the best of food, then beaten seven times upon his genital organs while flutes played! Then he was burned on a pyre of trees, and his ashes cast into the sea.[12] Please note that this was during the "golden age" of Greece that some homosexuals talk so much about. Also during this "golden age," women were second-class citizens; the most brilliant men did not know the function of the heart, liver, or brain nor did they know about the circulation of the blood. They believed the entrails of a chicken could predict the fate of a nation, and that the Greek "deities" really lived on Mt. Olympus! Golden age indeed!

When Marseilles was smacked by plague, a poor man would offer himself as a scapegoat! (He was not only poor, but dumb!) For a year, he was fed the best food and kept in comfortable surroundings, but after the year he was led through the city while prayers were made asking the gods to put all the people's sins upon the well-fed dummy. He was then taken outside the city walls and stoned to death. At times the volunteer would only be cast out of the city.[13]

The Athenians always kept hapless souls at public expense, and during times of pestilence, famine or natural disaster, two of them were sacrificed. Rome also resorted to scapegoats at times. (Isn't it interesting that all people have felt the need to have someone pay for their sins? Of course, Christ is our sin-bearer.)

TROUBLING TIMES

For thousands of years, mankind resorted to human sacrifices and with more enlightenment (and the teaching and preaching of the Bible), animals replaced humans. Whether human or animals, the sacrifice was to placate "the gods." Honest men know they are sinners and are in need of expiation, and being sinners they react to death staring them in the face. Some will confess and repent, while other will become callous and rebellious. I am convinced that we will see the same division following more terror in the U.S.

I'm afraid people will act as they always have in times of major disasters. Will we see even more depravity, drunkenness, child abuse, robbery, and murder as deaths from terrorism multiply? Will honesty, loyalty, kindness, honor, and compassion become obsolete and even suspect? Will those of us who profess normalcy exhibit major character flaws and not be true to our highest ideals? Will church members permit hatred, fear, and bigotry to take control instead of faith, hope, and love? Will real Christians get weary in the battle and surrender their long-held Bible principles to accommodate the soft, sinister purring of unbelieving liberals who tell us the Bible is antiquated and unreliable? Probably so! In times of distress, disease, and death, even good people often capitulate to evil to gain safety, succor, and success.

Consider that in A.D. 189, a great plague (thought to be smallpox) attacked the Roman Empire and 2,000 people died each day in Rome. Rome was in trouble at that time with internal strife, debased currency, encircling barbarians and demoralization of the populace. Those complex problems were made infinitely worse by so many daily deaths. The labor supply was dwindling, military campaigns were stopped or hindered, day-to-day business operations were paralyzed, and production of food almost ceased. The weakened Empire was grinding to a halt.

MUSLIM ATTACK

How long would it take for any major city to be crippled if 2,000 people died each day? If there were a massive attack upon a major American city, could the hospitals care for the injured or infected? Who would handle all the paper work for their deaths? What would it do to the insurance companies? Are there enough funeral homes to handle the dead? Are there enough grave plots presently available? How long would it be before the labor force could no longer supply workers to replace the dead? Would there be enough experienced people to train new workers, if workers could be found? What impact would those deaths have on the tax base? What would it do to the Social Security system?

What would follow a massive terrorist attack? Would law and order totally break down with looting and vandalism? Would stores close for the safety of the owners? If so, where would you get the supplies you need? If most stores closed, what would that do to our economy? Many financial advisors would tell you that a massive attack followed by a paralyzed economy would make the stock market plummet to the basement. What would that do to your retirement? Would the military take over police duties, and if so, how would that impact your daily life?

SOME QUESTIONS

There is no doubt that new, intrusive laws would be passed (or implemented) that would restrict our freedom of movement. There would be mandatory vaccination against smallpox and other infectious diseases. What if you think the shots would be far worse than the risk of getting the disease? What if you refused the shots? If a smallpox outbreak happens in your city, you will no doubt be quarantined. What about your travelling job? What about seeing your children in another city? Will you obey a law that restricts public meetings such as church services? If so, for how long?

Two of our major problems would be obtaining health care and eating. Where would the necessary nurses and physicians come from? What about hospital beds? How could we exist if only 30% of the farmers were no longer producing food? If politicians react as they have in the past to major disasters, they will freeze prices and wages and may even prohibit a person from changing jobs. Would you support a law that **requires** a man to stay in his present job? Well, what if he is a farmer, and if he doesn't farm, you won't eat? Would you support that law under that condition? How firm are your convictions when it affects feeding your family?

These questions must be faced now; however, our leaders give no indication that they are being considered, and some will question my loyalty for asking the questions! Patriotic Americans will ask some questions and demand answers from the people whose salaries they pay. Keep in mind that we are the masters, and the politicians and bureaucrats are the servants!

REACTION IN LONDON

People are basically the same everywhere in every age. It is most informative and interesting to look at how authorities reacted to the London plague.[14] It is worth noting that the London officials based their actions on law. When King James I came to the throne during a plague in 1603, the Parliament took action giving city officials authority to deal with the plague. When the plague sneaked into London in 1665, the officials of London then took action. Will we see the same kind of laws in America?

London officials appointed one or more "examiners" to inquire as to the status of every home in the parish. An examiner was to keep a list of the homes where plague victims lived, and those houses were to be "shut up" by the constable. If a man refused to become an "examiner" because of his family, job, fear, etc., he was to be imprisoned until he was convinced to do the work. "Watch-men" were to be appointed to watch every house where there was infection! There was to be a watchman for the day and one for the evening, and they were to keep anyone from entering or leaving the house. Any such person attempting to enter or leave was to be "severely punished."

"Searchers" were women who were appointed to identify the dead and ascertain whether they died of plague or some other disease. Such women were forbidden by law to "keep any shop or stall, or be employed as a laundress, or in any other common employment whatsoever." However, what if she had to work or was fearful of examining the dead? Too bad. Since some of the searchers were not very effective and the disease continued to spread, "chirurgeons" were appointed to provide a more precise accounting. "Chirurgeon" is an archaic word for surgeon. Some of those surgeons worked in the "pest house" or hospital for those with contagious diseases, while others were independent physicians. They were to be paid from the personal effects of those they examined! If that did not prove profitable, the city would pay the cost.

Citizens were required to report to the examiner any member of their family who showed signs of infection, and it had to be done within two hours! Any infected person was to be sequestered for 30 days following the first signs of plague. All burials were to take place either before sunrise or after sunset, and no friend or neighbor could accompany the burial under threat of imprisonment. There could be no funeral in the church during this time, no matter what was the cause of death. Each house where a person was infected was to be marked with a 12 inch red cross in the middle of the door over which these words were to be written: "Lord, have mercy upon us." All those who came in contact with the dead were to carry, in public, a red rod at least 3 feet in length in their hands. Nor could they go into any house but their own except on official plague duties.

HOW WILL WE REACT?

If America experiences a massive biological attack, look for similar laws to be passed. There will be limitations on personal liberty, but hopefully lawmakers will think these issues through, debate them, and implement only those most necessary.

Reasonable people will argue that, in times of emergency, extreme measures must be taken for everyone's good; however, there is always a problem. When extreme measures are taken "for the present time," some of them persist after the danger is past. There are many examples of that in our history. So ask questions and expect answers from the authorities.

In 1878, a deadly plague started along the Gulf Coast of the U.S., almost wiping out some towns. It caused horror and fear wherever it hit. It slowly worked its way up the Mississippi River to New Orleans, killing the poor and prosperous, ignorant and intelligent, and city-folk and country-folk alike. Its name was whispered in awe: yellow fever.

New Orleans in 1878 was a prosperous, proud, and prissy city. Cotton was king, food was an obsession, dueling was common, and gambling was rampant. The wealthy lived in opulent, antebellum homes nestled along the Mississippi. Everyone knew that yellow fever was working its way north along the river, and everyone knew it was deadly; however, New Orleans officials and media told everyone not to worry. Things would be all right. They wanted to believe that but had no reason to believe it. When the fever hit New Orleans, it was the worst plague to lash across the face of the city in its history. More than half of the inhabitants were killed and in fact, the city lost its charter and was not an official city until 14 years later. Public officials dallied, dawdled, delayed, and denied the danger thinking they were too smart, sophisticated, and special for such a thing to happen to them. It happened. They refused to take the warning seriously and paid for it.

New Orleans may be a prototype of America when massive terrorism smacks us again. We know further attacks are coming and are reacting in ineffective, even silly ways. Federal officials are making plans for their survival, but there is little concern about the mass of citizens. We must realize that we are not too smart, sophisticated, and special that such a thing could never happen here. It already has, and terrorists, no doubt, are invading our nation tonight with plans to cause more devastating attacks upon us.

We must react as concerned, committed, and compassionate Christians, not as people have reacted in past times of distress, disease, and death.

References:

1   Hans Zinsser, *Rats, Lice and History*, Boston: Brown and Co., 1935, p. 121.

2   Daniel Defoe, *A Journal of the Plague Years*. London, Everyman's Library, 1908, p. 7.

3   Ibid., pp. 29-30.

4   Ibid., 31.

5   Ibid., 32.

6   Ibid., 38.

7   William McNeill, *Plagues and People*, Garden City, NY: Anchor Press/Doubleday, 1976, p.121.

8   Defoe, p.18.

9   Defoe, p. 198.

10   J. L. Cloudsley-Thompson, *Insects and History*, New York: St. Martin's Press, 1976, p. 68.

11   Ibid., 69.

12   Ibid., 25.

13   Ibid., 25.

14   Defoe, pp. 43-48.

Chapter Fifteen

A New Direction for America!

A message must be sent to the terrorists worldwide, and the message must be clear, unambiguous, loud, and uncompromising: The U.S. will not be bullied, badgered, bulldozed, or bludgeoned; nor will we permit our citizens to be killed by any terrorist state, cultic religion, or extremist hate group. Any attack upon Americans anywhere in the world will trigger a sure, swift, and severe response. We will react as our strong leaders have in our past.

Hopefully our new president will follow Teddy Roosevelt's example in 1904 when American businessman (Ion Perdicaris) and his stepson were kidnapped by Muslim terrorists. They were taken from their home in Tangier by Raisuli, known as the "Last of the Barbary Pirates," and held for $70,000 ransom along with other demands. President Roosevelt (a progressive!) sent seven battleships to Morocco with a message: "This government wants Perdicaris alive or Raisuli dead." Perdicaris was released in a few days!

That international incident was an example of Teddy's "Speak softly and carry a big stick" philosophy. Obama speaks softly (when he has a teleprompter) and carries a wet noodle. Terrorists have not been impressed.

What is usually missed is the impact Roosevelt's action had on his political fortunes. The Republican National Convention was taking place in Chicago at the time, and Secretary of State Hay sent the delegates a copy of Teddy's message to the kidnappers. Teddy's reelection campaign was lackluster, lukewarm, and lifeless but when the telegram was read to the delegates, the convention exploded with excitement. Teddy got another term in the White House.

We don't want a "shoot from the hip" president; but we want one with a bone in his back, a brain in his head, and hair on his chest—assuming our next president is a man!

NEW SPEECH FOR THE PRESIDENT

Our new President should issue a statement on terror (don't hold your breath):

"My fellow Americans, as of today, this nation will follow a new foreign policy that will solve the problem of terrorism. We will return to our roots and follow the wise advice of our Founding Fathers. We will no longer become entangled in foreign alliances. We will no longer meddle in the affairs of other nations nor consider ourselves the policeman of the world. We will always consider first our national interests. We will not presume that we know best for other countries. What may be 'best' for us may not be best for them."

"Since we have been attacked repeatedly, we will go more aggressively after those responsible. We will not try to topple governments and set up democracies; however, we will always encourage liberty everywhere. We will not carpet-bomb cities filled with innocent civilians. We do not believe 'total war' is morally right or militarily justified if it means wiping out innocent civilians. However, be assured those culpable individuals will be punished as a deterrent to others."

"Americans don't hate Muslims or anyone else since it is wrong and unproductive to hate; however, we will no longer plead with Muslims, at home and abroad, to 'love us.' We will no longer express guilt and self-loathing. Federal officials will no longer try to prove that Americans are not racists. It is up to Muslims to prove they are not terrorists!"

"Our loose immigration policy for many years has resulted in us not knowing who is among our population. We will therefore stop all immigration for five years. Furthermore, we have decided to finish building the wall on our southern border. It will be manned by additional border agents with additional aid from manned and unmanned vehicles."

"Any U.S. business that hires an illegal alien will be heavily fined and a repeated offense will result in the business being put out of business."

"Furthermore, as of today, we have shut the welfare window. No more foreign aid to any nation. We may decide in the future that it is in our best interest to help some nation, but it will be as unusual as snow in August. Too often, financial aid to nations is like mob payments to keep them being nice to us."

"We will also start bringing our troops home from all over the world. They will be sent to foreign nations only in event of declared war or in the interests of the U.S. This is not isolationism but it is an 'America First' policy. Any other policy is insane."

"As to the Middle East, we and our advisors don't know what is best! The U.S. has vast disagreements with most of the factions especially with those who declare their determination to "drive Israel into the sea." However, we do not give unquestioned support for anyone, including Israel. They must settle their own affairs, with or without the assistance of surrounding nations. I pray to the God of the Bible that they will solve their differences, but they will do so without U.S. assistance, although we will always be available to act as mediator."

"As to our reliance on Middle East oil, we have already started drilling in Alaska, the Gulf of Mexico, and off the coast of California and will immediately expand the mining of our vast coal supplies. We will try to be sensitive to the environment; however, I believe that people are more precious than plants or bugs or snakes or fish or spotted owls. Our drilling equipment may cause a caribou here and there to abort her young or a bear may bruise its rear-end on our pipeline, but we will live with those tragedies.

American oil will flow. Moreover, of course, we will still buy oil from South America and even Middle East nations; however, we will not buy oil from states that support terrorists. They can pour their excess oil over their pancakes each morning for all we care. Or drink it! This government will no longer pretend that terrorists are gracious gentlemen, nor will American officials shake their hands while smiling like an idiot. Nor will we bow to them since real Americans don't bow to anyone–except God."

"We will encourage American entrepreneurs by tax incentives and other measures to pursue the development of alternative fuels."

"We have some difficult days ahead that will require an adjustment by all of us. Nevertheless, we see a bright future after a few years of sacrifice. The new administration will keep you informed since you are the Boss.

You pay our generous salaries as you do for all Federal employees."

"This new administration takes our jobs seriously; therefore, we promise that any further bill that comes to the Oval Office must meet five criteria to qualify for my signature: It must be constitutional. It must be necessary. We must be able to afford the proposed law. It must not expand government and limit individual liberty. The last criterion is that it must not undermine the family, decency, and general morality. If a bill does not pass those five criteria, it will not get the required signature."

"No doubt there are knees jerking all across America (left ones, of course) and those people can cast their vote for new leadership and different policies in the next election. Until then, learn to live with it. I am your President and will do as I have promised. And may the God of the Bible bless America! Good night."

Of course, like former Presidents Bush and Obama the new president may not have the convictions, courage, or character to make such a statement.

NO EXCUSE FOR TERRORISM

Yes, I think such a statement might defuse some Muslim terrorists throughout the world, and cause an epidemic of cardiac arrests among the entertainment industry, leftist politicians, and top honchos of the ACLU, Americans United for Separation of Church and State, etc. Muslim terrorists would have no justifiable reason to hate America. Moreover, this new policy would be the right thing to do! Hopefully, concerned citizens will hold the President's feet to the fire. Maybe then we will have America on a path for victory.

However, Americans must understand that Muslim terrorists' major compulsion is obedience to the Koran to establish a world caliphate so they would hate America whatever the political climate. Every Muslim is expected to contribute to the cause of world caliphate. However, they do understand force and will ridicule weakness which has been the perceived image of America for many years.

If decisive action is not taken soon by our public officials, I believe America's rivers and streets will run with blood. It is a fact: our government policies have influenced irrational people to do irrational things. (But that is no excuse for terror!)

On the day after Pearl Harbor, former President Herbert Hoover wrote to friends: "You and I know that this continuous putting pins in rattlesnakes finally got this country bitten." Friends, America has been bitten and while in the next years, we must "kill some rattlesnakes," we must also stop feeding the rattlesnakes.

DOES WAR EXCUSE EVIL?

While Americans demand that terrorists be caught, convicted, then executed, we do not want to be the proponents of government terror. All Federal officials take an oath to support and defend the Constitution, and nowhere is it suggested that they can abrogate that oath because of the circumstances. "But," we are told, "don't you understand that we are at war. Thousands of Americans have been killed." True, but hundreds of thousands of Americans were killed defending our Constitutional rights to live free. Must we live with a **little** U.S. authorized terror to stop terrorism? How much terror can we justify? How much does the Constitution justify? And if the U.S. becomes tyrannical, how are we much different from the terrorists? Are you satisfied to be less evil than the enemy? Is our difference simply one of degree? Or of kind?

The sacrifice others have made in our history requires that we maintain a free nation where we can disagree without shooting each other. We don't have to like or agree with each other, but we can respect opinions of others and defend their right to have them. After all, it is not unconstitutional, unreasonable, or unpatriotic to be wrong or even stupid! However, we will not remain free if we begin to act like the terrorists and terrorist-supporting nations we abhor!

It is about here that I should quote Benjamin Franklin's famous statement: "They that can give up essential liberty to obtain a little temporary safety deserve neither liberty nor safety."[1] He was right on target. We are fools if we don't look at the big picture. At this point I think what Alexander Hamilton wrote is appropriate: "The violent destruction of life and property incident to war–the continual effort and alarm attendant on a state of continual danger–will compel nations most attached to liberty to resort, for repose and safety, to institutions which have a tendency to destroy their civil and political rights. To be more safe, they at length become willing to run the risk of being less free."[2] Hamilton's statement requires a second reading! It is as if he were looking at our present situation.

ATTACK BY FEDERAL GOVERNMENT

In late July of 2002, the media was full of President Bush's plan to reorganize the Federal Government to make it more effective in the war on terror. For many months, even before the Muslim attacks upon us, this plan was in the feeble minds of those people not dedicated to the Constitution. It means more power for an expanded government and it means less freedom for citizens. One of the most dangerous parts of the plan is to nullify the 1878 *posse comitatus* act that basically prohibits the military from exercising police powers over U.S. citizens. Let me remind you that the military has been trained to kill, not investigate, arrest, and detain.

On Sept. 26, 2005 President Bush, in a knee-jerk reaction to Katrina hurricane disaster, urged Congress to consider revising federal laws so he or any future president could use the U.S. military without *posse comitatus* limitations. He wanted to use the military to seize control immediately in the aftermath of a natural disaster or terrorist attack. He noted that "it may require change of law." Presidents already had authority to use federal troops; however, there were limiting parameters.

Finally, it was done without a whimper from the citizens. With minimal media debate, at a time when Americans were celebrating the New Year with their loved ones, the "National Defense Authorization Act" H.R. 1540 was signed into law by President Barack Obama on Dec. 31, 2011. This was a direct attack upon average citizens. What's next? We may not see lodging of troops in American homes; we may "only" see soldiers trained to fight a war being used to keep order when select Americans protest government actions.

Whatever, it seems terrorism justifies anything. I predict that Americans will rue the day when *posse comitatus* was annulled.

MUSLIM ATTACKS

We know that Middle East terrorists have already attacked the U.S. many times before and have admitted there will be further attacks, so why not take them at their word? After all, they may be dastardly killers, but that doesn't mean they don't occasionally tell the truth.

Following are **some** of the attacks Muslim terrorists have made upon our nation and our response:

- The 1983 U.S. Embassy bombing in Beirut that killed 63 and injured 120.

- The 1983 bombing of the Beirut barracks that killed 307 Americans and Frenchmen and injured 75.

- There was the 1993 World Trade Center bombing that killed six and injured about 1,042 people. You may remember that President Clinton promised that those responsible would be pursued into their darken dens and would be punished. It didn't happen.

- After the 1995 bombing in Saudi Arabia which killed five U.S. military personnel, Clinton promised that those responsible would be hunted down and punished. It didn't happen.

- Then there was the Khobar Towers bombing in 1996 in Saudi Arabia which killed 20 and injured 372 U.S. military personnel; Clinton again promised that those responsible would be hunted down and punished. It didn't happen. So are you beginning to see a pathetic pattern?

- In 1998, U.S. embassies in Africa were bombed, killing 224 and injuring about 5,000 people. Yet again, Clinton promised that those responsible would be punished. And yet again, it didn't happen. However, it gets worse and worse.

- After the bombing of the USS Cole in 2000, which killed 17 and injured 39 U.S. sailors, Clinton promised that those terrorists would be pursued and prosecuted. And surprise, surprise, surprise, it didn't happen. By this time, the terrorists were convinced that the U.S. was a "paper tiger" without claws and fangs.

- On Sept. 11, 2001 four airliners were hijacked by 19 al-Qaeda fanatics and crashed them into the Twin Towers of the World Trade Center. One also flew into the Pentagon and another crashed near Shanksville, Pennsylvania failing to hit Washington. D.C. There were 2,996 killed.

- During October of 2002, John Allen Muhammad and his young acolyte killed 16 and injured 9 in a series of Washington, D.C. sniper attacks.

- On November 5, 2009, Major Nidal Hasan killed 13 and injured 33 at Fort Hood, near Killeen, Texas.

- On September 11, 2012, Muslim terrorists attacked the U.S. Consulate in Benghazi killing four Americans including our Ambassador.

- On April 15, 2013, two Muslim terrorists killed 3 and injured 183 during the Boston Marathon.

- On July 16, 2015 a Muslim terrorist attacked a recruiting station in Chattanooga killing five military men and injured one.

- On December 2, 2015 two Muslim fanatics killed 14 people and injured 130 at a party in San Bernardino, California.
- On June 12, 2016 an American Muslim of Middle East heritage killed 49 and injured 53 patrons at a homosexual night club in Orlando, Florida. Omar Mateen, age 29, was the killer and has been reported to have been a homosexual.

Some of us think that if those cases had been followed up and the killers brought to justice the terrorists might not have become as bold. However, our government officials were busy doing other things. Of course in a few recent incidents, local officials did their job rather quickly.

COMMON SENSE

One of the most vacuous arguments I have heard in the last 25 years is that illegal aliens in the U.S. (about 15.7 million) have some protected rights in America: taxpayers are responsible to educate them and their children! That they have a "right" to free medical treatment! That we must be very careful not to abuse or bruise their civil rights–even though they are law-breakers! Such people, once it is proved that they are illegal, should be fingerprinted and returned to the border and told that if they return illegally, they will go to prison. No ifs, no ands, no buts.

Some of us can remember when President Eisenhower was elected in 1952 that he expelled all illegal aliens under a program known as Operation Wetback! There was very little objection; after all, those people had illegally entered our nation. Imagine the response if I recommended that our President do what Eisenhower did and announce "to the nation he was launching Operation Wetback II."[3] The politically correct fools would gasp and call for me to be drawn and quartered. It's interesting that liberals have more concern for the criminals than for those of us who try to obey the laws. It has nothing to do with their culture, color, education, religion, or politics. It has to do with law and common sense.

IMMIGRANT SENSITIVITY

Even so, I do believe strongly that if people are going to emigrate to America, they should be required to guarantee that they will not become dependent on taxpayers; they should learn our language, they should be assimilated into our society, at least by the second generation. After all, that's what the Germans, Irish, Italians, Jews, and others did. Of course, each major city has its Chinatown, but those areas were formed by masses of people who came to do the "grunt" work for our first railroads. Upon their arrival, they were without funds, friends, or family, and it was natural and desirable for them to congregate in one area. Future generations usually were absorbed into the melting pot. Few Muslims are "melting," and many are waiting for a time to strike.

New immigrants must understand that they are coming to America, and it is basically a "Christianized" nation. It has never been "Christian," since only a person can become a Christian through faith in Christ. They cannot expect us to be supersensitive to their mores, customs, religion, etc. Since we made room for them, they should be sensitive to us and not antagonize us. Moreover, it would help if they showed a little gratitude.

Immigrants need to understand that our money screams our affirmation: "In God we trust." Now that is not some god of eastern religions nor is it the main god worshiped in Arabia during the sixth century known as Allah. It is the God of the Bible, whom our earliest settlers believed in and followed. This nation was built and defended by people who wanted it to remain "American" and "Christianized." Not African, Hispanic or Arabic nor Hindu, Buddhist, or Muslim.

REASON FOR COMING

Just to set the record straight after so many years of distortion about religion and the church in American's past: America was founded upon the premise that its citizens would be Christians adhering to Biblical principles. Yes, I know, we have come a long way from that, but people look at me like a calf looking at a new gate when I speak about America's historic Christian roots.

In the *Mayflower Compact*, said to be America's birth certificate, it is clear that the original founders thought they were planting a "Christian" nation. They wrote, "Having undertaken for the Glory of God advancement of the Christian Faith and honor of our King and country...." Note that it was not some fuzzy, ambiguous god somewhere, but the God of the Christian faith.

This line of thinking continued in that first generation of leaders as expressed in the *New England Confederation* which affirmed: "We all came into these parts of America with one and the same end, namely, to advance the Kingdom of the Lord Jesus Christ." Can it be any clearer? After all, the people writing were first generation Americans. They should know their purpose for coming!

Even **after** the U.S. Constitution was passed, some states insisted that their lawmakers be Christian! In Maryland, the state constitution, as late as 1864, required office seekers to have a "belief in the Christian religion, or of the existence of God, and in a future state of rewards and punishments." In New Hampshire there was a requirement of senators and representatives as late as 1877 that they be of the "Protestant religion." Gasp!

PURPOSE OF FIRST AMENDMENT

We are told that the First Amendment forbids preferring one religion over another, but that is not true. Supreme Court Justice Joseph Story was a leading jurist who served on the U.S. Supreme Court from 1811 to 1845. Story was a Unitarian and he wrote in his *Commentaries on the Constitution:* "The real object of the (first) amendment was not to countenance, much less to advance, Mahometanism [Islam], or Judaism, or infidelity, by prostrating Christianity; but to exclude all rivalry among Christian sects, and to prevent any national ecclesiastical establishment which should give to a hierarchy the exclusive patronage of the national government."[4]

Story was saying that the purpose of the First Amendment was not to equate Christianity and other religions, but to exclude the establishment of a national church, i.e., Baptist, Methodist, Congregational, etc. Of course, the enemies of Christ and common sense have twisted that fact like a pretzel until it is now illegal to pray and to read the Bible in school, to place a nativity scene on public property, and other ridiculous prohibitions.

Justice Story further commented on this issue about equating all religions in 1833: "At the time of the adoption of the Constitution...[an] attempt to level all religions and to make it a matter of state policy to hold all in utter indifference, would have created...universal indignation."

When foreigners visit national monuments, they can see numerous references to the God of the Bible and what our founders believed.

The proponents of the salad bowl theory tell us that one culture or religion is just as good as another. The 300-member, Stone Age culture with all its barbarism, brutality, and backwardness is just as viable as our modern, urbane, sophisticated society with elevators, airplanes, automobiles, hospitals, MRI machines, computers, etc. Likewise, the voodoo cultures practicing witchcraft, shamanism, demonism, pantheism, etc., are as acceptable and on par with Christianity! "After all," we are told, "there is strength in diversity." However, history proves the opposite: There is strength in unity!

IMMIGRANTS CAN LEAVE

Black Muslims, Sunni Muslims, Hindus, and others should take off their robes and turbans and assimilate as some are doing. We must stop calling people Arab-Americans, Afro-Americans, Jewish-Americans, etc. Why not simply be "Americans"? It doesn't mean one cannot appreciate some of the good things that were left in the old country, but if one is in a new country, he should love it and never be ashamed to profess it.

Many Muslims have identified with the terrorists and have told journalists and pollsters that Americans are anti-Muslim! What did they expect? Are Americans expected to be pro-Muslim when Muslims, for the most part, don't speak our language; dress in sixth-century, desert clothing; treat women like possessions; and seem to look for opportunities to criticize the nation that has opened its arms to them? They seem to be determined to change America to be like the country they left! Why did they leave?

I am tired of immigrates who demand that we be so sensitive to their feelings when they don't give a flip about ours. We have our own language, lifestyle, culture, music (such as it is), and I am weary of foreigners who enjoy all the many benefits of our nation and are not sensitive to our feelings. In the name of multiculturalism and non-discrimination, we opened our collective arms and invited anyone and everyone to our shores with no questions asked and no obligations required. We have been fools and have watched our sworn enemy invade our nation.

NATIONAL IDENTITY

I think my grandchildren have a right to live in a nation similar to what I grew up in. I don't want to see our culture changed to that of the sixth or seventh-century Arabian Desert. It is not unreasonable to expect America to reflect the America I grew up in! I would like a return to the relative innocence of the 1950s; however, that won't happen. But we can have a return to Bible truth practiced by Christians, and impact society by walk and talk. If Christians are the salt and light Christ told us to be, we will make a difference. We will once again believe that there is a difference in right and wrong, and we have a moral responsibility to choose the right. We will discriminate in that we will make value judgments about cars, music, television shows, politics, and even religion.

With the massive increase in legal and illegal immigration, we are going to lose our national identity. Some think that is not bad. I'm **not** one of them. People from Europe emigrating to the U.S. are much easier to assimilate than those from Latin American, African, and Middle Eastern nations. Moreover, as people come and hold loyalty to former homelands, it erodes our society. It weakens our sovereignty. If we have to assimilate a million new Americans here, do you think it would be easier to assimilate a million British or a million Zulus?

I suggest that we put a moratorium on all immigration for at least five years, multiply our efforts to stop illegal aliens at our borders; vigorously pursue foreigners with expired visas (then send them packing); and generally enforce the laws to protect America.

A new report by the Department of Homeland Security has added urgency to the problem. It found that nearly half a million people overstayed their visas last year alone.[5] They have settled into our society and will affect our national identity and our national security.

Do you understand the ramifications of the above? It means that last year over half a million **additional** foreigners are living here illegally! And the federal government admitted that while they had an entrance program they do not have an exit program! I believe Larry, Curly, and Moe are running this government! The government insists that you have proof of citizenship when you apply for a driver's license, passport, etc., but they don't know what happened to 500,000 visiting foreigners last year!

At the same time, we must stop getting involved in every barroom brawl around the world, cut all foreign aid, and hold Jews and Muslims to the same high standard. After all, we will never get rid of the symptoms (terror) unless we cut out the infection! Send out a message that this "watchdog" will not only bark but will bite the rear end off any that threaten our safety.

START PROFILING TODAY

Should we profile people in our efforts of apprehending terrorists? The liberal mantra is that we must never offend anyone, especially fanatics who want to kill us! Especially when what they want to do is subdue and then offend us as a way of life! Moreover, the leftists in the media and academia tell us to keep on strip-searching 80-year-old ladies, eight-year-old kids, and making congressmen and others take off their pants at airports! Not me. It will mean jail time for this Georgia cracker!

Let's think about profiling. If there were a string of killings done by a man that matched my description, should I be offended if I am stopped and checked out by police looking for the killer? No, I will answer their questions, prove my identity, and move on hoping they catch the killer.

If a black man robs a bank, killing three people, and drives off in a red Ferrari, it is not unjust, unfair, or unreasonable to stop every black man in a red Ferrari. It amazes me that any person can say otherwise, without bursting out in belly-bobbing laughter. Now, if the police stop all Blacks driving expensive cars, then I would come to their defense. In such a case, probable guilt is assumed against a whole race of people, and that is not right.

Young Middle Eastern men have committed horrendous terror so if those having the same profile are stopped and questioned, they should realize that is the price to pay. Airport officials should treat them kindly (as they should everyone), become satisfied that the men in question are innocent citizens, then apologize to them and even give them first class seats on their next flight if possible. That's profiling and it's good sense.

REMINDERS

Let me remind you that in 1979 when the U.S. embassy in Iran was taken over and our people were taken hostage, it was not done by Christian high school students from Dallas, Elvis and his buddies, or a senior citizens' group from Lakeland, Florida. It was done by Muslim male extremists, mostly between the ages of 17 and 40.

In 1983, when the U.S. Marine barracks in Beirut were blown up, it was not done by a pizza delivery boy; crazed feminists angry that their biological clock keeps ticking; or Geraldo Rivera making up for a slow news day. It was done by Muslim male extremists, mostly between the ages of 17 and 40.

In 1988, Pan Am Flight 103 was not bombed by the Tooth Fairy; Madonna, wearing only her underclothes; or the Indianapolis Pacers; but by Muslim male extremists, mostly between the ages of 17 and 40.

In 1998, the U.S. embassies in Kenya and Tanzania were not bombed by Mr. Rogers; Jerry Falwell and his singing group from Liberty University; or the right-wingers at *Fox* television. It was done by Muslim male extremists, mostly between the ages of 17 and 40.

On September 11, 2011, the four airliners were not hijacked and destroyed by Wiley E. Coyote, Daffy Duck, and Elmer Fudd; or Donald Trump and Ted Cruz. It was done by Muslim male extremists, mostly between the ages of 17 and 40.

On January 7, 2015 after the *Charlie Hebdo* magazine published sketches of Mohammed, the editor and eleven others were not killed by Jerry Springer, Mickey Mouse or a local chapter of the Girl Scouts, or Concerned Women for America, but by Muslim extremists, mostly between the ages of 17 to 40.

On Nov. 13, 2015 when Paris experienced multiple terrorists killing 130 people it was not done by Jeb Bush, Bugs Bunny, or the Mormon Tabernacle Choir, but by Muslim extremists, mostly between the ages of 17 to 40.

On Dec. 2, 2015 when a couple invaded a party in San Bernardino and killed 14 people it was not done by Mitt Romney, Donald Duck, or Ken Ham and his creationist workers at his Creation Museum, but by Muslim extremists, mostly between the ages of 17 to 40.

Now, let me write very slowly so television addicts can understand: do you see a pattern that is beginning to develop? Is it unreasonable to expect that the next terrorist attack will be carried out by Muslim male extremists, mostly between the ages of 17 and 40? So, do you think it reasonable to check out all people in that category? If not, why not?

Case in point: Suppose you were waiting to board a plane and at the last minute, in walk two groups of three men. One group consists of Baptist preachers and the other group is made up of Middle Eastern men between the ages of 17 and 40. There is time to search only one group (a second time) so which group do you want searched? All but insane bigots will choose the Middle East men! How can I justify that when I would not support stopping all Blacks driving expensive cars after a bank robbery? Because all bank robbers are not black. We must stop playing "Let's stop the terrorists" game and get serious. Start the profiling today because lives are at stake.

NOT PROFILING COSTS LIVES

In fact, lives have already been lost because of reluctance to look realistically at the world of terror. There were witnesses who reported that the Washington area snipers were "dark skinned," "Hispanic," and a "black" man; so wouldn't most sensible people start looking for men who fit that general description? No, not in the world of super-sensitivity whenever race is involved. Montgomery County Police Chief Charles Moose (a Black) didn't want to release a composite sketch of the suspects because he didn't want to "paint some group." So he painted all **white** men, but then we are also a group! The problem is we are not a recognized minority.

On Oct. 3, the two black snipers were stopped by Washington, D.C. police but were released because D.C. Police Chief Charles Ramsey said, "We were looking for a white van with white people." There was zero information to suggest that the snipers were white and at least three eyewitnesses who identified them as other than white! It is possible, even probable, that all deaths after October 3 could have been avoided had Moose used common sense and profiling to do his job. Did he think he was Public Relations Director for the NAACP instead of a law enforcement officer? If the two snipers had not basically surrendered (by boasting about the Alabama murder) Moose would still be looking for an angry white male. We do know that cops were told to search only vehicles driven by white males. Sounds like profiling to me, but since it was white men, that's all right!

Chief Moose has been praised profusely by almost everyone; however, a *WorldNetDaily* column bravely said praising Moose was rewarding and validating incompetence.[6] That it does, whatever the color. I say to all state and Federal authorities, "Stop assuming loyal Americans are the bad guys and go after the terrorists and use common sense to put them away."

This is my idealistic message for our people and leaders. Some of these principles will be implemented, but most will not. They will not because politicians are not principled people and that is one reason we must never put our trust in politicians. Our confidence is in Christ alone, and when politicians make a decision that is principled, we thank God and move on.

References:

1 Benjamin Franklin, *Historical Review of Pennsylvania, 1759.*

2 *Federalist,* number 8.

3 Pat Buchanan, *WorldNetDaily,* Jan. 11, 2002.

4 *Constitutional History*, New York: Harper Torchbooks, 1965, p. 133.

5 Isaac Daniel and Catherine Renner, "The next wave of the biometric revolution," *The Hill,* Feb. 15, 2016.

6 *WorldNetDaily*, Nov. 8, 2002.

Chapter Sixteen

Keep America American!

America–first, last, and always! Liberals will scream "bigotry"; but most sane, sensitive, and sincere Americans believe that we don't have to apologize for putting our national interests first and wanting to keep America, America! It does not mean that we are, by nature, superior to anyone else, nor does it mean that we wish anyone else ill. It simply means that we like what we have here, although we would like to remove the crime, hatred, perversion, abortion, etc., but it would be abnormal if we did not want America to continue to be America. No one suggests that we are perfect or close to it, but I prefer America to any place I have been. What is wrong with that? Let me prompt your answer: nothing is wrong with it.

We identify with America as we identify with our family. I don't identify with your family but with mine. I don't wish you ill will or failure. I just identify with my family. Because, well, because it is my family. As with a family, so with a nation. If that were not true, then there would be no nations. But then, maybe that's exactly what the globalists want: one massive "family" in one big world with no boundaries where all cultures would be equal.

Immigration is changing North America before our eyes every day and one indication is that New York City public schools have students that speak 176 different languages! Moreover, the Nashville schools have students speaking 120 different languages! Furthermore, as of April 15,

2016, America's public schools are a snapshot of a changing America because for the first time in America's history, a majority of those in public schools are students of color! I see a trend here! American is quickly getting less white! A partial explanation is that maybe more white students are going to non-public schools.

It is natural to resist change as one gets older. He or she becomes nostalgic about the past. In reality, things were usually not as bad or as good as we imagine them. Even with that understanding I maintain that America is only a shadow of its former self and my grandchildren will live and die without knowing the nation that once was.

My grandchildren will never know the America I knew as a boy in a small West Virginia town and they are poorer because of that.

Realizing that America was and is a multicultural nation and there have always been good guys and bad guys in our midst, there were some things generally true. Innocence is one of the first things that comes to mind. We had confidence in our leaders and were shocked when a crook was revealed now and then. We trusted and respected anyone in uniform, even the mailman.

I REMEMBER

I remember an America where teachers were obeyed, respected, and even feared. We knew that if we received a paddling at school, we would get one at home. That was before the graduates of Columbia took control of the educational system. My three most respected and loved teachers were the ones who were the most demanding.

I remember when the Bible was read and prayers said each morning in the public schools. Today, the schools are nut factories often filled with uneducated, unprincipled, and uncaring teachers and rebellious, resentful, and raucous students. Some kids go on to college but only 55% receive a degree within six years and often that degree is useless. One reason for the 45% drop out is that most college freshmen read on a seventh grade level.

I remember an America when every high school graduate had basic knowledge about America, the world, and their obligations to work hard to make a good life. I remember when every student in elementary school learned basic math, historical events, about dangling participles and split infinitives, facts about government, memorized the *Preamble to the Con-*

stitution, the *Gettysburg Address,* the *Bill of Rights,* the *Wreck of the Hesperus, Inchcape Rock,* and was familiar with Poe, Hawthorne, Coolidge, Irving, etc. And a weekly book report, written and read, was the norm.

I remember an America when men stood when a woman entered the room; when you tipped your hat to a lady; when you removed your hat when entering a building and would not even think of eating while wearing a hat; and when a gentleman always asked a lady, "Do you mind if I smoke?" Moreover, if a crude man carelessly cursed in a woman's presence, he would often blush and ask to be forgiven. How quaint. And, even in West Virginia, smoking and cursing women were as scarce as white dinosaurs in Manhattan.

I remember an America when we walked quietly and respectfully by a home with a gold star hanging in the window. We knew that some father, brother, or son had been slaughtered on faraway battlefields with strange names such as Iwo Jima, Corregidor, Coral Sea, Battle of the Bulge, Anzio, Heartbreak Ridge, Inchon, Pusan, and many others.

I remember an America when we never locked our doors day or night and the iceman had access to our back porch icebox for ice deliveries.

I remember an America when neighbors bossed anyone's kid around and even provided a swat on the rear when needed. This was before the fanatics at Child Protection Agency, trying to do good, took control and destroyed a vast number of families with the help of our culture.

I remember an America when families could watch any television show together and never be embarrassed. The most risqué show was when Milton Berle, dressed as a woman, hit other stars with his purse.

I remember an America when men—even myself—would shake hands on a $50,000 business deal and both kept their word—without a written contract.

I remember when no man suggested he had a woman in his body. It never happened. And if anyone had suggested the possibility of same-sex "marriage," he would have been certified insane.

I remember an America when a girl got pregnant (a very seldom occurrence) she was a shame to her family (but was not rejected) and visited grandma for a few months. The baby was often reared as a sibling or cousin or was adopted by a deserving family.

I remember an America when every life was sacred and it was a major shame, scandal, and sin if a woman had her own child butchered within her womb. And a crime.

I remember an America when a politician, who disgraced himself, his family, and his party, quickly apologized, resigned, and took the next plane or train to his backwater town to live in obscurity until his death.

I remember an America when you could discuss serious issues with people who believed the opposite yet would remain friends.

I remember an America when we loved our dogs, always stray mongrels, but when they got old or sick, we shot them and lamented it for a few days but realized that they were just animals.

I remember an America when parents were loved, respected, if not feared and the thought of talking back was never a possibility.

I remember when your family name was almost sacred and the thought of bringing disgrace to it was anathema.

CHANGING SOCIETY

No, my America was not perfect but it was pleasant, peaceful, and proper and my grandchildren and great-grandchildren will only see some glimpse of it from their own principled family but not from the nation as a whole.

So, I believe we should retain as much of old America as possible and we can do that without harming or offending other cultures or races. However, old America is being challenged, changed, even crushed by Islamic and Hispanic immigration, legal and illegal.

Islamic and Hispanic immigration is overwhelming America. State and Federal officials, so enamored with political correctness, are determined to totally change our society into a multicultural hodgepodge where no one is better off than any other. Instead of raising everyone through free enterprise, they are determined to lower everyone with programs that would make Marx, Lenin, and Stalin stand up and cheer.

Recently I saw video of a young Martin Luther King Jr. declare, "I am proud to be black. Black is beautiful. Someone needs to say it." Why is it right for him to say it about being black but wrong for me to say the same thing about being white? I will expect an answer from my critics.

Non-thinking racist liberals are now defending their racism by calling me a racist! That's like a skunk accusing a rabbit of having bad breath! Not too swift but no one says racists liberals are very sharp or honest people. They are fanatics and totally committed to their radical agenda.

WHITE PEOPLE

This is an issue that no one wants to deal with: how do we defend and promote our culture, whatever it may be, without being thought of as haters? Our heritage is under attack by Somalis in Minnesota, Iraqis in Dearborn, Michigan, and unvetted Syrians all over America.

Of course, there are times when we are embarrassed with what white people have done and are doing, but that would be true of every group. Does affirming that fact make me a racist? Overall, white people have contributed enormously to make the world a better place–yes, even Christianized white people–that is, people who aren't Christians but who have been influenced by the Bible.

The desire to keep America the way it is with our language, customs, religion, mores, etc., is admirable and nothing to be ashamed of. Why should we want a major shift in the racial ratio, language, customs, religion, etc.? The desire for keeping America in its present state is a reason to be skeptical of mass immigration. Of course, there is no question regarding illegal immigration although liberals and Democrats (but then I repeat myself) usually try to justify that criminal activity.

My being proud of being a white Christian does not reflect badly on those who don't fit that description, and my love for my wife and family and my considering them the best does no harm and is no criticism of others who don't agree. Just because you think your wife is more beautiful than mine and your children and grandchildren are the brightest and most loveable does not make you a bigot. You are simply wrong, since mine are! (I have their test scores and photos to prove it!) Most sane people would agree that that attitude is desirable and completely normal. It would be abnormal if that were not true.

THAT CHANGE NOT GOOD

Massive immigration should be halted for a few years although I think exceptions should be made for those Americans who marry foreigners.

If it is noble, kind, and compassionate to take in an unlimited number of foreigners, then let the other advanced nations get the "blessings" of immigration. Furthermore, if immigrants are offended when I sing patriotic songs, fly the American flag, and pray to Christ, then tough luck. This is a big world so they can find somewhere else to live. There is plenty of empty space on the Arabian Desert to put up a tent!

If America continues as it is: permitting massive legal and illegal immigration, we will eventually become a banana republic—without bananas and without a republic!

It is not racism to suggest that the racial ratio of America is being changed, and while some think the change is good, I don't. Why must white people apologize for being white? Is there an advantage for losing national "whiteness"? Because we think being white is just as good as being black, brown, etc., is that *prima facia* evidence that we hate other people? What is the advantage of changing the national hue?

Blacks, Indians, Latin Americans, Arabs, etc., should be proud of their race, after all God made them that way. So would you mind if I believe that Whites should feel the same about being white? Would the racists out there forgive me for pointing out that white Christians (along with some scoundrels) came to this continent and discovered a land of forests, swamps, and tribes of warring Indians? There were no roads, no businesses, no churches, no hospitals, and no factories.

OUR ANCESTORS

Our ancestors drained the swamps, built log cabins and churches, planted crops, dug copper, coal, gold, and silver from the ground, built railroads, attempted to civilize the warring Indians (and made friends of the friendly Indians) and established a land of freedom and incredible opportunity like nowhere on earth. My critics will point out the mistakes and excesses which I am willing to admit; but I will add the many failures of the Indians and others, proving mankind's fallen nature. Yes, Blacks made a contribution to our success and their enslavement is a source of embarrassment to all honest people. However, that does not mean I share any guilt for wrongs done to Blacks in the past since I had nothing to do with it. I admit to being embarrassed but harbor no guilt.

Moreover "former slaves" will get reparations from me when shrimp learn to whistle "Dixie" in unison and pigs learn to fly in formation over the White House.

Moreover, I will point out that for thousands of years nothing had been done to develop the land, forests, rivers, and mining opportunities. Indians lived as they had for more than a thousand years, sitting around their campfires while their children and elderly died unnecessary and often early deaths.

Whites have had their share of scoundrels but generally have made an incredible contribution to civilization often having to fight the system.

Justin J. Moritz, a white, retired police officer, with no criminal record was refused a patent for "White Pride" by the U.S. Patent and Trademark Office because it "is considered offensive and therefore scandalous." There is no justification for the USPTO to reject a patent for "White Pride" after **approving** Black Pride, African Pride, Asian Pride, Chippewa Pride, Gay Pride, Indian Pride, and many other "prides." Can anyone defend such offensive policies and obvious discrimination? Only a racist would defend such a practice and only a fool would try.

MINORITIES

I have defended minority people and groups all my life. I have demanded that people be treated like people. If all people are treated with respect, kindness, thoughtfulness, and graciousness, then everyone benefits. I do not endorse or support the NAACP because they are racist in seeking the benefit of "colored" people. Why not seek the advancement of people? Must civil rights leaders be reminded that the "Jim Crow" days are long gone? If we seek the advancement of everyone, that will cover Blacks, Hispanics, Whites, Indians, etc.

All my adult life I have detested unfairness, discrimination, narrow mindedness, political correctness, and cowardice. I am ashamed to say that national and state politicians, plus those in academia and the media, plus many evangelical Christians are guilty of all the above.

I don't share the liberal politicians' dream in changing America because I don't want to see American culture altered to that of the sixth or seventh-century Arabian Desert or a third world African or South American nation. It is not unkind, unreasonable, or unpatriotic to expect America to reflect the America I grew up in, especially since we have abolished systemic segregation! I think my grandchildren have a right to live in a nation similar to what I grew up in. However, young people under 40 have no idea what America was like with a strong emphasis on faith, family, and freedom. It was a great country, but of course, not perfect.

I would like a return to the relative innocence of the 1950s; however, that won't happen. I would like to see us respecting women as very special people who deserve deference and appreciation. I would like to see us love and respect innocent, unborn children. I would like to see us able to blush at crude and lewd behavior and once again able to believe that there is a difference in right and wrong with an accompanying moral obligation to choose the right. I would like to see us discriminate in that we will make value judgments about cars, music, television shows, politics, and even religion. I would like to see us even run a business using our own rules, not the government's or the customer's rules!

NATIONAL UNIQUENESS

With this massive invasion of alien peoples we are losing our national uniqueness. Many radicals have taught that is good, even desirable. They have been very critical of Christian missionaries who have gone to a tribe of stone-age people and totally transformed the tribe by preaching the Gospel of Christ. I think that is what a sovereign God desires and has commanded us to accomplish.

Moreover, I don't think God is pleased with the massive change that has taken place in European nations and the change that is taking place in America because of a massive infusion of people of different languages, beliefs, practices, and cultures.

The proponents of the salad bowl theory tell us that one culture or religion is just as good as any other. We are told that a 300-member, Stone Age culture with all its barbarism, brutality, and backwardness is just as viable, valuable, and virtuous as our modern, urbane, sophisticated society with elevators, airplanes, automobiles, hospitals, MRI machines, computers, etc. Likewise, the voodoo cultures practicing witchcraft, shamanism, demonism, pantheism, etc., are as acceptable and on par with Christianity. I don't believe that either.

I do believe that some immigration is acceptable although I would stop it for at least five years, and people who want to blend with our culture should have priority. Most Americans want a cultural and national melting pot, not a salad bowl. However, there should be rules, restrictions, and requirements for immigrants. In addition to limiting immigration we should raise our standards requiring future immigrants to sing in English all the verses of the National Anthem and whistle "I'm a Yankee Doodle Dandy" at the same time–with a mouthful of saltine crackers!

Well, maybe not quiet that extreme, but almost!

AMERICAN CULTURE

My critics whine that people are suffering all over the world, and many of the gate-crashers only want a better life. That is true; however, does that mean that America must become the social welfare system for the world, as well as the world's policeman? After all, is there not a limit to what one country can do? Moreover, let me remind you that Saudi Arabia has not accepted any "refugees" from Syria or anywhere else.

I am tired of immigrates who demand that we be sensitive to their feelings when they don't give a flip about ours. We have our own language, lifestyle, culture, music (such as it is), and I am weary of foreigners who enjoy the many benefits of our nation and are not sensitive to our feelings. It would also be delightful if they said, "thanks" now and then. In the name of multiculturalism and non-discrimination, we opened our collective arms and invited anyone and everyone to our shores with no questions asked and no commitments required. We have been fools and are watching American culture being denounced, denigrated, and destroyed in front of our eyes. That must stop!

So long, goodbye, farewell, cheerio, and if you don't understand English then adios amigo!

GATE-CRASHERS

We are told that there are up to 15.7 million (maybe 35 million) illegal aliens in the U.S.! Many or most of those people may be hard workers and love their families, but they broke our laws to get here. They pushed in line ahead of others who respected our laws, followed our procedures, filled out the paper work, paid the fee, and eventually qualified to be citizens of this great country. The 15 million thumbed their noses at our laws and decency and crawled across the Rio Grande (or whatever) to get here.

The fact that many or most of those people are now making a contribution to America does not change the facts. They broke the law and need to be removed. Furthermore, I would remind you that if a field worker can slip into America, terrorists can do so just as easily. More easily. Of the millions of illegal aliens in the U.S., how many are terrorists? Of course, the killers on September 11 were here legally, as were all the other terrorists!

Most Americans don't know that there are more than 2.5 million from **Muslim** countries in America today according to a report from the Center for Immigration Studies![1]

The best estimates of the number of illegal immigrants in the U.S. is 15.7 million, about half coming from Mexico.[2] Most Americans think that the Mexican illegal aliens are only farm workers; they are wrong. The report reveals that illegal Mexicans are in garment-making, meat-packing, construction, and manufacturing. Furthermore, **none** of those were checked for criminal records, contagious diseases, ability to provide a living, or if they had any Middle East connection with terrorists!

UNLIMITED IMMIGRATION?

May I suggest that authorities make a concerted effort to apprehend all those people and jail those who are known criminals and expel all others who are "only" gate-crashers? If we picked up only one terrorist in the group, it would be worthwhile. After all, he may be the one planning on dropping a bomb over your city or poisoning your water supply! But how could we remove them? Load the Mexican illegal aliens in a ship off the California (or Florida) Coast sail to the Mexican Coast, and dump them for Mexican officials to deal with. Then give each of the remaining illegal aliens a one-way ticket to the country of their origin or to one of the nations whose leaders whine about the U.S. immigration policies.

My critics whine that people are suffering all over the world, that many of the gate-crashers only want a better life, and that is true; however, does that mean that America must become the social welfare system for the world, as well as the policeman of the world? After all, is there not a limit to what one country can do? Moreover, most Americans don't realize that we take in over half of the immigrants of the world! Wait a minute, what about England, Spain, France, Australia, etc.? If immigration is good for America, then it would be good for other nations, so let's spread it around to all nations.

Pro-immigration voices will accuse me and others of wanting to pull up the ladder once we have climbed aboard the ship. Yes, all nations are nations of immigrants, but just because we have been generous in the past does not mean that we must have no restrictions in the future. After all, every ship has a limit as to the number of passengers it can carry. Pulling up one more passenger may sink the boat! I ask pro-immigration advocates: Should America permit an unlimited number of immigrants? No sane person believes in **unlimited** immigration so it is a matter of agreeing on the number of immigrants we should accept.

AMERICA FIRST

When a country is young and in need of farmers, artisans, tradesmen, etc., then immigration is reasonable and desirable. When the U.S. western frontier was the Alleghenies in the 1700s, we needed more people and had plenty of room for them, but our frontier has been pushed to the Pacific. In addition, when a nation is at war, there is a need to raise a fighting army. However, that is not the situation at this time in American history. It is time to call a halt before permitting further immigration to allow for a time of balance to be established.

The bleating hearts will almost always sob: "But what about the Statue of Liberty?" What about her? The statement on the base of the statue is compassionate but not constitutional. It is not in the Constitution or any other major American document. The words are commendable: "Give me your tired, your poor, your huddled masses yearning to breathe free, The wretched refuse of your teeming shore." The statue was not "given to us by France" but paid for by French and American citizens in honor of our centennial, and the full name is "The Statue of Liberty Enlightening the World." Emma Lazarus, a young Zionist, was reacting to the assassination of Czar Alexander II in 1881, and she wrote the words added to the base. Commendable thought but hardly a constitutional mandate.

When immigration is continued, it should be based on our needs, not the needs of others. There is nothing wrong with saying, "America first, last, and always." There is everything right in putting our interests first. We can't be compassionate to others if we become a third world nation. We should accept immigrants who have skills to offer in the furtherance of strengthening America. It is interesting that Mexico requires **their** immigrants to have useful skills and a pension plan from their nation of origin! If the U.S. required that of Mexican immigrants, the Mexican officials would scream like a stuck pig! How do you say "hypocrites" in Spanish?

QUALITY NOT QUANTITY

In recent years, the U.S. has attracted a large percentage of low-skilled people from Mexico and South America. That is understandable since there is no large middle class in that area; it is only natural that they would look north where there is freedom and opportunity. Therefore, we get the lowest skilled workers from those areas. After all, why would a lawyer, physician, or highly successful person want to leave his homeland to take up life in a foreign, sometime hostile land?

In a high tech age, we may want to allow highly qualified people to emigrate since they have much to offer us. What should count is not the quantity of people but their quality–and the quality of their ideas. Selfish? No, it is a sane, sensible policy, one the U.S. is not following.

We must insist that those immigrants are not carrying diseases that could explode into our native and unprotected population. The *Washington Post* reported that Virginia State health authorities announced that "tuberculosis continues to rise" and that "immigration is fueling the spread."[3] The Virginia State Health Department released figures showing an increase of almost 5 percent in TB cases in the state between 2000 and 2001. As the *Post* reported, "Health officials say the rise of TB....is largely a consequence of the migration of people from parts of the world where the disease is common. It is thought that two-thirds of the cases of TB brought into the United States originated in just three countries: Mexico, the Philippines and Vietnam."

The media reported on May 17, 2016 information from the Minnesota Department of Health that the one of every five refugees resettled in Minnesota by the federal government tested positive for latent tuberculosis in 2014! That is not a disaster waiting to happen. It has already happened and officials should go to prison!

Immigration officials are criminally reckless if they don't inquire as to a person's health, and it is criminal to permit people to enter the U.S. if they are carriers of plague, tuberculosis, pneumonia, Ebola, Zita, AIDS, typhoid, and other contagious diseases.

AMERICA'S CHANGING FACE

It is irresponsible to suggest that a huge influx of low-skilled, under-educated, often hostile gate-crashers will not have a long term, adverse effect on America. Your nation is being changed as you sleep. Now if you don't mind that and your bleating heart demands that we open our borders to permit anyone access, then so be it. Don't whine when you can't get a job or when your taxes are double what they are now, when your kids can't be educated in an overcrowded public school (they shouldn't be there anyway), when you see signs in Spanish (or Arabic!) everywhere you look, when workers who are supposed to serve you don't speak clear English, etc.

Those of us who demand a balanced immigration policy (and unashamedly argue for an "America First" policy) are characterized as bigots, xenophobes, haters, etc., but those who would change the face of America do not give us any reason to think a change is wise, compassionate, thoughtful or economically prudent. I maintain that we don't have to debate the issue; I choose to keep America, American. I know there are people who would like to emigrate here and who would make good Americans, but the boat is full. One more person may sink the boat.

As previously stated, I want my grandchildren to experience the America I experienced. Of course, they will not since globalists have taken over the media, academia, and politics; however, there is still a semblance of America. Nevertheless, if we are flooded with people of a different religion, culture, work ethic, language, race, etc., that semblance of America will be gone. Let's keep America, American and apply some common sense to our future immigration policies.

IS WHITE PRIDE WRONG?

We have observed environmental fanatics, in collusion with the Federal government, who go to outrageous efforts to preserve the snail darter, spotted owl, and the yellow belly sap sucker, so is it unreasonable to preserve America as the land of the free and the home of the brave? Why is it commendable for Blacks, Hispanics, and others to loudly proclaim their ethnicity, but when a **white** person does so, everyone treats him like a bigot? This is an issue that no one wants to deal with. It is as if there is an elephant sitting in a formal living room that no one admits is sitting there! While I don't want to be identified with the white supremacist crowd, I do think it is not only right but also desirable to be proud of our heritage.

Blacks, Latin Americans, etc., should be proud of their race, after all God made them that way. So would you mind if I believe the same thing about being white? Moreover, why make America into another Hispanic country? Aren't there enough of them south of America? There are far more nations populated by people of color than white nations. Why not have a mainly white nation here and there around the globe? Why do we need another Spanish-speaking nation? Moreover, those who emigrate here should learn to speak English! That is the least they can do. Teddy Roosevelt suggested that any immigrant who did not learn English within five years of his arrival should be shipped back home!

WHEN OUR CULTURE IS LOST

When the apostles of open borders with help from assorted progressives, liberals, do-gooders, America haters, etc., get their way and America is invaded by massive hordes of immigrants with alien customs, language, religion, etc., our nation will be lost. Once it is gone, it is gone for good. So, where do we go to reclaim our heritage? We will yell, vote, cry, demand, but it will be for naught. After all, the culture will be decided by the vast number of aliens. It will not matter that White Christians basically developed this nation; that we controlled and molded it for hundreds of years; that history supports us. It will not matter. We will be a minority and the issue will be closed.

Arthur Kemp reminded us that political power does not depend on historical rights or title deeds or morality but only on physical occupation. He wrote, "Those people who occupy a territory determine the nature of the society in that region."[4] It won't matter what's "right." Those who occupy our nation will decide what is "right."

South Africa was a nation made up of blacks and whites although the white people controlled the nation. The Blacks demanded self-determination and after many years of bloodshed, sabotage, and espionage, the Blacks took control with Nelson Mandela as their first president. He came to power as a leader of the African National Congress (ANC), an admitted communist organization that controls South Africa at this time. In April of 2016, the ANC refused to remove their president even though a black court found him guilty of raiding the public treasury. South African whites have seen their culture, language, and way of life disappear so they organized a town of their own called "Orania."

Orania consists of about a thousand people and is located on the Orange River. They do all their own work and everyone must agree to the Afrikaner culture. They expect to become a separate nation someday. They declare that they don't hate Blacks but want to perpetuate their own language, customs, and heritage. Maybe someone will tell why it is wonderful for a stone-age tribe in the Amazon to continue their backward, brutal, and barbaric ways but it is bigoted, hateful, and unreasonable for South African Whites to do the same.

SOME SUGGESTIONS

An observation: Illegal farm workers don't pay $50,000.00 to come into the U.S. to pick tomatoes or strawberries! Terrorists do. It's time to plug

242

the holes in our walls; however, the invasion has been taking place for many years. Even though there are an unknown number of terrorists in the U.S. who want to wreak havoc upon us, it is possible to limit their success. Some suggestions:

- Authorities should immediately close all jihadist training camps in more than 35 locations across America as reported by a 2006 Department of Justice report! Are U.S. officials idiots or incompetents or traitors? Young jihadists, many of them Blacks, are being trained in explosives, kidnapping, weapons use, and guerrilla warfare and are linked to a Pakistani militant group known as Jamaat al-Fuqra.

- No more immigration for at least five years. Only exceptions would be if a military man marries a foreigner, then she would be accepted.

- Plug all holes in the borders even using the military.

- Assess large penalties to any employer who hires an illegal alien.

- Recognize that non-citizens do not have the rights that Americans have. Deport all who are here illegally. Fingerprint and photograph them and imprison them if they return.

- Fingerprint and photograph all visitors who come to America from Islamic nations. Fine them heavily if they overstay their visas.

- Go on record that we are no longer the world's policeman. We will not get involved in every brawl. Nations will handle their own problems. Our stated purpose of U.S. foreign policy is to protect the freedoms of U.S. citizens.

- Also go on record that there will be no more national (or international) welfare. All foreign aid will stop.

- Reject multiculturalism as anti-American and anti-common sense. We will no longer have a guilt complex for being successful.

- Any American citizen who joins any terrorist group will lose his or her citizenship.

- All Muslim immigrants must publically renounce *sharia* Law or will be deported.

- Any group that has ties or public sympathy to ISIS and similar groups will be dissolved

- Any mosque that does not disavow terrorism in all forms would be closed and their leaders deported.

- Since most U.S. mosques are financed by Saudi Arabia's extremist Wahhabi sect, all plans to build others should be suspended.

- Saudi Arabia must permit the building of churches or synagogues equal to the number of mosques in the U.S.

- Any religion that requires death for any members who leave should not be permitted to operate in the U.S.

- All federal and state Muslim employees should be required to take an oath as to their loyalty to the U.S. and rejection of former citizenship.

- Anyone practicing female circumcision will be prosecuted for sexual child abuse and lose custody of such child.

UNFAIR

The above suggestion to fingerprint and photograph all visitors from Muslim nations has caused left-wingers to scream like a stuck pig. Egyptian physician, Hany Fares, said that if it is done, it should be done to all visitors. He said, "Muslims and Middle Easterners don't have to be terrorists. This is an insult." Hey, Hany, you are right and wrong. Muslims don't **have** to be terrorists, but all the terrorists who have attacked America have been Muslims!

Others have said that such documenting of Muslim visitors is "unfair"! Can you believe that? We lost over 3,000 innocent Americans; children are orphans; spouses are alone; massive financial problems exist, and Muslims talk about **us** being unfair! That's like Donald Trump accusing Ben Carson of being brash, bold, and boastful. It's not unfair, but it is unbelievable that we have not been documenting all visitors from nations that foment terror as a way of life.

We must be vigilant that we don't become haters of good and decent people who are different from most of us. Such a result of terror would mean that they have been successful in destroying America, and it would no longer be America.

We must also hold public officials' feet to the fire and chain them to the Constitution (notice how smoothly I go from one metaphor to another?). We must be careful not to become un-American in our desire to remain American! Questionable anti-terrorist legislation has already been passed with more to follow. Much of it is only feel good legislation with no positive results.

NEUTRAL AMERICA

Finally, let's return to our roots and become a truly neutral nation like Switzerland. I have been to Switzerland many times and have a great appreciation for the Swiss. A Swiss writer expressed his nation's position very well: "Switzerland is a neutral country. It has made permanent armed neutrality, a concept of preventing war, the maxim of its foreign policy. By doing so Switzerland guarantees four permanent objectives. It will never begin a war, it will never enter a war on the side of a warring party, it will never one-sidedly support warring parties, but it will vigorously defend itself against any attacking party."[5] That is where America used to be. Switzerland goes a step further and requires each homeowner to possess and know how to use a gun. Every adult is expected to defend the nation if attacked by another. But why would any nation want to attack a nation that will defend itself and adheres to the above four principles of neutrality?

It is past time to start facing reality about terror. Ayn Rand reminded us that "You can ignore reality, but you cannot ignore the consequences of ignoring reality." American officials had better get serious about terror, beyond doing things to make us all feel warm and cozy. We must recognize the enemy as the enemy; remove him from our shores; restore our nation to a nation of free people living under a Constitution. It's late, and we must get started today!

References:

1   Matthew Boyle, *Breitbart,* Sept. 24, 2014.

2   Wikipedia, "Illegal immigrant population of the United States."

3   *Washington Post,* March 18, 2002

4   Arthur Kemp, *Nova Europa: European Survival Strategies in a Darkening World,* Ostara Publications, 2013.

5   Matthias Erne, *Current Concerns,* "Reflections from Switzerland–Neutrality: Protection against Terror," Sept/Oct., 2001.

Epilogue:

What Kind of America Do You Want?

There is no doubt that I have been misunderstood by many people reading these pages; however, that was not my intent. Yes, I have used sarcasm and have been forceful at times in presenting my position, but difficult times demand strong and decisive action. I repeat my question for those who think I have been too hard, harsh, or even hateful: What if terrorists drop a nuclear bomb over one of our major cities resulting in the deaths of 100,000 Americans from the blast with another 300,000 dying of radiation; plunging the stock market to the basement; devastating our economy for a generation; putting millions of people out of work; producing fear and anxiety up and down every street in the nation; would you still think me to be too harsh? Many national leaders think the above could happen, with millions being killed. Or major populations might be infected with a biological or chemical weapon! Government officials **have** distributed gas masks to Washington lawmakers in the past!

I am firmly convinced (as I hope you are by now) that we are in a war. It is a clash of cultures and of religions, and even though we don't like religious wars, they do happen. We must remember that this war was not of our making. A large host of Muslims decided on this war. And war it is. It started even before September 11, 2001 and will never end until Christ returns! We are in another Hundred Years' War.

FORCES OF FREEDOM

If the U.S. and the "forces of freedom" are to win, then we must be dauntless, decisive, and determined. We must understand, if we have not already, that our world has changed forever. We will not be able to remove all Muslims from our country, and we should **not** remove those who are sincere, hardworking, assimilating Americans. However, those who aid and abet terrorists are the enemy, even if they deplore extreme activities. Honest, kind, gracious Muslims must understand that if they are not for us, they are against us.

Muslim immigrants to the U.S. must be willing to melt into our society. No, they don't have to forget and reject everything from their home country, but they must love America if they choose to move here. Obviously, they think America is better than their former home. If not, why come here? They should have a love affair with America. If not, they should go home. Theodore Roosevelt said, "The man who loves other countries as much as his own stands on a level with the man who loves other women as much as he loves his own wife."[1] So Muslims should be proud, appreciative, grateful Americans who happen to have been born in a foreign land, a land they have rejected when they moved to our shores.

To the moderate Muslims out there who are trying to walk the fence, I would ask: What will you do if you must decide between the Koran and the U.S. Constitution? The great majority, even those who say they abhor terror, will choose the Koran. Informed people will say, "But you Christians believe that the Bible must be obeyed above everything else." That is correct, but we don't fly planes into buildings and walk into restaurants wearing body bombs! You see, we have proved over hundreds of years that we don't believe in violence, except in self-defense.

In recent years, Muslims have proved that if they are true to the Koran and Hadith, they cannot be both good Muslims and good Americans.

Christians follow the Bible's command in II Timothy 2:24 that says, "And the servant of the Lord must not strive; but be gentle unto all men, apt to teach, patient." The Koran teaches anger, hatred, adultery, slavery, murder, oppression of women, etc., and while some **professing** Christians are guilty of some of those sins, they are disobedient to Christ and His Word. Nor do thinking Christians seek to defend professing Christians who disobey Christ.

WAR BETWEEN CHRIST AND MOHAMMED

In closing, I must make a major point: We have a major problem in America even if none of the terrorist attacks were done by Muslims! Assume there has been a massive mistake, conspiracy, whatever, and no Muslim was involved in the attacks on America. We still have a problem with our whole society being subjugated by a foreign religion that is determined to completely change our nation by coercion, if necessary. You must ask if that is what you want. What kind of America do you want for your children and grandchildren? It will be changed because of the Muslim invasion and even a "peaceful" Islam is a threat to America staying America!

I will be the first to demand that Muslims be treated kindly and with respect, even though they ridicule Christ and what we stand for. As Americans, they have the right to do that. We don't have to like what they do and say, and they must not be humiliated, harmed, or harassed in any way unless they break the law. Then, like you and me, they must pay the penalty for law-breaking.

Some Muslims have complained that they do not feel comfortable going to their mosques and about their everyday duties since the many terrorist attacks. Some of them have been cursed and intimidated by American thugs. I am ashamed of those Americans; however, it is interesting that few Muslims have demanded their former homeland guarantee religious freedom to Christians living there. Furthermore, none of the heads of state in Muslim nations have called for religious freedom in those states.

Whether we like it or not and whether politicians recognize it or not, there is a war between Christ and Mohammed. And Christ's cross will be victorious over the crescent moon. When men of the cross, with the mark of the cross, take the message of the cross (without making it a holy horseshoe), we will be "more than conquerors" through Christ.

Christians must win the Muslims to Christ while Muslims seek to win America to Islam! Maybe if we had been more aggressive in telling them the good news, we might not have the terror we have today. We must tell them that the bad news has a cure, and it is Christ. Everyone must hear the bad news, that all of us are sinners, but the good news is that there is a remedy for the bad news. It is faith in Christ. We will win them if we go after them in unreserved, unselfish, and unconditional love, telling them that repentance of sin and placing simple faith in

Christ will produce the New Birth that Jesus said is the requirement to enter Heaven. Even those terrorists inside the Trojan Horse can have that life-changing, eternity-deciding experience. Let's get to it! After all, we are running out of time; the fuse is burning!

Jesus Christ is still the hope, the **only** hope for this world!

References:

1 "The Indomitable President," The American President website.

INDEX

n indicates entry in reference notes

CPSIA information can be obtained
at www.ICGtesting.com
Printed in the USA
FFHW020704080219
50440243-55643FF